EMPIRE ™

EARTH

THE ART OF CONQUEST

BRC AGE	COPPER AGE	BRONZE AGE	DARK AGE	RENAISSANCE	INDUSTRIAL AGE	INFORMATION AGE
25,000 BC	5000 BC	2000 BC	800 BC	0 AD	900 AD	1300 AD	1500 AD	1700 AD	1900 AD	2000 AD	2100 AD
STONE AGE		BRONZE AGE		MIDDLE AGES		IMPERIAL AGE		ATOMIC AGE		NANO AGE

PRIMA'S OFFICIAL STRATEGY GUIDE

An
Incan
Monkey God
Studios Production

Prima Games

A Division of Random House, Inc.

3000 Lava Ridge Court

Roseville, CA 95661

(800) 733-3000

www.primagames.com

EMPIRE EARTH
THE ART OF CONQUEST

PRIMA'S OFFICIAL STRATEGY GUIDE

~∞~ Credits ~∞~

IMGS Writers
Melissa Tyler, Tuesday Frase

**The Theory of
Scenario Design**
Gordon Farrell

Campaign Walkthroughs
(Original Campaigns)
Chris McCubbin
Jim Heath
(Expansion Campaigns)
Chris Bold
John Cataldo
David Fielding
Dan McClure
Tom Murray
Matthew Nordhaus

Statistics and Editing
David Ladyman
Beth Loubet

**Layout Blood,
Sweat and Tears**
Tuesday Frase
David Ladyman
Raini Madden
Sharon Freilich

Expert Multiplayer Advice
Damon "Stratus" Gauthier
Sunny "Crexis" Sihota
Nate "REDLINE" Jacques
Mike "YoungGunZ" Echino
Richard "Methos" Bishop

Expert Scenario Advice
Chris "Eggman" Theriault
GJ Snyder III
Ben Schneider
Chris Bold
John Cataldo
David Fielding
Dan McClure
Tom Murray
Matthew Nordhaus

**Wonderful Sierra Facilitators
(second time around)**
Steve Beinner
JonPayne

Mad Doc Heroes
Ken Davis
Matthew Nordhaus
and the rest of the crew

ORIGINAL EDITION

Oceans of Information
Ryan "AgeOfEgos" Geiler

Stainless Steel Heroes
Dara-Lynn Pelechatz
Jon Alenson
Rick Goodman
James Hsieh

Stupendous Artwork
Steve Ashley
Josh Buck
Jeff Carroll
Jason Childress
Cory Strader

Wonderful Sierra Facilitator
Charles Holtzclaw

**People Who Appeared Out of
Nowhere to Help**
Lisa Nonog
Chad Martin
Gary Stevens

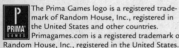
ISBN: 7615-3981-6

Library of Congress Catalog Card Number: 2002112363

Printed in the United States of America

04 05 DD 10 9

Incan Monkey God Studios and the IMGS logo are trademarks of IMGS, Inc.

∽∽ **Table of Contents** ∽∽

EMPIRE EARTH
THE ART OF CONQUEST

PRIMA'S OFFICIAL STRATEGY GUIDE

Contents

World Statistics

The Theory of Scenario Design

EMPIRE EARTH
THE ART OF CONQUEST

PRIMA'S OFFICIAL STRATEGY GUIDE

∽∽ Key Commands ∽∽

View Keys

↑	Scroll Up
↓	Scroll Down
←	Scroll Left
→	Scroll Right
⌐⌐	Zoom in
⌐⌐	Zoom out
>.	Follow Unit
F2	Cycle through Perspective Zoom modes
F5	Cycle through 3 Show Hidden Units modes
F9	Screen Shot with UI
⇧Shift F9	Screen Shot w/o UI
Ctrl F9	Low Resolution Screen Shot of Entire Map
Alt F9	High Resolution Screen Shot of Entire Map
Spacebar	Move to location of last player event (keep pressing to review the queue of recent events)

Selection Keys

Tab	Idle Citizen
Ctrl Tab	All Idle Citizens
<,	Idle Military Unit
Ctrl <,	All Idle Military Units
A	Idle Atomic Bomber
B	Idle Bomber
D	Idle Fighter/Bomber
F	Idle Fighter
S	Idle Space Fighter
W	Idle Planetary Fighter
Ctrl #	Create group #
⇧Shift #	Add selection to group
Alt #	Select and center group #
#	Select group # (Press the group's number)
# #	Select and center group # (Press number twice)

Select and Center ...

H	Town Center
Ctrl A	Archery Range
Ctrl B	Barracks
Ctrl C	Siege Factory
Ctrl D	Dock
Ctrl F	Tank Factory
Ctrl G	Granary
Ctrl M	Market
Ctrl I	Missile Base (campaign)
Ctrl N	Settlement
Ctrl Q	Airport
Ctrl R	Cyber Factory
Ctrl S	Stable
Ctrl U	University
Ctrl V	Naval Yard
Ctrl X	Cyber Lab
Ctrl Y	Temple
Ctrl Z	Hospital
Ctrl \	Missile Base
Ctrl /	Priest Tower

Game Commands

| +Numpad | Increase Game Speed |
| −Numpad | Decrease Game |

Speed

Esc	Cancels Current Input or Action Mode (exits cinematics in scenarios)
Enter	Chat
F1	Return to Scenario Editor (When in Test Mode)
F3	Pause
F4	Quick Save
F4	Quick Load
Ctrl F4	Auto Save Load
F10	In-Game Options
F7	Toggle Display of Game Clock/Speed and Frame Rate
Alt F	Enter Flare Mode
Page Up	Display Previous Messages
Ctrl Shift Z	All out "Banzai" computer player attack — allied computer players will assist you (single player)
Ctrl Alt Z	All out "Banzai" computer player attack — allied computer players will not assist you (single player)
;	Just-in-Time Manufacturing ON
	Just-in-Time Manufacturing OFF

Unit Commands

| Shift | Show Goal Queue / Add Goal to Queue (with other key) |
| B | Unit Behaviors |

[D] Conscription (single player)

[F] Fanaticism

[F] Flaming Arrows

[G] Garrison /Populate a Building

[L] Explore

[M] Formations

[M] Meteor Storm

[P] Stop

[D] Unload Transport or Fortress

[Z] Patrol (Land Military Units only)

[Del] Kill First Selected Unit

[Shift Del] Kill All Selected Units

Behaviors

[Alt][A] Aggressive

[Alt][D] Defend (Stand Ground)

[Alt][G] Guard (Guards a location)

[Alt][S] Scout

Bomber

[T] Attack Ground

Capital Ship

[C] Devastating Beam of Death

Citizens

[A] Build Archery Range or AA Gun

[B] Build Barracks

[C] Build Siege Factory

[D] Build Dock or Space Dock

[E] Build House

[F] Build Tank Factory

[J] Build Granary/Farms

[M] Build Market (U.S.)

[N] Build Settlement or Expansionist Town Center (Ottoman Empire)

[O] Build Fortress

[Q] Build Airport

[R] Build Cyber Factory or Radar Center (single player)

[S] Build Stable or Transporter

[T] Build Tower or Space Tower

[U] Build University

[V] Build Naval Yard or Space Turret

[W] Build Wall or Space Wall

[X] Build Cyber Lab

[Y] Build Temple

[Z] Build Hospital

[?/] Build Priest Tower (Babyln.)

[~] Build Bundeswehr (Germany)

[|\] Build Missile Base (Novaya Russia)

[:;] Build Palisades

[`] Build Palisades Tower

Conquistadors

[C] Increase Line of Sight

Cyber Ninja

[C] Logic Bomb

Mechs

Tempest

[A] Anti-Matter Storm

[R] Resonator

Key Commands

Hades

[E] Teleport

[T] Time Warp

[V] Nano-Virus

Apollo

[C] Ion Pulse

[E] Repair

[S] Diffraction Shield

Furies

[D] Self-Destruct

Poseidon

[C] Assimilate

Priests & Crusaders

[C] Convert

Prophets

[A] Plague

[C] Hurricane

[E] Earthquake

[F] Firestorm

[R] Malaria

[V] Volcano

Radio Man

[A] Drop Units (single player)

Riot Police

[C] EES Mind Control (single player)

Roman Legionary

[A] Pilum Attack (single player)

SAS Commando

[C] Plant Explosives

EMPIRE EARTH
THE ART OF CONQUEST

Siege Weapon

`T` *Attack Ground*

Strategist Heroes

`C` *Battle Cry*

Transports

`D` *Unload*

Buildings

`I` *Set Rally Point*

Aircraft Carrier

`F` *Build Fighter/Bombers*

Airport (`Ctrl` `Q`)

Set rally points for. . .

`V` *Atomic Bomber*

`X` *Bomber / Helicopter*

`Z` *Fighter*

`A` *Build Atomic Bomber*

`B` *Build Bomber*

`C` *Build Gunship Helicopter*

`E` *Build (AT) Helicopter*

`F` *Build Fighter*

`G` *Build Sea King (Anti-Sub)*

`O` *Place Paratrooper Rally Flag (Italy)*

`Q` *Build Paratroopers (Italy)*

`R` *Build Transport Helicopter*

`S` *Build Fighter/Bomber*

`T` *Build (AT) Airplane*

`W` *Build Planetary Fighter*

Archery Range (`Ctrl` `A`)

`A` *Train Foot Archers*

`C` *Train Chariot and Cavalry Archers*

`E` *Train Ranged Spear Throwers*

`F` *Train Elephant Archer*

`X` *Train Crossbow*

Barracks (`Ctrl` `B`)

`A` *Train Ranged Shock (Gun) Units, Sampson or Watchman*

`B` *Train Grenade Launcher or Bazooka*

`C` *Train Medic or Centurion (single player)*

`D` *Train Elite Guard*

`E` *Train Pierce (Spear) Units or Flame Thrower*

`F` *Train Hand Cannoneer or Mortars*

`G` *Train Machine Gunner or Gallic Warrior (single player)*

`J` *Train Cyber Ninja (Japan)*

`N` *Train Barbarian*

`P` *Train Riot Police (single player)*

`R` *Train Sharp-shooters or Snipers*

`S` *Train Melee Shock (Sword) Units, Stinger Soldier or Standard Bearer (single player)*

`T` *Train Partisan*

`V` *Train Viking*

`W` *Train Rock Thrower*

`X` *Train SAS Commando (Great Britain)*

Cyber Factory (`Ctrl` `R`)

`A` *Build Ares Cybers*

`C` *Build Pandora Cybers*

`R` *Build Hyperion Cybers*

`T` *Build Minotaur Cybers*

`Z` *Build Zeus Cyber*

Cyber Lab (`Ctrl` `X`)

`A` *Build Apollo Cyber*

`D` *Build Hades Cyber*

`E` *Build Poseidon Cyber*

`F` *Build Furies Cyber*

`T` *Build Tempest Cyber*

Dock (`Ctrl` `D`)

`B` *Build Battleships*

`C` *Build Cruisers (Anti-Air)*

`D` *Build Frigates*

`F` *Build Fishing Boats*

`G` *Build Galley/Galleons*

`T` *Build Transports*

Granary

`F` *Research Techs to Increase Farming Rate*

`R` *Replant Farms*

Hospital

`A` *Research Techs to Increase Citizen Attack and Hit Points*

`C` *Your Pop Cap*

`H` *Damage Control*

`R` *Hospital Healing Rate*

`S` *Citizen Speed*

Market

- Q *Buy Food*
- W *Buy Gold*
- E *Buy Stone*
- R *Buy Iron*
- A *Sell Food*
- S *Sell Gold*
- D *Sell Stone*
- F *Sell Iron*

Missile Base

- M *Build ICBM*

Naval Yard
(Ctrl V)

- C *Build Aircraft Carriers*
- G *Build Sea Kings (Anti-Sub)*
- S *Build Attack Submarines*
- T *Build Nuclear-Powered Missile Submarines*

Priests Tower

- C *Convert*

Space Dock

- B *Build Space Capital Ship*
- C *Build Space Corvette*
- F *Build Space Fighter (on Space Carrier)*
- G *Build Space Carrier*
- T *Build Space Transport*

Stable (Ctrl S)

- C *Train Shock (Melee) Cavalry*
- E *Train Pierce (Spear) Cavalry*
- F *Train War Elephant*
- G *Train Gun Cavalry*
- S *Train Persian Cavalry*

Siege Factory
(Ctrl C)

- A *Build Anti-Tank (AT) Guns*
- B *Build Artillery*
- C *Build Siege Weapons*
- E *Build Field Cannon*
- G *Build Siege Cannon*
- R *Build Rams*
- S *Build Field Weapons (pre-gunpowder)*
- T *Build Siege Towers*

Tank Factory
(Ctrl F)

- A *Build Mobile AA Unit or Anti Missile Battery*
- M *Build Mining Unit (single player)*
- S *Build Armor-Piercing (AP) Tanks*
- T *Build High-Explosive (HE) Tanks*

Temple (Ctrl Y)

- E *Train Priest*
- R *Train Prophet*

Research Techs to Increase . . .

- A *Temple Range*
- D *Prophet Speed*
- F *Priest Hit Points*
- M *Priest Recharge Rate*
- N *Prophet Range*
- P *Prophet Hit Points*
- S *Priest Speed*
- T *Priest Range*

Research Tech to Allow . . .

- B *Conversion of Buildings*
- C *Conversion of Priests*
- F *Faith Healing*
- P *Quantum Technology*

Key Commands

Town Center / Capitol (Ctrl)

- C *Create Citizen*
- E *Train Strategist Hero*
- X *Upgrade Strategist Hero*
- R *Train Warrior Hero*
- Z *Upgrade Warrior Hero*
- B *Produce Spotting Balloon or Spy Satellite*
- D *Train Canine Scout (Dog)*

Research . . .

- A *Epoch Advance*
- G *Gold Mining Technologies*
- K *Cloaking (Rebel Forces)*
- N *Hunting Foraging Technologies*
- S *Iron Mining Technologies*
- T *Stone Mining Technologies*
- U *Wall and Tower Upgrades*
- W *Wood Cutting Technologies*

University

- S *Build Zero-G Engineers*

Research Techs to Increase . . .

- B *Building Line of Sight*
- E *EES Mind Control Technology (single player)*
- F *Building Hit Points*
- R *University Range*
- S *Rate of Repair at Dock*

Research Tech to Decrease . . .

- T *Cost of Tributes*

Wall

- G *Make Gate*

EMPIRE EARTH
THE ART OF CONQUEST

PRIMA'S OFFICIAL STRATEGY GUIDE

∼∼ Introduction ∼∼

There's something deeply satisfying about playing a Real Time Strategy (RTS) game. It's the mental challenge of strategy, the instant gratification of being in the right place at the right time, combined with the forbidden pleasure of firmly, completely and utterly grinding to a pulp anyone who dares challenge your rule.

Empire Earth delivers the whole package like no one else can. The in-box manual tells you everything you need to know to play. This book tells you how to *win*.

BASICS

The Basics chapter is intended for the player who is for the first time experimenting with the RTS genre, it establishes the correct "mind set." It talks about the infrastructure, the military set up and how much preparation is too much and how much is negligent.

CAMPAIGNS

There are seven campaigns: Greek, British, German and Future, plus the new Roman, War in the Pacific, and Asian campaigns.

Each campaign scenario is discussed in three sections.

The **Map** is the world revealed.

The **Stats** section discusses the basics of the scenario, and gives what you start with, what your goals are and essentially what you are up against. There are a few hints as to what might be useful for the successful completion of the scenario, but nothing too revealing.

The **Walkthrough** gives step-by-step instruction on how to successfully get through the scenario. It starts at the beginning and takes you through the process to a successful win. Of course there is more than one way to win a scenario. This is the way that worked for both us and the testers at Stainless Steel Studios.

MULTIPLAYER

Playing against real people is so utterly different from playing against the computer that it's almost like two different games. Thus we have a section devoted to the multiplayer experience. We provide a variety of different multiplayer philosophies straight from the award-winning Real Time Strategies players/game balancers. Are you a rush-n-crush personality? You're not alone, so learn the best way to bash first and bash hardest. Are you a build-defend-build kind of player? We've got tips for you.

NUMBERS

Each civilization has its advantages and disadvantages. Knowing who you are and who you are up against is vital in launching a successful career.

Similarly, knowing the myriad **Statistics** that keep the game running will help you stay ahead of disaster. How much food do you need to build the optimum army? How many resources will it take to rule the skies? The cold hard facts are listed in the stats section. Play the numbers, and make the system work for you.

ᘓᘓᘓ **Basics** ᘓᘓᘓ

Great leaders have only one goal: to make their people strong. Their reasons for wanting to be strong are as different as their situations. Strength keeps your people fed. Strength holds hostile neighbors at bay. Strength is the power to do what you want, to have what you need, to live your life the way you wish to live it.

Being strong in Empire Earth *means having two things: a thriving economy and a robust military. Each and every game you play in* Empire Earth *is somehow related to these two things.*

ᘓᘓᘓ **Infrastructure** ᘓᘓᘓ

START SMALL, THINK BIG

The goal for each game you play is generally established at the start of the game. In the campaign scenarios, you're usually instructed to go to a certain place or to accomplish a certain task. In multiplayer you have one of two paths: conquer everyone on the map, or build a Wonder and hold onto it. In nearly all of these, you need to establish a healthy economy. Almost always, this is followed by some sort of military action. The faster you accomplish the first one, the more successful the second will be.

Empire Earth is a military game. Successful battles are integral to winning the game. Building a defensible environment with happy workers and meticulously spaced buildings may be satisfying to build and pleasant to look at, but it isn't going to pass muster in the long haul. Building walls is good, erecting buildings is great, but don't lose track that the end goal is to marshal your troops and send them out to conquer and claim anything that stands against them.

This is your ultimate goal: preparing for the conflict.

> **⊷TIP**
>
> Go ahead and get it out of your system. Take a few games to putter around, learning the interface and exactly what everything looks like. Marvel at the graphics and your industrious minions. Then start over and concentrate on building your empire. Remember, that's what the other guy is hard at work doing.

Work Smarter

What's the best way to prepare? The answer is "time and resources management." As wimpy as it sounds, the difference between good commanders and great commanders is not their knowledge of combat, but their ability to control people and resources. In other words, a great commander is a great manager.

What do you need to do to manage well? You need to keep your people working in the most efficient way possible.

EMPIRE EARTH
THE ART OF CONQUEST

The first thing to do is to assign tasks to the new citizens that come out of your town center. This is a little time - consuming at first, when your focus is more on building up your resource-gathering potential, but it's definitely worth it. (Follow the team sequence as it appears in **Go Forth and Wander**, next. After a while you'll shift from building the work teams to building your military, at which point it isn't so "hands on" anymore. You'll just send them to the barracks, archery range, etc. and let them build up in numbers.)

> ## ☠WARNING☠
> What you don't know *can* kill you. If you don't send out a scout, you're playing blindfolded.

Go Forth and Gather

Scout. You need to send someone out to investigate the terrain. Canine scouts are excellent for revealing terrain. As soon as you can, select a dog and hit the Explore button. Don't worry about watching him to make sure he stays safe — consider him expendable. Use one at a time.

Scouts can move through trees, which make them useful in late-game situations for establishing Line of Sight.

Work Teams. Work goes faster when a lot of citizens are working together. Since speed is of the essence, always try to keep your citizens in teams of six (the maximum number that can work a mine, field, etc.). Drag over or select them as a group when you assign them to a new task. If a job is important enough to do, it's important enough to do quickly.

Food Team. Unless you have a store-house of food already established, you're going to need to provide food in order to build up your population. Establish a work team of six people, and have them concentrate on the local food supply, be it foraging for vegetables, fishing, hunting or farming. As your Pop Cap (population capacity) rises, use the new citizens to do other things.

As long as your food is abundant, keep at least one food team hunting/gathering until all the resources are exhausted. It takes a lot of wood (and thus, time) to build all the farms you eventually need, and you never want to have too few people because you don't have enough food.

Foraging. If there are multiple foraging patches around your home base, go ahead and deplete them entirely in the early stages of the game. Part of what lets you pull ahead of your opponent is getting your population numbers up as soon as possible. It takes time to build a farm or hunt or fish. Farms are better in the long haul, of course, but it's better to build a farm with the extra people your population can afford if you've been busy getting food.

> ## ➥TIP
> It is *critical* that your gatherers not have to carry resources more than 10 steps to get to the settlement! Wherever the action is, put down a settlement. If they clear out an area and move farther on, build another settlement close to the new harvesting area.

Basics

Hunting. Hunting actually brings in about 30% more food than farming. Don't stop because it's not "modern" enough — more food is always good. Keep your eye on the hunting teams. Don't let them get discouraged because they can't see anything to kill ... move them to better hunting lands.

As with other forms of food, you should put a settlement close to the richest grazing grounds. For your hunters, you can be a little flexible with the "no more than 10 steps away from a town center" ... but not much. Keep track of how long it's taking them to make the return trip. For hunters, a town center should be no more than a slow 10-second count away.

> **➥ TIP**
> Even thriving civilizations rarely need more than twelve farms; don't get over-enthusiastic with your development plans.

Fishing. If you're near the water, fishing is a good opportunity to pick up some steady, cheap food. Build a dock at a convenient point near the best fishing spots. Because the dock serves as a drop-off point, you don't need to worry about building a town center nearby. However, you do want to build a dock close to every fishing spot you can find. You can't really set up fishing "teams" like you have for building or hunting, but you can build multiple fishing boats to fish from the same fishing hole. Six is the maximum number. When you have depleted the fish in that area, build a dock close to the next fishing hole and move all your fishing boats over.

Farming. Farming is *the* way to go. It doesn't have the high yield that hunting does, but you can build more to make up the difference, plus it takes less micromanagement.

Farms are automatically near granaries and vice-versa. Building a farm includes the foundation location for your granary. Populating a granary with 8 people provides a 20% bonus to food gathered there.

Lumber Teams. It doesn't matter how many resources you have nearby if you don't bring them in. Look at your environment and goals, and decide where to allocate your civilian efforts (after food). Usually wood is your next priority, followed by stone, gold and iron. Wood is integral in nearly every structure, and stone is necessary for the best defenses, including walls and towers. Iron allows for armed military units, and gold allows for advanced military units.

You should always have at least one full work team (six citizens) working on lumber. If there is not an immediate threat nearby, you should also aim to have full work teams on gold, stone and iron. If there is danger nearby, cut production down to one full team on wood, one full team on stone and at least a half-team (three people) on each of your other resources.

Cut with a plan. The first place to clear is your main settlement area. Trees take up space where you could otherwise place valuable buildings. Find a nice, defensible place and have your lumber team clear out any miscellaneous trees. Work from the capitol — or soon-to-be center — outward.

| COPPER AGE | DARK AGE | RENAISSANCE | INDUSTRIAL AGE |

| 5000 BC | 2000 BC | 500 BC | 0 AD | 900 AD | 1300 AD | 1500 AD | 1700 AD | 1900 AD |
STONE AGE   BRONZE AGE   MIDDLE AGES   IMPERIAL AGE   ATOMIC AGE

EMPIRE EARTH
THE ART OF CONQUEST

Once you have a nice place for your buildings, take a look at how the trees add to the defensibility of your territory. Most enemy troops cannot travel through forest — the exceptions are barbarians and partisans — so a line of trees is nearly as valuable as a wall and a whole lot cheaper. Don't cut your way through any long line of trees that might be standing between you and your enemies. Instead, find a grove of trees that isn't serving any sort of tactical purpose, and use those as your wood resource.

Don't underestimate the value of wood. Lumber is essential for everything from farms to frigates. Only when you start relying on aircraft and other highly advanced equipment does it begin to lose its value. Look ahead not only to what you want and need for this epoch, but what you're going to want for the next one down the road.

Mining Teams. There are three types of mines in *Empire Earth*. There's stone, which yields the materials for towers, fortified walls, etc. There's gold, which allows you to have the things that only money can buy — which is pretty much everything from advanced military units to universities. There's also iron, which is used in the manufacture of nearly all advanced units.

Stone. Invaluable through most of the ages, its value drops sharply in the modern epochs, when anti-aircraft units provide more protection than walls do. It's still necessary, just not nearly the priority it was earlier.

Iron. Fairly useless in the beginning, iron winds up being absolutely vital to a successful career. Like the old adage about bringing a knife to a gunfight, you don't want to find yourself only able to afford tanks when your opponents have bombers.

Gold. Cold hard bullion is always useful, always necessary. Gold is the key to advancement in nearly all things, from the beginning to the conclusion. In addition, the need for gold in quantity increases as the game progresses. That's not so much of an issue with the campaign scenarios, but it's a serious tactical consideration in long-term multiplayer situations. If you know you're going from the semi-primitive to the higher-tech epochs, be careful about bulking up on things that take a lot of gold. This is one of the most difficult elements in long-term multiplayer games ... how do you stay alive long enough in the earlier periods while you save up your pennies for the be-all, end-all army of the future?

In all cases, you want to set up a town center and tower close to the mines. Treat mines like the incredibly important resource that they are. Unless you're just mining for fun, you want to station at least five military units nearby to act as the first line of defense in case of attack. In the case of gold, you can always expect an attack! Throw up a wall and don't even bother about a gate. If and when the alarm is sounded, don't hesitate to send troops to defend the mines. A civilization with no money is an extinct civilization in no time.

Basics

Build for the Future

The moment you have enough resources to build with, you need to start getting things put up, and fast. After your lumber team has tackled the local wood, your next team of six citizens should be devoted to using it. Consider them the local construction crew, and keep them busy.

Basic Building Checklist (if you don't have the structure and can build one):

⊕ Settlement near a resource

⊕ Settlement near a food supply

⊕ Barracks, preferably in the direction that the enemy is most likely to appear (not too far out, just "in that direction")

⊕ Granary and farm (or dock and fishing boat), preferably in the direction the enemy is least likely to appear

⊕ Tower, near town center, on the side the enemy is most likely to appear

⊕ Two more granaries (or fishing boats)

⊕ Advanced military buildings (such as archery ranges, stables or factories)

⊕ Wall between you and the enemy

⊕ Gate, and tower near the wall

⊕ New settlements near any resources that are farther out

⊕ Towers near the new settlements.

Obviously, this is only a start, and must be adapted to epochs that have other needs.

> ⊷**TIP**
>
> There eventually comes a point when you no longer need as much food to purchase your different military units — but don't stop making food. Food remains an important ingredient for going up an epoch.

> ⊷**TIP**
>
> If you can find an enemy mine near your territory, take it! Stealing their gold and iron is the same as stealing their future. Unlike stone, which is probably not worth sticking your neck out for, gold and iron need the extra effort to find, claim and retain.

Save for a Better Tomorrow

The first "epoch up" in a game will cost 50% of the regular price (20% if you're playing tournament). The second will cost 80% the regular price (50% in tournament). Note that Epochs 2 and 3 will never cost full price — the earliest you can start is Epoch I, so II and III can't be your third or later "epoch up."

EMPIRE EARTH
THE ART OF CONQUEST

PRIMA'S OFFICIAL STRATEGY GUIDE

Epoch	Food	Gold	Iron
II	850		
III	750	400	400
IV	1000	500	500
V	1200	625	625
VI	1450	725	725
VII	1650	825	825
VIII	1750	850	850
IX	1800	900	900
X	2200	1100	1100
XI	2250	1150	1150
XII	2350	1175	1175
XIII	2675	1350	1350
XIV	2700	1375	1375
XV	3000	1500	1500

Guarantee a Good Start

Campaign scenarios start you in the middle of the adventure, but in regular games you have to do all the dirty work yourself. As there are some things that you always need, so there are some steps you always take. You can feel comfortable starting any game with a few swift and sure steps.

1) Send your canine scout out to reconnoiter. By placing waypoint flags in ever-widening circles, you reveal important terrain features. The dog will probably be killed by the first tower he approaches, but that means you've revealed the enemy, and that's all you wanted from the scout, really.

2) Command your town center to produce people. The hotkeys are [H] and then [C]. Don't worry about how many times you should click, but don't queue up more than five at a time. It may come to the point when you need the food for something else, and you won't want to have to stop and de-queue citizens to free up the food.

3) Send your first six people out to gather food at any local patches. Is it far from your town center? Have your first gatherer concentrate on building a new settlement near the patch.

4) Send your next six people to harvest wood. Need a new settlement? Build one.

5) Send a citizen to look for gold and iron. Send six people to gather gold. Do you need a new settlement? Build one.

6) Send a citizen to look for a stone mine. Assign your next six people to harvesting the lumber from solitary trees near your town's center. Remember not to let them harvest long stands of trees that can be used for defense later.

➡ TIP

It's an important thing to keep your citizens busy. While you're getting your basic civilization running, do an occasional check for Idle Citizens. Grab them and set them to work harvesting whichever of your resources are lowest.

COPPER AGE		DARK AGE		RENAISSANCE		INDUSTRIAL AGE		INFORMATIO
BC	2000 BC	500 BC	0AD	900 AD	1500 AD	1500 AD	1700 AD	1900 AD	2000 AD
	BRONZE AGE		MIDDLE AGES			IMPERIAL AGE		ATOMIC AGE	

Basics

7) Build a barracks if you find iron, a stable if you find gold. Send your first unit out to the enemy to kill as many of his citizens as he can.

8) Keep assigning the new citizens tasks.

9) Immediately begin converting your resources to something useful. Don't hoard resources; spend them. Buy an upgrade.

10) When you have the opportunity to advance to the next epoch, build the two buildings necessary, concentrate on getting any other resources necessary to "buy" your way in, and advance as soon as possible.

> ☠ **WARNING** ☠
>
> Computer AI has no delay in assigning roles to new citizens. As soon as they come out, they know what they are supposed to do. You need to be about that fast.

Populate for Bonuses

Populating a building with citizens takes those citizens out of the game. They're dropped from your Pop Cap, and you don't get them back. It's worth it for the increase in productivity, though!

When 5 citizens populate a settlement, it turns into a town center.

A town center within two tiles of a stone, gold or iron resource site (for reference, a house is one tile) gives a 25% bonus on the resource gathered there. There is no bonus for wood.

For every additional citizen (up to 10) populating a town center, the bonus goes up 2%.

When 10 citizens populate a town center, it becomes a capitol. A capitol gives a 35% bonus to the resources gathered there.

For every additional citizen (up to 15) populating a capitol, the bonus goes up 1%. The max bonus is a 50% capitol bonus.

LOOK AHEAD

Real-world commanders never know what the next big advance in technology will be, or how they will need to adapt. Tomorrow brings nothing but surprises. You have a huge advantage over them: all future inventions are laid out on the Technology Tree poster that came in the box. Take the time to look at what the next epoch has to offer.

Don't worry that it's "cheating" to look ahead to the final epoch of whatever scenario you'll be playing. It's not. It's called planning ahead and playing well.

For instance, if you're going to want siege engines, that takes a lot of gold but very little iron. In fact, nothing much in the Middle Ages requires much iron at all. (There are, of course, some things such as long swords. Still, there isn't much.) If you aren't going to go past the Middle Ages, you don't need to spend much time on iron at all. However, advancing just one more age to the Renaissance opens up a variety of iron-based options. (Cannon are a very important element of the Renaissance.) Anyone who's spent the Middle Ages slowly hoarding up iron has an immediate advantage over less-prepared players. Don't use a lot of citizens to gather something you don't need yet. One or two is plenty to get a good head start.

EMPIRE EARTH
THE ART OF CONQUEST

PRIMA'S OFFICIAL STRATEGY GUIDE

> **➤ TIP**
>
> Planning ahead for multiple epochs is more of a multiplayer game issue than it is for a campaign scenario. You cannot take surplus supplies or advancement from one scenario to the next, only Civ Points. Multiplayer allows you to decide what you want your strengths to be, and to plan toward that goal. Campaigns are more "realistic" in that your situation is usually set out by the game, and while you'll often "epoch up" in a scenario, one scenario never spans more than two epochs.

Upgrading

Getting upgrades costs money. This is a fact of life, not just a game mechanic. Very few truly revolutionary ideas came from a factory worker who managed to discover a new kind of math on his lunch breaks. In real life it takes funding dozens of inventors, staffing and stocking their laboratories *and then* setting up the facilities to actually put their new ideas to use. No wonder *Empire Earth* requires you to fork over a formidable amount of resources in return for a technology upgrade.

In fact, it might be tempting not to upgrade. You wind up thinking "my farms are doing fine, who needs a Wheeled Plow" or "why should I spend my hard-earned resources on Human Anatomy when I don't plan for my citizens to be a fighting force?" Actually, often people wind up not thinking about them at all, and just missing the opportunity to take advantage of all a new epoch has to offer.

People who don't learn to love upgrades are merely "dabblers" in the game, which in this context rhymes with "vanquished" as well as "crushed," "destroyed" and "defeated." Upgrades are an edge, and that's what gets you ahead.

Pop Cap. First of all, anything that raises your population capacity (Pop Cap) is a Very Good Thing. Sanitation, Chemical Drugs, Vaccinations and Anti-Aging Pills are your friends. Why? Because the time-proven best way to defeat an opponent is to swarm them with superior numbers. The more people you have, the more chances you get.

Citizen Speed. This is also valuable, because it translates into getting your resources more quickly. That's always a good thing, since falling behind in available resources can be crippling.

Personal Style. After Pop Cap and Speed, upgrades should be chosen according to what your personal playing style is. Do you feel best shoring up your defenses before going out to conquer? If so, upgrading your farms is a good thing, and so might be upgrading your priests' attributes as insurance against early attacks. Do you tend to scatter some farms, throw up a wall or two and take your military out a-pillaging? You might want to invest in some better towers and walls, but mostly concentrate on military-based advantages, such as upgrading your Iron Gathering or Dock Repair rate.

Be an observant player. If you notice that once your home wall is breached, you die a dismal death, concentrate more on

UPPER AGE		DARK AGE		RENAISSANCE		INDUSTRIAL AGE		INFORMATION
BC	2000 BC	500 BC	0AD	900 AD	1500 AD	1700 AD	1900 AD	2000 AD
BRONZE AGE		MIDDLE AGES		IMPERIAL AGE		ATOMIC AGE		

Basics

upgrading the walls next time. If superior numbers always spell defeat for you, look into speeding up your agriculture.

Wonders

The ultimate upgrade is building a Wonder. As long as you have a Wonder, you have the benefits that Wonder gives. For instance, having a Lighthouse lifts the fog of war from the oceans.

In a multiplayer game, building and sustaining a certain number of Wonders is one of the ways to win. It's not as easy as it sounds, because once you erect a Wonder, suddenly you are the subject of intense interest from all the other players. It takes about 10 real-time minutes *after* you create the last Wonder before you can claim a victory. That gives your enemies plenty of time to try to take you out. People who were bitter enemies a moment ago will put aside their differences for however long it takes to batter down your walls and destroy your Wonders ... and usually your entire civilization while they're at it. In the same vein, it's usually a good idea for you to temporarily forgive your fellow combatants, and join them in taking out whichever of your neighbors has started a Wonder countdown.

Obviously, before you build a Wonder you should ensure you have enough walls, military units, anti-aircraft emplacements, upgrades and so forth to defend it.

In a campaign scenario, sustaining a Wonder does not give you a win. Scenarios have specific goals that must be met, and those are the only things that buy victory. Building a Library of Alexandria is all well and good, but it doesn't mean Wellington can ignore the fact that Napoleon is marching across the globe.

In fact, that brings us to the next important element of success ....

Building a thriving infrastructure is fun and enormously satisfying, but let's face the facts ... a thriving economy does not make an empire. A thriving economy makes a target. You need, want and must have a military to defend what's yours. It takes a military to go out and claim the wilderness. You especially need a military to storm the enemy walls and make what's theirs, yours.

The name of the game is *Empire Earth*. The whole point of your carefully constructed economy is to produce an unstoppable military force with which you can spread your empire across the map. If your idea of fun is making the farms line up symmetrically and imagining the workaday life of your people, there are other games that cater to that. *Empire Earth* is for building empires.

Now that you know the basics of building an infrastructure, it's time to put it to use.

••TIP

Always have your Wonder near the town center and a tower. Obviously, serious defenses need to be arrayed nearby, but just being near the town center gives local citizens higher morale — which translates to higher HP — which means they are better at defending it.

| STONE AGE | COPPER AGE | BRONZE AGE | DARK AGE | MIDDLE AGES | RENAISSANCE | IMPERIAL AGE | INDUSTRIAL AGE | ATOMIC AGE |

0 BC   5000 BC   2000 BC   500 BC   0 AD   900 AD   1300 AD   1500 AD   1700 AD   1900 AD

PRIMA'S OFFICIAL STRATEGY GUIDE

EMPIRE EARTH
THE ART OF CONQUEST

～ The Military ～

SCOUTING

The very first thing you need to do is to learn who's out there and what they're up to. Make a canine scout, send it out and keep it moving.

In multiplayer, you always have a canine scout. In campaign scenarios without a scout, send out a unit to figure out what's where. There is nothing to gain and absolutely everything to lose by wandering around unaware of your surroundings.

- Find out what civ you are up against. Each civ has its weaknesses and strengths. They attack with their strengths; you can count on it. Think to the future ... what works well against the troops that your enemy is most likely to have or build?

- Look at the terrain. Is there something that makes your area more defensible? Is there some high ground you can claim? Build walls nearby so that the enemy is funneled into the place where you have the upper hand. Do you have to cross dangerous territory to get where you want to go? Think about what would make your task easier.

- Where is the gold/stone/iron? Can you claim and defend some of the resources that are near your neighbors? Is there nothing to be had, so that you have to survive on what you start with?

ATTACKING

A defense-minded player can win this game, but it's hard to do. Nine times out of ten the game goes to the aggressive, get-in-your-face kind of player. Even if you don't like to play in an aggressive way, you should cultivate it as a skill that can come in handy.

In a campaign scenario, you might not have time to build an army — you may need to work with what you have at the beginning. In either case, unless it is a very unusual scenario, you want to have as many units ready to go as early as possible. The goal is to hurt your opponent as early as possible, as much as possible.

Tactics

Regardless of multiplayer or scenario, good tactics are vital to success.

Note. The difference between strategy and tactics is time. Strategy is long-term: building an army, using resources, going up in epochs. Tactics are short-term: using units to their best advantage in battle.

- Always try to outnumber the enemy. Swarming the other guy with superior numbers may seem a little crude, but it's the time-tested best method of winning a battle.

- Learn the Unit Relationships. (These are described on the in-box poster, or pp. 228 –235.) Know what you're facing, and send the appropriate response. Don't send gun cavalry against gun infantry, for instance. Use sword cavalry or field cannon.

Basics

Take the high ground. If you have the opportunity, you can wall off the lower ground and force the enemy to fight uphill.

Try to flank the enemy (attack from the side as well as the front). Take out their heroes whenever possible.

Don't underestimate a pinpoint strike. Ambush when you can. One good crossbowman can do a surprising amount of damage if placed in an unexpected location.

Try to have a variety of kinds of units — for instance, battleships *and* frigates or sword cavalry *and* gun infantry. Keep them organized by type, and attack according to the best unit relationship.

Whenever possible, try to find a range where your units are effective, but cannot be reached by enemy attacks. If you have a ship that can attack land units from the far side of the map, by all means put it on the far side of the map.

Don't spend your units las if they're disposable. Only bad commanders send their troops to certain death.

Upgrade your military capabilities when you can, and in the manner most likely to hurt your opponent.

Keep your hero near your units. Strategists (healing heroes) should be carefully kept on the side away from the fighting, if possible.

Retreat when you're losing. Go all the way home and heal, if that's what it takes.

Never leave your home base completely undefended. No matter how strong your walls, a siege weapon can always get through and wreak havoc.

Don't lose your focus. Never get distracted by details while the battle's going on.

And, of course,

Practice.

> **⇥ TIP**
>
> In multiplayer, you can expect to need your military up to snuff by the tenth minute of gameplay.

FUTURISTIC COMBAT

Don't forget to use the Capitol Ship's Devastating Beam of Death! It's extremely powerful, plus you can attack ground troops with it (not just buildings).

If you find your planet penned in by enemy spaceships, remember that you can use Planetary Fighters and the Prophet's Meteor Storm to clear away enemy ships.

It's possible to build huge quantities of Robotic Farms because they don't require citizens to work them. Combining this massive supply of food with Just In Time Manufacturing or a Market works really well.

In space combat games, be sure to research Damage Control in the hospital, and Zero G Engineers in the university. This will keep your ships in good repair, even when on the attack.

Teleporters, other than providing a way to conduct small raids, are also good for sending small groups of citizens to establish colonies (possibly on an enemy's home world).

Hades Cybers provide an easy way to get line of sight (LOS) for Missile Bases.

PRIMA'S OFFICIAL STRATEGY GUIDE

EMPIRE
EARTH
THE ART OF CONQUEST

∽∽ Greek Campaign ∽∽

A cold wind blew off the Anatolian mountains. In the foothills below, the young trib-al chief, Hierakles, looked over the remaining members of his fading village. Despite their courage, they appeared ragged, tired. He knew they would not last through another bitter winter if they remained here. But where was there to go?

Thank the gods! The village shaman, Kalkas, had the answer. It was why he had gathered his people here today.

In a recent dream, Kalkas had envisioned a way to traverse the western sea. He believed the Anatolian people could cross the water to a land called Thessaly, and there they would prosper. Now, it was time for Kalkas to share his wisdom. The leg-endary story of the Greek peoples begins here.

THE EARLY HELLADIC PEOPLE

"My people, I have gathered you here to listen to the words of Kalkas, our wise high priest. He has seen, in a vision, a way to lead us to a land where we may prosper."

"My people! We must travel west to a hostile village called Troas. From them we shall steal the secret of traveling upon the deep waters. Lead me to their Dock, and I will convert it for our own use. The time for emigration has come, for we will surely perish if we remain here!"

Legend

- **F** Forage
- **S** Stone
- **D** Dock
- **I** Iron
- **G** Gold
- — Wall

Greek Campaign / The Early Helladic People

Players

Anatolians (you; blue;
Prehistoric ➜ Stone)

Troas (enemy; orange; Stone)

Dorians (a.k.a. Thessaly; annoyance;
green; Copper)

Required Objectives

Gain control of the Troas dock
(by taking Kalkas to it)

Transport Hierakles, Kalkas and
citizens to Thessaly

Build barracks, settlement
(or town center) and temple near
Acropolis in Thessaly

Initial Resources

400 Food   500 Wood   500 Stone

500 Gold   500 Iron

Optional Objectives

Defeat Troas (stops clubmen)

Defeat Dorians (stops horsemen)

Civ Point Opportunities

5	Control Troas dock
5	Destroy two Dorian stables
15	Victory

Tech Opportunities

Dock (war raft, transport raft)
        (Control Troas dock)

Temple   (Build barracks or settlement
at Thessaly; take Kalkas to Acropolis)

Stone Age technology (When you
epoch up)

You Lose If

Hierakles dies

Kalkas dies

You don't have any citizens left and you
can't produce any more

Troas dock is destroyed before you gain
Dock technology

Scenario-Specific Stats

Kalkas

HP	150
Attack	–
Speed	9
Armor	6 (Ar, Pr), 10 (Gn)

Dorian Raiders

HP	240
Attack	17
Speed	16
Armor	6 (Ar)

Walkthrough

When you gather enough resources,
you're able to advance an epoch. By all
means do so. When you attack Troas,
you want to have as many warriors as
you can afford, of course (and enough
citizens to take you all the way up to
your population limit). Also, before you
attack, have enough wood stockpiled to
build your raft as soon as you get control of the dock.

Don't try to raze Troas to the ground —
in particular, don't go after the defensive
towers. That's a huge waste of time and
resources. Instead, just blow through the
town as quickly as possible and go
straight to the dock. Build your raft
immediately and take off for the new
land. (The only advantage to eliminating
the Troas populace is that it stops their
raids on your resources.)

EMPIRE EARTH
THE ART OF CONQUEST

Watch out for patrolling warships just off the dock. You can try to outrun them (which is entirely doable), you can build your own warships to defend your raft(s), or you can get Kalkas to take out the bad guys with a hurricane.

Epoch up as soon as you can — you'll be glad you did.

Once you take the dock at Troas and set sail for Thessaly, jump back to your original settlement, and build six-to-ten new citizens (you probably took more casualties than that crossing Troas). Put these homeboys to work hunting and chopping wood for your new settlement. Don't worry how the resources get across the ocean; it's enough to know you can use them.

You want to land on the new island with at least three or four warriors (not counting Kalkas and Hierakles) and at least five citizens. You'll have to deal with some hostile locals, but they shouldn't be a big problem if you have a few fighting men (spearmen are favored against the Dorians). If you choose not to take out their stables right away, don't dally with your urban construction — every few minutes they send a few more horsemen to harass you. Your own five locals are enough to turn your first settlement into a town center so you can build new citizens at the new town. If you don't have five citizens left by the time you're ready to build your new city, you might be able to get a second wave of colonists across from the old country, or you might just want to revert to a save and try again.

Once you get your barracks and settlement up you may want to hold off a bit on building the temple, and instead go hunting the Dorians. You get a few extra civ points if you wipe them out.

———— ∾ ————

"The future of our new village is secure! Let us tame this land and call it our own!"

WARRIORS FROM THE SEA

While the people of Thessaly prospered, another warrior race was fleeing towards the coast of Crete.

King Pelops and his three sons sailed northward in their swift galleys. Having been driven from Egypt, they hoped to find a land more ripe for conquest, somewhere across the Mediterranean.

The first island they had encountered was Crete, but it was already under the control of the advanced Minoans. They were forced to flee again, and the Minoan fleet had not yet given up their pursuit.

Legend
- **F** Forage
- **S** Stone
- **D** Dock
- **I** Iron
- **G** Gold
- — Wall

Pelops and his sons now needed to locate a haven somewhere in Crete where they could remain undetected long enough to regain their strength. Then they would be ready to press further north, and continue their search for a new home. The prosperous people of Thessaly are about to have company.

Greek Campaign / Warriors From the Sea

Players

Danaans (you; blue; Stone ➔ Copper)

Minoa (enemy; pink; Copper)

Achaia (enemy; yellow; Copper)

Messenia (enemy; red; Stone)

Initial Resources

500 Food   1000 Wood   100 Stone

500 Gold   1000 Iron

Required Objectives

Build capitol and dock on Crete

Take Pelops to Argos (Peloponnesia)

Destroy two (out of three) enemy town centers

Build capitol in Argos

Optional Objective

Destroy third town center

Civ Point Opportunities

5 x 3   Destroy enemy town center (can be won for each TC)

5   Build capitol in Argos

5   Victory (Argos capitol built and town centers destroyed)

Resource Opportunities

100 Wood   When you build town center on Peloponnesia, if you have less than 100 Wood

Tech Opportunities

Copper Age technology (When you epoch up)

You Lose If

Pelops dies

All three of Pelops' sons die

You no longer have enough wood and people to expand

Scenario-Specific Stats

Pelops		Pelops' Sons	
HP	1180	HP	865
Attack	17	Attack	15
Speed	16	Speed	12
Armor	1 (Ar), 4 (Pr)	Armor	6 (Ar)

PRIMA'S OFFICIAL STRATEGY GUIDE

Walkthrough

There are two ways to go at the start of the game. You can dig in on Crete and try to build the best army and navy possible before making the crossing, or you can get off quick — build a transport or two and a couple warships, then use the warships to engage the Minoan navy (your warships are toast, but all you need is a diversion while the transports squeak through to the new world). Once you're on the new island, Pelops and his sons should be enough to defend your citizens while you get your city established.

If you do decide to build up on Crete before moving, work fast ... you have one hour (real time) before the game sends the main body of the Minoan army down on your sorry butt. Even if you take them out, they keep sending more, every few minutes. Oh, and did we mention the earthquakes and volcanoes? Someone *really* wants you off of Crete, someone important.

If you don't camp out on Crete, the invasion happens as soon as Pelops lands on Greece, so the moral here is don't leave anything behind on Crete if you think you might need it later.

Whether it happens on Crete or on the mainland, you definitely want to Epoch up as soon as possible. Hunting is very limited around your new home. There's some good fishing grounds just south of your city, but the fish will run out too if that's all you have. Bottom line, you really need a granary (plus all the other nifty new stuff you get for graduating from the Stone Age).

Once you've got your basic city infrastructure up and running, build as many troops as you can (which won't be many, because your resources are limited) and go take the nearest village. You may lose a couple sons in this fight, particularly if you didn't bring an army over with you from Crete. That's OK, you have more. (You may want to leave Pelops and a couple of sons behind when your army goes on campaign — they can guard the home front and you don't risk hosing your victory conditions if a battle goes sour). Taking this first village will give you access to the resources you've been missing, allowing you to build your army up to full strength.

The big secret of this scenario is to take the nearest village and the furthest. Leave the one in the middle alone, because it's a bear. (Although if you do take the time and energy to destroy all three town centers, you get extra civ points.)

If you hold off on building your new capitol to destroy the third village, make sure your capitol on Crete survives. Otherwise, you'll get a free capitol on the mainland before you want it.

The citadel at Argos is complete. In the coming centuries, the power of Pelops' people will grow and extend across the entire land. The first great Age of the Greeks has begun.

COPPER AGE	DARK AGE	RENAISSANCE	INDUSTRIAL AGE	INFORMATION
BC 2000 BC 500 BC	0AD 900 AD 1300 AD	1500 AD 1700 AD	1900 AD 2000 AD
BRONZE AGE	MIDDLE AGES	IMPERIAL AGE	ATOMIC AGE

Greek Campaign / The Trojan War

THE TROJAN WAR

"My lord Agamemnon, you must kill the sacrificial goat in the sacred pit, marked by the stones. Only then can I determine what the gods demand of you ..."

"I cannot be bothered with such menial tasks. Have one of my nobles do the bloody deed."

"Aahhh ... yes ... I have interpreted the signs from the offering, Sire, and the will of the gods is clear. You must travel to Sparta, Achaia, and Ithaca.

"In each city, the ruling king will ask for a specific favor. When you accept, each will then agree to join you in a war against Troy. They can provide ships and men, and each king must accompany you on this quest."

Legend

- **F** Forage
- **S** Stone
- **D** Dock
- **I** Iron
- **G** Gold
- — Wall

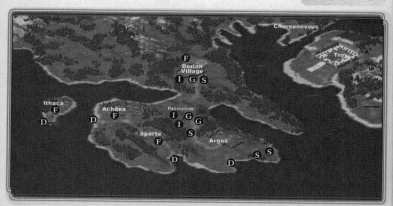

Players

Argos (you; blue; Copper)

Sparta (ally; red; Copper)

Achaia (ally; yellow; Copper)

Ithaca (ally; pink; Copper)

Troy (enemy; orange; Bronze)

Dorians (annoyance; green; Copper →
Bronze)

Initial Resources

1000 Food   1000 Wood   1000 Stone

500 Gold   500 Iron

Required Objectives

Make a deal to ally with
Menelaus/Sparta, Achilles/Achaia and
Odysseus/Ithaca

Attack Troy

Build temple to Athena in
Chersonessus

Pray to Athena for assistance

Kill Priam

Destroy Trojan palace

Optional Objectives

Avoid killing deer at Chersonessus
(to avoid calamities)

STONE AGE		COPPER AGE		DARK AGE		RENAISSANCE		INDUSTRIAL AGE	

0 BC   5000 BC   2000 BC   500 BC   0 AD   900 AD   1800 AD   1500 AD   1700 AD   1900 AD

STONE AGE   BRONZE AGE   MIDDLE AGES   IMPERIAL AGE   ATOMIC A

EMPIRE EARTH
THE ART OF CONQUEST

PRIMA'S OFFICIAL STRATEGY GUIDE

Civ Point Opportunities

5	Ally with all three kings
5	Destroy Dorian village
5	Build Chersonessus temple
10	Victory

You Lose If

Agamemnon dies

Achilles dies

Menelaus dies

Odysseus dies

Trojan Horse is destroyed before entering Troy

Any Trojan temples are destroyed

Scenario-Specific Stats

Menelaus

HP	1400
Attack	41
Speed	16
Armor	2 (Sh, Pr)

Morale

Achilles

HP	2300
Attack	52
Speed	12
Armor	3 (Sh, Pr)

Morale

Priam

HP	1575
Attack	16
Speed	16
Armor	4 (Sh, Pr)

Heal

Battle Cry

Trojan Walls

HP	15,500
LOS	1

Agamemnon

HP	1735
Attack	14
Speed	16
Armor	3 (Sh, Pr)

Heal

Battle Cry

Odysseus

HP	1325
Attack	52
Speed	12
Armor	3 (Sh, Pr)

Heal

Battle Cry

Greek Elite Troops

HP	215
Attack	15
Speed	12
Armor	6 (Ar)

Walkthrough

This scenario represents a major step forward in both complexity and difficulty for the campaign.

First, you have to collect your allies. Go west to Sparta first to meet Menelaus, then north to Achaia. Achilles will give you a transport to cross the channel to Ithaca and recruit Odysseus.

You now have a solid core of elite warriors, but do not try to attack Troy directly with this force! First, you need resources, which can be found northwest of your capitol. Unfortunately, they're guarded by a walled city full of tough Dorian barbarians.

You need to get the Dorians out of the picture before you move on to Troy. Destroying their city is a tough fight, and you'll probably lose some elite warriors in the process, but you get extra civ points for it. Another option is to build a wall between the Dorians and the resource patch. Your call.

The next phase of the war is the naval campaign. Move your warships north towards Troy, taking out all the Trojan opposition. If you keep you ships tightly grouped and concentrate your fire when you find enemy forces, you should be able to clear the route to Troy without having to build any more ships. The Trojans don't have a working dock, so once the Trojan navy is gone, it's gone for good.

Make sure your invasion force includes at least five citizens. Once you hit the beach at Troy, build yourself a serious camp: town center, barracks, archery range and stable, plus a hospital and at least a couple towers. You might want a temple too.

Now you better clear the outskirts of the city. (Technically speaking, you can

Greek Campaign / The Rise of Athens

ignore them, or at least try to. Don't depend on them ignoring you in return, though.) There are two fully-garrisoned fortresses outside the city gates. Those are your primary objectives. Try to lose as few elite warriors as possible during this phase of the battle — you may want to keep them in the transports unless there's a real emergency. Send as large a conventional force as you can muster against a fortress, lure some Trojans out and try to pull them back to your towers and hospital, then rebuild your forces and attack again. Lather, rinse, repeat. Eventually, you'll want to send in an attack force to pull off the remaining Trojan defenders, then send in a brute squad of sampsons to pound on the fortress itself. Eventually, they'll go down.

When your army makes it to the actual gates of Troy, it doesn't take long for Odysseus to realize that the walls are too strong to fall to conventional siege tactics. (The Trojans can repair their walls just as fast as you hammer on them.) Divine intervention is called for.

Send some citizens (on transports, with a warship escort) north to the sacred grove at Chersonessus. (Hopefully you cleaned out the northern waters during the naval campaign ....) The only tricky thing here is, do not kill any of the deer in the grove. They're sacred to Athena,

and if you kill one she'll definitely ruin your whole day (not to mention that she's the one you need help from, in the first place ...). Just have your citizens build a temple and the Trojan Horse will magically appear on the beach by Troy.

Hopefully you know the rest of the drill. Load your kings and best warriors into the horse (don't hold back the elite warriors — this is the moment you've been saving them for). Move the horse to the gates of the city. The Trojans, of course, being chumps, fall for it.

Inside the city, let your troops out and kill King Priam, who's hanging around outside the palace. Move the horse over next to the gates and they'll open. Bring the rest of your army in (you might not even have to do this ... your horse crew may be plenty). Destroy the palace, but remember your promise to Odysseus not to destroy any of the temples.

After you win, Helen explains that the gods made her do it and Menelaus, amazingly, buys it. They sail off together back home.

———————— ⌁ ————————

Troy has fallen! King Priam is dead! Agamemnon has honorably kept the promises he made to his fellow kings.

The tale of the Trojan War shall not soon be forgotten.

THE RISE OF ATHENS

The Sons of Pelops were long gone. But north of Argos, on the Saronic Gulf, their descendants continued to rule in the city of Athens. Though at first little more than a sleepy village, Athens was poised to take control of the entire Attic Region.

No one believed in that vision of Athens more strongly than her king, Theseus.

Theseus has assembled the leaders of Athens at the Hill of Ares. Here, he will share his plan for expanding the city ... one that he hopes will secure forever the future of Athens.

The legendary Greek city-state is about to emerge.

Legend

F	Forage
S	Stone
D	Dock
I	Iron
G	Gold
—	Wall

STONE AGE	COPPER AGE		DARK AGE		RENAISSANCE		INDUSTRIAL AGE	
	BRONZE AGE		MIDDLE AGES		IMPERIAL AGE		ATOMIC AC	

| 0 BC | 5000 BC | 2000 BC | 500 BC | 0 AD | 900 AD | 1300 AD | 1500 AD | 1700 AD | 1900 AD |

EMPIRE EARTH
THE ART OF CONQUEST

PRIMA'S OFFICIAL STRATEGY GUIDE

Players

All – Copper Age

Athens (you; blue)

Aphidna (town; enemy turned ally; orange)

Eleusis (town; enemy turned ally; green)

Pallene (town; enemy turned ally; purple)

Sparta (invaders; red)

Thebes (invaders; yellow)

Initial Resources

500 Food	800 Wood	150 Stone
400 Gold	200 Iron	

Resource Opportunities

500 Gold, 500 Iron   From each defeated town

Required Objectives

Defeat Aphidna's defenses, and ally with it

Defeat Eleusis's defenses, and ally with it

Defeat Pallene's defenses, and ally with it

Defeat invading Spartans (up to 5 can survive if they're hidden)

Defeat invading Thebans (up to 5 can survive if they're hidden)

Civ Point Opportunities

10	Ally with all three defeated towns
15	Victory (defeat Spartans and Thebans)

Tech Opportunities

Aphidna gets javelin, macemen and priests when it declares allegiance to you.

Eleusis gets javelin and spearmen when it declares allegiance to you.

Pallene gets spearmen and macemen when it declares allegiance to you.

You Lose If

Temple of Athena destroyed

You have only one noble left before you ally with all three towns

Theseus dies before all three towns declare allegiance

Any town center destroyed before becoming an ally

Greek Campaign / The Rise of Athens

Scenario-Specific Stats

Theseus

HP	1800
Attack	52
Speed	12
Armor	3 (Sh, Pr)
Morale	

Athenian Noble

HP	845
Attack	15
Speed	12
Armor	6 (Ar)

Temple of Athena

HP	5000
LOS	3

Sparta, Thebes Towers

HP	4350
Attack	204
LOS	8
Range	4

Walkthrough

Conquering a town means eliminating all its military units, or reducing it to under five total units (military and civilian). Try for the military kill — it leaves more citizens to rebuild the town and support your later needs. Take Aphidna first. It's the easiest, and taking it will give you access to important resources.

Ideally, you want to take out the enemy's army without destroying any of their buildings. That allows them to rebuild faster, making them stronger allies in the end game. You can set a flare to tell your current allies to come fight for you against another city, but be careful with this tactic — your allies tend to be enthusiastic, and you have no direct control over their actions. They can annihilate the foe when you'd really prefer to make friends. (Don't forget, if an enemy town center is destroyed, you lose.) In general, it's better to take your time, build up your forces and don't send a boy to do a man's job.

Remember to keep at least two Athenian nobles alive through all this. (You're limited to the nobles you begin with — you can't create any more.) You must have a couple of nobles to accompany Theseus on his goodwill visits after each town conquest.

When all three cities have gone down, Theseus will return to Athens and the gods will come down and give him an on-the-spot promotion to divinity. This is supposed to mark the transition from mythical to historical Greece (in other words, don't expect the gods to keep sticking their noses in your business from this point forward).

Once Theseus is gone, Sparta and Thebes will both invade. Make sure you're well prepared for the siege. Your allies will come to help you fight, but you can hurry them along with a flare. One good tactic is to let your allies take the brunt of the attack outside the walls, while you pack the city with archers firing over the walls. Prophets can also come in very handy during the siege. Important note — any enemy soldiers who breach your walls head *immediately* for the Temple of Athena and start banging on it. They know as well as you that you've lost if you allow the temple to be leveled.

Once the armies of both Sparta and Thebes are destroyed, you win. Again, you don't have to take them all out, as long as the remaining units are wisely hiding from you.

The Spartan and Theban armies have been annihilated! The power of Athens has been established once and for all on the Greek peninsula. From this day forward, greatness — and greater enemies — assuredly await.

EMPIRE EARTH
THE ART OF CONQUEST

PRIMA'S OFFICIAL STRATEGY GUIDE

THE PELOPONNESIAN WAR

Pericles narrowed his eyes in the glare of the afternoon sun, taking note of the hard-set jaw of the Spartan King who faced him.

The survival of Athens depended on bringing in food from the west. But negotiations with Sparta regarding land routes had failed, and war was now inevitable.

The Athenian army could never hope to beat the Spartans in the open field, and so it was that Pericles gave the order to bring the citizens residing north of Athens safely within the city walls. There they would hold out against the impending siege for as long as was necessary.

And, somehow, Pericles swore he would find a way to lead Athens to victory.

Legend

F Forage
S Stone
D Dock
I Iron
G Gold
— Wall

Players

All – Bronze Age
Athens (you; blue)
Sparta (enemy; red)
Taras (potential ally; pink)
Rhegium (potential ally; green)
Segesta (potential ally; orange)
Corinth (neutral; yellow)

Initial Resources

(you actually receive these after Pericles goes to the Parthenon)

1000 Food   2000 Wood   1000 Stone
1500 Gold   1500 Iron

Required Objectives

Bring countryside citizens into Athens (at least 9)

Take Pericles to Parthenon

Ally with Taras (send diplomatic ship)

Ally with Rhegium (send diplomatic ship)

Ally with Segesta (send diplomatic ship)

Defeat Sparta

Optional Objectives

After receiving grain, keep at least 10,000 food in Athens (to avoid further plague)

Civ Point Opportunities

5   Import 15,000 food (all 6 shiploads of grain)

5   Repulse attack on your new ally, Segesta

15   Defeat Sparta in final battle

Greek Campaign / The Peloponnesian War

Resource Opportunities

400 Gold, 400 Iron	Alliance with Taras
7500 Food	Alliance with Taras*
400 Gold, Iron	Alliance with Rhegium
7500 Food	Alliance with Rhegium*

* 2500 on each of 3 frigates; each frigate must arrive safely for you to claim its food

Tech Opportunities

Diplomat	Pericles arrives at Parthenon
Citizens	10,000 food in Athens
Bronze Transport	10,000 food in Athens

You Lose If

You fail to get at least 9 citizens into Athens

You fail to get at least 10,000 food (4 shiploads from your new allies) into Athens

Pericles dies before he gets to the Parthenon

Scenario-Specific Stats

Pericles

HP	1960
Attack	14
Speed	16
Armor	3 (Sh, Pr)
Heal	
Battle Cry	

The Parthenon

| HP | 1000 |
| LOS | 3 |

Athens Walls

| HP | 7750 |
| LOS | 11 |

Sparta Buildings

All have double HP

Diplomatic Ship

HP	1200
Attack	1
Speed	15
LOS	4
Range	0.5

Grain Shipment

HP	1000
Attack	1
Speed	14
LOS	4
Range	0.5

Walkthrough

To start out you're told to move your citizens into town to ride out a siege by Sparta. Do it. Don't dink around, just grab everybody, military or civilian, and move them in. Note that even inside town your citizens can still gather wood and stone, so keep them working. The wood will come in very handy later.

When Pericles gets to the Parthenon, he orders diplomatic envoys sent to Taras and Rhegium. Create three diplomats and hold the third in reserve. Send the diplomats to the docks and they'll be given their own ships (non-attacking, but fast with high hit points). Build up as many warships as you can afford to protect the diplomats. (A diplomat is replaced by a diplomat ship at your dock; each diplomat ship is replaced by three grain shipments.)

Using your warships to provide a diversion, run your diplomats through the Spartan fleet to Taras and Rhegium. Shortly after your diplomats leave, a plague will start in Athens due to the lack of food reserves. You can minimize the damage by running sick citizens to the hospital, but the best thing to do is just get the food relief back to town as quickly as possible.

EMPIRE EARTH
THE ART OF CONQUEST

PRIMA'S OFFICIAL STRATEGY GUIDE

When you ally with each town you'll get more resources (which can be used to build more warships) and each town will give you three transports loaded with grain, which you have to successfully navigate back home. You have to get at least four of the transports home or you lose the game. If you get all six through, you get extra civ points.

You can use the docks at any allied city to repair your ships. You can also build the Temple of Zeus, which will heal all your units, including ships. This means you have fewer resources for warships, but might be worth it anyway.

At this point you're told that Segesta wants to ally with you as well. Send your third diplomat on to Segesta. (If you want, you can send your third diplomat to Segesta ahead of their call; if he's at the Segesta dock when they request him, the alliance takes place immediately.) Once you're there you'll get access to gold and iron, but make sure you station a garrison at Segesta as soon as possible, because a medium-sized Spartan attack is coming (about six to eight minutes after you make the alliance). If you can lure the invaders to the shoreline, you can get useful artillery support from your navy. You get Civ Points if you successfully defend Segesta.

Now it's time to build up your ground forces for the final battle with Sparta. You'll face the Spartan army at Corinth. Build as large and powerful a force as you can muster, and don't forget to bring Pericles along, so he can heal your forces between assaults. When the Spartan army is defeated, you win.

***

The Spartans have been vanquished! Athens, through expert leadership, has ensured her freedom.

YOUNG ALEXANDER

"Ignorance and superstition," Aristotle once grumbled as he rooted among the wild herbs growing near the coast in Mytilene, "They're like twin idiots running rampant through the land ..."

After her eventual loss to Sparta in the Peloponnesian Wars, the city of Athens lost faith in herself. And, in the rising tide of fear and mysticism that followed, the old philosopher-scientist had chosen to head for higher ground. Here in Mytilene, Aristotle had commenced his studies in natural science, observing and recording the myriad characteristics of the flora and fauna.

But a new storm of militarism was about to sweep across the land. A young prince named Alexander was next in line to rule the Kingdom of Macedon. And a certain philosopher-scientist would soon be appointed to tutor the up-and-coming general in the ways of power.

Legend

- **F** Forage
- **S** Stone
- **D** Dock
- **I** Iron
- **G** Gold
- — Wall

Greek Campaign / Young Alexander

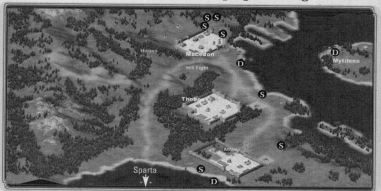

Players

Macedon (you; light blue; Bronze)

Athens (enemy; potential ally; blue; Bronze)

Thebes (enemy; potential ally; yellow; Bronze)

Sparta (enemy; red; Bronze)

Mytilene (neutral; orange; Bronze)

Hill Tribes (enemy assassins; purple; Copper)

Initial Resources

500 Food   500 Wood   250 Stone
500 Gold   250 Iron

Required Objectives

Kill assassins

Alexander is trained and becomes known as King Alexander

Defeat and ally with Athens

Defeat and ally with Thebes

Defeat Spartan invaders

Optional Objectives

Aristotle discovers interesting herbs in Mytilene (which can trigger calamities)

Civ Point Opportunities

5	Aristotle discovers interesting herbs in Mytilene
5	Defeat and ally with Athens
5	Defeat and ally with Thebes
10	Defeat Spartan invaders

Resource Opportunities

500 of each	When King Alexander appears
300 Iron, 500 Gold	Defeat and ally with Athens
300 Iron, 500 Gold	Defeat and ally with Thebes

Tech Opportunities

Earthquake	From Aristotle's herbs
Firestorm	From Aristotle's herbs
Malaria	From Aristotle's herbs
Volcano	From Aristotle's herbs
Canine Scout	When King Alexander appears
Citizens	When King Alexander appears
Byzantine Transport	When King Alexander appears

EMPIRE EARTH
THE ART OF CONQUEST

You Lose If

Alexander or Aristotle gets too close to Thebes too soon (triggering an attack that kills Aristotle)

Alexander dies

Aristotle dies before training Alexander

Macedonian palace destroyed

Scenario-Specific Stats

Aristotle

HP	150
Attack	Calamities
Speed	9
Armor	6 (Ar, Pr), 10 (Gn)

Young Alexander

HP	545
Attack	15
Speed	12
Armor	6 (Ar)

Macedonian Palace

HP	1000
LOS	3

Philip of Macedon

HP	1800
Attack	46
Speed	16
Armor	3 (Sh, Pr)

King Alexander

HP	1960
Attack	14
Speed	16
Armor	3 (Sh, Pr)
Heal	
Battle Cry	

Macedonian Palace

HP	1000
LOS	3

Assassins

HP	130
Attack	11
Speed	11
Armor	4 (Sh)

Walkthrough

The last three scenarios of this campaign form a trilogy on the life of Alexander the Great.

You start out by hooking up Alexander and Aristotle. Nearby, Alexander's dad, Philip, is fighting off some hill tribes. Go to the hill with Aristotle and watch, but don't try to take any action. After the fight Aristotle wants to go hunting for wild horses. When you get to the horses they'll take off on their own to your stable.

While you're on your way back to town, Alexander's father is murdered near the stable by assassins. Alexander has to go and engage the murderers, after which Philip's guard pours out of the city to help finish off the rest.

When Alexander goes into the town center, he vanishes. Click on the capitol and press the hero button to finish Alexander's preparation for rulership.

While Alexander is cooking, Aristotle has a bright idea. He remembers some flowers he saw in Mytilene, and thinks he knows a way to use them to spread disease against the enemy. Put him on the transport to Mytilene, walk him out to the flowers and bring him back.

Greek Campaign / A Conqueror is Born

There are some hurricanes waiting out in the open sea, but they shouldn't be a problem if you steer the transport carefully. When Aristotle gets back, he has a prophet's power to cast calamities on the enemy (not just plague, but some others, too).

Once Alexander's ready to take charge, build up your forces as much as you can afford (concentrating on Alexander's new Companion Horse unit) and march south to Thebes and Athens. Don't forget to use Alexander's battle cry and Aristotle's new tricks against the enemy. Each city will surrender when you defeat its army, and you'll get some additional resources, which you can use to rebuild your forces.

As soon as Athens goes down you'll get the word that Sparta is attacking Macedon. Hustle your forces back home, and start building new troops with the resources you got from Athens. The Spartans will attack from the forest south of Macedon. (If you have towers guarding the clearing between the forest and the city, you'll really appreciate them about now.) Have your forces hug the wall and just work your way around the city, killing Spartans as you go. The only time you should let your back get away from the wall is when you sortie to attack the Spartan's siege engines.

The Spartans will attack in two waves, so make sure you have something left for the second assault. You might want to save Aristotle's powers so he can disrupt the Spartans as they attack, and don't forget to deploy those replacement troops you started building when Athens surrendered. When the second wave of Spartans is dead, you win.

Sparta, Athens, and Thebes have all been defeated by Alexander's armies. Greece is now united under strong Macedonian rule — and greater conquests lie ahead. Soon, all the world will know the name "Alexander the Great!"

A CONQUEROR IS BORN

The great warhorse flinched and shied beneath her rider, as if aware of the danger presented by the enemy troops across the river. Alexander soothed her with a firm hand and quiet voice. Beside him rode Parmenion, his most trusted general.

They had crossed the Hellespont with their army, along with the seasoned Greek generals Craterus and Meleager. The Emperor Darius III had mounted his defense on the far bank of the River Granicus, where his own generals waited, confident in their ability to smash the Greek upstarts.

The battle would soon be joined … King against Emperor, general against general. At stake, nothing less than control of the Persian Empire!

Legend

- **F** Forage
- **S** Stone
- **D** Dock
- **I** Iron
- **G** Gold
- — Wall

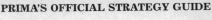

EMPIRE EARTH
THE ART OF CONQUEST

Players

Macedon (you; light blue; Bronze)
Persia (enemy; yellow; Bronze)
Tyre (enemy; orange; Bronze)
Antioch (potential ally; blue; Bronze)
Issus (innocent bystander; red; Copper)

Initial Resources

1500 Food 1500 Wood 500 Stone
1200 Gold 600 Iron

Required Objectives

Defeat Persians at Granicus
Defeat Persians at Issus
Destroy Tyre's capitol

Optional Objectives

Occupy Antioch and acquire its benefits
Destroy ships protecting Tyre

Civ Point Opportunities

5   Defeat the first half of the
    Persian army (Granicus)
5   Defeat the second half of the
    Persian army (Issus)
15 Destroy Tyre's capitol

Resource Opportunities

2000 Gold   If any Hero visits Antioch

Tech Opportunities

Hospital	If any unit visits Antioch
Catapult Ships	If any Hero visits Antioch

You Lose If

Alexander dies	Philotas dies
Craterus dies	

Greek Campaign / A Conqueror is Born

Scenario-Specific Stats

Alexander the Great

HP	1960
Attack	14
Speed	16
Armor	3 (Sh, Pr)
Heal	
Battle Cry	

Craterus

HP	2100
Attack	52
Speed	12
Armor	3 (Sh, Pr)
Morale	

Philotas

HP	1750
Attack	41
Speed	16
Armor	2 (Sh, Pr)
Morale	

Meleager

HP	915
Attack	16
Speed	14
Armor	2 (Sh, Pr), 4 (Ar)

Memnon (Persian General)

HP	900
Attack	12
Speed	16
Armor	2 (Sh, Pr)
Heal	
Battle Cry	

Arsames (Persian General)

HP	2775
Attack	75
Speed	12
Armor	5 (Sh, Pr)
Morale	

Catapult Ship

HP	765
Attack	85
Speed	10
LOS	6
Range	9
Armor	–

Catapult

HP	160
Attack	85
Speed	8
LOS	8
Range	5
Armor	8 (Ar), 6 (Pr), 4 (Ms)

Walkthrough

This scenario breaks down into two very different sections. The first offers a short course in staying on the offensive despite limited resources.

You start out with a large force, but the Persian army across the river is even larger. You have to win while limiting your losses. Attack from the north, and try to engage the Persians one unit at a time. Fortunately, you only have to destroy half of their forces before they lose their nerve and run.

However, you don't get any replacements between this battle and the next one, at Issus. The only break you get between the fight is access to the hospital at Antioch, which allows you to heal up your heroes. Once again, send your cavalry across the river a few at a time, and try to pull the enemy to your force in small groups. Try to kill the enemy heroes as quickly as possible.

Once the Persian army is eliminated, you hook up with Meleager at Tyre, where he's waiting with a few reinforcements. At this point, the scenario shifts into a naval engagement. You get access to the shipyards at Antioch (just send one of your heroes up to Antioch to accept their surrender), and can start building ships to attack Tyre. Don't try to take Tyre from the front; you definitely want to use your navy — at this point ships are a renewable resource, and ground troops aren't.

Build the Pharos Lighthouse. You'll find the intelligence it provides about Tyre's navy and defenses invaluable. Then just keep building ships as fast as you can. Once you've cleared out the waters all around Tyre, move a couple of catapult ships into range and start taking down the defensive towers that ring the city.

EMPIRE EARTH
THE ART OF CONQUEST

Catapult ships have better range than the towers, but it can be a bit tricky positioning them just right. A good way to set a target for a catapult ship is to send a frigate in ahead to act as a forward observer (the frigate will take substantial damage, probably, but you can always build more). Once the frigate spots the target, set the catapult ships on it and retreat the frigate. This will insure that the catapult ships only attack from their maximum effective range.

The key word for this phase of the game is patience. Just keep building ships and keep destroying defenses. Eventually you'll be able to either destroy the two ports of Tyre, or Tyre will run out of resources to build new ships. Beware of

a desperate Tyrean attack against your ground forces as the battle progresses.

Once all the outer defenses of the city are down, move your ground forces into place, knock down the city gates and move in. You should be able to handle whatever's left inside, particularly if you continue to use your navy to support your troops with offshore bombardment. Once the Tyrean capitol goes down, you win.

The spirit of the Tyrean people has been broken! The island city is prepared to surrender, and the entire Palestinian coast will come under Macedonian control. Where will Alexander's hunger for conquest take him next?

AND ALEXANDER WEPT

The cities of Tyre and Gaza have been captured. The Kingdom of Egypt has surrendered without a fight. And when Alexander made a pilgrimage to the Shrine of Ammon in the Western Desert, the high priests there hailed him as a living God-King — Son of Ra — anointing him the new Pharaoh of All Egypt.

But Persia remains a thorn in your side. Persian forces, reformed and still led by Emperor Darius, are threatening to renew their hostilities. They must be dealt with once and for all.

As if the Persians weren't enough, ugly rumors of an assassination plot have reached Alexander's ears. Though uneasy, he knows he must press forward — for there is no other direction he would even consider to go.

Somewhere in Asia, your destiny awaits.

Legend

- **F** Forage
- **S** Stone
- **D** Dock
- **I** Iron
- **G** Gold
- — Wall

Greek Campaign / And Alexander Wept

Players

Macedon (you; light blue; Bronze)

Gaza (ally; blue; Copper)

Imperial Persian Army (enemy; yellow; Bronze)

Persepolis (Persian capital defense; red; Bronze)

Gaugemela (Persian army; pink; Copper)

Babylon (potential enemy; green; Bronze)

Hill tribe (potential enemy; orange; Copper)

Oasis tribe (a.k.a. Bedouins; potential enemy; white; Stone)

Initial Resources

2000 Food   1000 Wood 1000 Stone

700 Gold   300 Iron

Required Objectives

Defeat Persians at Gaugemela

Defeat Persians at Persepolis

Defeat assassins

Optional Objectives

Destroy all buildings in Hill tribal village

Conquer Hill tribal village (destroy town center)

Destroy all buildings in Oasis tribal village

Conquer Oasis tribal village (destroy town center)

Conquer Babylon

Civ Point Opportunities

10   Kill both Darius and Bessus at Gaugemela

15   Conquer Hill tribal village and build your own town center

15   Conquer Oasis tribal village and build your own town center

10   Alexander enters Babylon

Resource Opportunities

300 Gold, 300 Iron	Destroy Hill tribal village
300 Gold, 300 Iron	Destroy Oasis tribal village
750 Gold, 750 Iron	Alexander enters Babylon

You Lose If

Alexander dies   Philotas dies in battle

Craterus dies

Scenario-Specific Stats

Alexander the Great

HP	2160
Attack	14
Speed	16
Armor	3 (Sh, Pr)

Heal, Battle Cry

Craterus

HP	2200
Attack	52
Speed	12
Armor	3 (Sh, Pr)
Morale	

Philotas

HP	1850
Attack	41
Speed	16
Armor	2 (Sh, Pr)
Morale	

Darius (Persian King)

HP	900
Attack	12
Speed	16
Armor	2 (Sh, Pr)

Heal, Battle Cry

Bessus (Persian General)

HP	1800
Attack	46
Speed	16
Armor	3 (Sh, Pr)
Morale	

Persian Assassins

HP	290
Attack	23
Speed	16
Armor	5 (Sh), 2 (Pr)

EMPIRE EARTH
THE ART OF CONQUEST

Walkthrough

You have a large army but limited resources. This is the final scenario, and the action is entirely military, so spend all your Civ Points on land forces upgrades.

Take off due east from Gaza. Along the way, you'll find two enemy towns, one at an oasis and one in the hills. In each, you're offered the choice of destroying the town (resources) or just destroying the town center and building one of your own to conquer the town (Civ Points). Given where we are in the campaign, we recommend the resources, but your call.

Although it's not required for victory, you want to capture Babylon. This will give you a whole pile of resources.

You'll engage the Persians near a river crossing, a natural choke point that you can use to your advantage. Station your infantry at the crossing with your archers behind. Run your cavalry across to pick up a few of the enemy and have them chase you back to the trap you've set. Do this a few times and you should have the field. Once again, the Persians will run when you've reduced their forces by half. You can chase them if you want, but there really isn't much point. Better to wait and regroup.

From this point you'll need siege engines — we hope you saved up for them. A couple catapults are particularly handy. The Persians have fortified the approach to their capitol, Persepolis. At the fortifications, you'll have to face the rest of the Persian army, including the king, Darius, and his foremost general, Bessus. You

should be able to kill at least Darius here, and possibly both. Once you've broken the Persian army again, knock down the gate and begin the advance down the canyon that leads to Persepolis.

Although you've killed their leaders, there's still plenty of Persians hoping to make your approach to Persepolis an unpleasant trip. Your siege engines will help you deal with massed enemies, but keep your siege engines safe at all costs. Take out the towers at the city gate and defeat the rest of the army; you don't have to destroy the gate itself.

Alexander now has to enter Persepolis to make a symbolic visit to the tomb of Xerxes. Take a few troops with you, because at the tomb you'll be attacked by a few assassins. Dispose of them and you win, the campaign is over and Alexander the Great has conquered the known world.

———— ⌘ ————

The assassins are dead and the Tomb of Xerxes has been captured. Alexander's triumph in Western Asia now is complete, though darkened by one realization: Philotas, the commander of the Companion Cavalry, was part of the conspiracy. This once-trusted friend must now be put to death. History claims Alexander wept when he had no more lands to conquer. But perhaps, as he stood alone at the height of his power, there was another reason behind the tears.

PPER AGE	DARK AGE		RENAISSANCE	INDUSTRIAL AGE	INFORMATION A
2000 BC	500 BC	0AD	900 AD	1500 AD	1500 AD	1700 AD	1900 AD	2000 AD	21
BRONZE AGE		MIDDLE AGES		IMPERIAL AGE		ATOMIC AGE		N.

English Campaign / The Return of Young William

∼∽ English Campaign ∼∽

For hundreds of years, beginning in the 11th century AD, England and France battled for land, honor and eminence in Europe and around the world. Conflicts ranged from minor infantry skirmishes to all out war, but even a decisive victory seldom stopped the fighting for long. Take control of England and command her forces in one of the greatest international rivalries in history.

THE RETURN OF YOUNG WILLIAM: 1040

William stared through the thick of the trees, squinting his eyes in the early morning light to detect the enemies he knew were nearby. Motioning for his small band of men to follow, he slipped silently through the trees, moving forward, always listening, always watching.

Torn from his rightful place as heir to the Dukedom of Normandy, William had been forced to remain in secret for years, outcast and rejected. But now the time had come to return, to make his presence known throughout all of Normandy. William was ready to seek revenge for the injustice done to him by Lord Toustain, Governor of Falaise. He would have Normandy ... and perhaps even more.

Legend

- **F** Forage
- **S** Stone
- **D** Dock
- **I** Iron
- **G** Gold
- — Wall

EMPIRE EARTH
THE ART OF CONQUEST

Players

All – Middle Ages

William (you; red)

Lord Toustain (enemy; yellow)

Normandy (neutral; blue)

Bandits (enemy; orange)

Siege Workshop (neutral; blue)

Initial Resources

400 Food   300 Wood   400 Gold

200 Iron

Required Objectives

Raise troops by going to two allied towns

Go to Falaise, talk to mayor

Build up resources and buy trebuchet, ballistae, ram

Destroy Toustain's castle

Civ Point Opportunities

5   Save town from bandits

5   Get Falaise

5   Destroy gold mines

10   Destroy Toustain's castle

Tech Opportunities

Crossbow – range 3 (Given by first town)

Siege Weapons   (Purchased from
                 Siege Factory)

You Lose If

William dies

Scenario-Specific Stats

William

HP   2450

Attack   39 (Ms) / 2;
          54 (Ms) / 2 after first town saved

Speed   16

Armor   5 (Sh, Pr)

Heal

Battle Cry

Ram Missile Armor

HP   275

Attack   125 (Sh) / 4

Speed   10

Walkthrough

The first three adventures in this campaign deal with the life of William the Conqueror and the Norman Invasion.

Go east to raise troops in the first village, then go north. Of course, Toustain's troops will be harassing you along the way. Between the two villages is a hamlet being attacked by bandits. Kill off the bandits and you'll get all kinds of goodies: 10 Civ Points, an attack upgrade for William, and any of the local crossbowmen that survived the battle.

Once you've raised all the troops you can from the land, head for the bridge leading to Falaise. You'll have to defeat the guards at the bridge and at the gate. When you enter Falaise, talk to the mayor and he'll surrender the town.

Now you can settle in and raise resources for the final battle. You can't build siege engines, but there's a castle owned by an engineer nearby, and he'll trade you siege engines for stone. You can get the stone from a stone mine a bit north of the engineer's castle. When you arrive, they'll hand you 1500 stone to get you started. You can send your own miners to get more if you want it.

English Campaign / William Duke of Normandy

A bunch of bandits have established a well-defended gold mine at the far south. Get a couple siege engines and all your troops together and go down and take it over. Now you have all the resources you need. Build up your forces until they're maxed out and you're ready to take the battle to Toustain.

When you go to Toustain's castle, make sure you have at least two trebuchets.

The bulk of the defending force will rush out as soon as you attack, so be ready to defend the siege equipment. Move into the castle slowly, behind your trebuchets, taking out defensive towers as you go. When the castle falls, you win.

───────── ⌘ ─────────

"The keep is in ruins! Toustain has been defeated!"

WILLIAM DUKE OF NORMANDY: 1047

Gollet the Jester shivered as he emerged from the house in Bayeux, but there was more than a mere chill in the air this evening. A rebellion against his master, William, Duke of Normandy, was brewing and Gollet knew it would not be long before the conspirators acted. Even with the pledged assistance of King Henry of France, the outcome for William was far from certain.

Pulling his cloak tighter, Gollet set off for the town gate, eager to return to his master's side. Hushed voices from a nearby alley stopped him in his tracks. The manner and tone of the conversation, especially at this time of night, seemed anything but innocent. Curiosity piqued, Gollet crept closer to the voices.

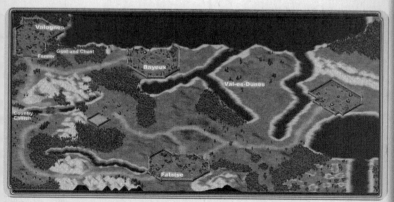

No resources found on this map

EMPIRE EARTH
THE ART OF CONQUEST

PRIMA'S OFFICIAL STRATEGY GUIDE

Players

All – Middle Ages

William (you; red)

Rebels (enemy; yellow)

Normandy (neutral; blue)

King Henry (ally; light blue)

Initial Resources

None

Required Objectives

Get disguise for Gollet from farm

Get Gollet to William in Volognes

Reach Falaise

Defeat champion and get troops

Slay Guy of Burgundy

Optional Objectives

Get chest — refills Gollet's HP and raises his attack +30

Civ Point Opportunities

5   Gollet finds Henry

5   Henry reaches Falaise

15   Guy of Burgundy killed

Tech Opportunities

Upgrade archers' attack +2

Upgrade longswords' attack +3

You Lose If

Gollet dies before finding William

William dies or is captured

Henry dies

Scenario-Specific Stats

William

HP	3,150
Attack	59 (Ms)/2
Speed	16
Armor	5 (Sh, Pr)
Heal	
Battle Cry	

Henry

HP	2,775
Attack	75 (Ms)/2
Speed	16
Armor	5 (Sh, Pr)
Morale	

Gollet

HP	715
Attack	35 (Sh)/2
Speed	16
Armor	6 (Ar); 26(Sh)

Sir Tesson

HP	1950
Attack	19 (Ms)/2
Speed	16
Armor	5 (Sh, Pr)

Guy of Burgundy

HP	7,938
Attack	60 (Ms)/2
Speed	16
Armor	5 (Sh, Pr)

Champion

HP	1,270
Attack	90 (Ms)/2
Speed	16
Armor	6 (Sh, Pr)

Mayor

HP	40
Attack	3 (Ar) / 2
Speed	12

Rebels

Infantry Attack +2

Archer Attack +2

Knight Attack +4

Walkthrough

This isn't the toughest scenario in the game, but it's one of the most complex, with many tasks that have to be performed in the right order.

You start out as Gollet, William's jester. In Bayeux, you overhear a plot to assassinate William, and have to flee the city by night to warn your master in Valognes, due

46

English Campaign / The Battle of Hastings

west. Shortly after you leave town, you'll be ambushed by a couple of conspirators, run away from them and take a sharp right that leads to a clearing to the north of the main road. In the clearing are a wolf and a chest. Open the chest and you'll find a sword that will upgrade your attack and heal your wounds. You should have no trouble handling the wolf and the troops chasing you now. You'll have to deal with one more group of conspirators before you reach Valognes. At the gate, the guards won't let you in. Go northeast around the wall until you meet a peasant that will offer you a disguise. Now you can enter town and find William. (You can go back to Bayeux if you need help — the guards and the towers are on your side.)

Now you have both Gollet and William. Don't try to leave through the city gate. On the eastern side of the city there's a secret passage that leads to the clearing where Gollet found the sword. Run south. You'll meet and have to fight some more bad guys, but shortly thereafter you'll come to a church. If William goes in, he'll be healed. As soon as William leaves the church, hide on the other side of the road until some mounted bandits pass. Continue south dealing with enemies as they arise. You'll come to the house of an old knight named Sir Hubert, who offers to let his three sons escort you to Falaise. You'll pass a couple of unreachable archers, then run into a large force of enemy soldiers. Let the sons of Hubert sacrifice themselves for you — have them attack to the south while you and Gollet sneak around to the north. Finally, you meet up with your old pal the mayor of Falaise.

Now you have to gather your troops for the big fight. There are two villages you have to visit, one northwest of Falaise, and one east. There are also some volunteers waiting due north of Falaise. At the northwest village you'll have to fight the town's "champion" one-on-one before the villagers will sign up. Use a little Battle Cry on him to speed things up.

Now you and your new army get to march out to join up with King Henry. As soon as you meet, a rebel force appears, but it's led by Sir Tesson, who wants to quit the rebellion and turn his forces over to you. Now at last you're ready to face the enemy. Try to find and kill Guy of Burgundy as soon as possible, and make sure you keep King Henry alive until the end of the battle. When Guy's army is defeated and Guy is dead, you win.

"You have conducted yourself well on this day, William. I hereby bestow upon you the title of Knight. From this day forth, let none doubt that you are the true Duke of Normandy."

THE BATTLE OF HASTINGS: 1066

The King of England, Edward "The Confessor," was dead. Reneging on his pledges, Harold Godwinson claimed the throne, which Edward had promised to William, Duke of Normandy.

Standing on the shore of the Channel, William stared out over the dark waters. To any casual observer, he would have appeared calm and composed. Yet inside, many thoughts raced through his mind. He busily considered what had happened, what to do about it, and just how to go about doing it. He had been betrayed, but all was not lost. With enough resources, enough men, and enough ships, he could take back what he had been promised. The throne of England could still be his.

EMPIRE EARTH
THE ART OF CONQUEST

PRIMA'S OFFICIAL STRATEGY GUIDE

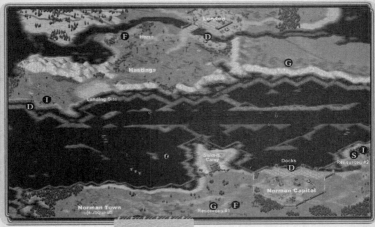

Legend
- **F** Forage
- **S** Stone
- **D** Dock
- **I** Iron
- **G** Gold
- — Wall

Players

All – Middle Ages

William (you; red)

England (enemy; yellow)

Normandy (ally; blue)

Bandits (enemy; purple)

Vikings (enemy; orange)

London (neutral; yellow)

Initial Resources

Food 1000

Wood 1000

Stone 1000

Gold 1000

Iron 1000

Required Objectives

Build up for invasion

Go to England

Fight battle with English army

Get William a horse and go to London

Optional Objectives

Talk to Norman villagers, then rescue their children from the slavers

Civ Point Opportunities

10   Save the Norman children

15   Defeat Harold, return to London

Tech Opportunities

Cavalry Archer	Archery	Stables
Siege	Temple	Knight
Cataphract	Longbow	Pikeman
Longsword	Priest	Prophet

You Lose If

William is killed

English Campaign / The Battle of Hastings

Scenario-Specific Stats

William

HP	2,450
Attack	19 (Ms)/2
Speed	16
Armor	5 (Sh, Pr)
Heal	
Battle Cry	

Harold Godwinson

HP	2,775
Attack	60 (Ms)/2
Speed	16; 20 during battle
Armor	5 (Sh, Pr)

Harold Hardegraad

HP	3,270
Attack	90 (Ms)/2
Speed	16
Armor	6 (Sh, Pr)

Docks

Range +2

Walkthrough

The first thing you have to do is build up your forces for the invasion of England. Watch out for bandits that will attack your citizens gathering resources. On the far west of the map there's a Norman village. Find them and they'll tell you that their children have been taken by slavers. Go to the slavers' camp to the north and defeat them and return the children home, and you get 10 Civ Points plus ongoing tribute.

You can only build 15 archers for the invasion. When your population reaches 60, you're told to go select a dock to start the invasion. Once you've clicked on a dock, you lose your ability to create any more military units. As you cross the channel, you get word that a gang of Vikings has attacked the English army waiting for you, making the enemy more vulnerable to your attack.

Once you're in England, the battle cannot begin until William is off the boat and with his forces. When you find Hastings, to the esat of the beach, your army will charge the enemy, ready or not. When half their army has been killed, a message will appear that William has been killed, but actually he's only lost his horse. William has to get to the top of the indicated hill right away, to keep his troops from losing morale. Between the time he loses his horse and the time he gets to the top of the hill, William can't use his battle cry.

If Harold (the English king) is injured (-50% hit points), he retreats and the English army is demoralized, making them easy to finish off. However, after he retreats, Harold is still surrounded by an elite guard of "huskarls," and this is a tough fight, especially with your forces diminished. Try to kill off Harold quickly. If he dies, the remaining huskarls become demoralized.

Now all you have to do is enter London. Of course, William will need a new horse before he can enter town in triumph. Fortunately, one waits for him near the gate to London. Ride into town and claim your kingdom.

———————— ∽∾ ————————

"We have reached London! England is ours! A new era has dawned upon the world!"

EMPIRE EARTH
THE ART OF CONQUEST

PRIMA'S OFFICIAL STRATEGY GUIDE

THE HUNDRED YEARS WAR: 1340 - 1346

King Edward looked gravely at his royal councilors. He shook his head, knowing they had not the slightest idea of the danger they faced — that all England faced.

"Gentlemen," the King began, "our fight against the French does not progress well. If the situation is not remedied, the crown may be in jeopardy."

"Your Highness," said a young advisor, rising cautiously to his feet, "with all respect, only minor skirmishes have been fought thus far, how can one say ..."

Edward glared at the man, silencing him instantly. "If you can hold your tongue, I shall endeavor to explain." The advisor quickly seated himself and Edward continued. "The French have a larger navy, a formidable army, and an abundance of resources. Moreover, they are pushing to control the Channel, which you all know," he said, looking again at the impulsive councilor, "is the only route to Normandy. Should their stratagem succeed, my son shall have no way to carry the fight back to French soil." The King paused and drew a heavy sigh. "There is, however, one chance. We must destroy the French Fleet before it is too late!"

Legend

- **F** Forage
- **S** Stone
- **D** Dock
- **I** Iron
- **G** Gold
- **—** Wall

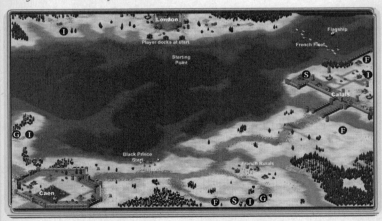

Players

All — Middle Ages
The Black Prince (you; red)
Caen (enemy; yellow)
Calais (ally; purple)

French Rurals (enemy; green)
England (neutral; dark red)

Initial Resources

| Food 400 | Wood 1000 | Stone 0 |
| Gold 100 | Iron 100 | |

English Campaign / The Hundred Years War

Required Objectives

Destroy French ships

Destroy Caen and build a town center in its ruins

Destroy Calais' Town Center

Optional Objectives

Kill French flagship to demoralize (HP −50%) French Navy

Civ Point Opportunities

10   Caen Town Center, University, Barracks and Church destroyed

10   Calais' Town Center destroyed

Tech Opportunities

Archery Range	Barracks	
Docks	Farm	Granary
Siege Factory	Stable	Temple
University	Tower	Walls

You Lose If

Your navy is defeated

Black Prince dies

Scenario-Specific Stats

Black Prince

HP	2,450
Attack	19 (Ms) / 2
Speed	16
Armor	5 (Sh, Pr)
Heal	
Battle Cry	

Caen Navy

HP	All ships' HP +75%

Player Navy

HP	All ships' HP +75%

Walkthrough

This scenario starts out with a short naval battle. You can't take out the French fleet head-to-head, so don't try. However, what you have to do is made pretty clear. Build as many ships as you can with the resources you have, then throw your fleet at the French. Try to draw the French forces down to the south. Then, take your special demolition ship and, hugging the coastline, sneak it around until you have a straight shot at the enemy flagship. If you get the demolition ship to the flagship, they both blow up and the French fleet becomes demoralized. Draw the French back to your docs (so you get the healing) and finish them off as they come.

With that done, the rest of the scenario becomes a land campaign in France. You're given an invasion force and dropped on the coast of France with the job of taking Caen. Fight a small force shielding the town, then take out its four towers. The four buildings in the middle of town collapse to form stone mines. You're given a work party of citizens, and when you gather the proper amount of stone to send back home, England responds by sending you an architect, who turns your settlement into a town center and gives you the ability to make most buildings and units.

Now you can prepare for the next battle. There are gold and iron resources on a peninsula along the western edge of the map, as far north as you can go. Watch out for raiding parties of French rurals. There's a fortified town about halfway between Calais and Caen, and when it's destroyed the attacks will stop.

EMPIRE EARTH
THE ART OF CONQUEST

PRIMA'S OFFICIAL STRATEGY GUIDE

When you max out your forces, march on Calais. This is a tough fight, because Calais will keep building units to oppose you until it falls. You'll probably need to rebuild your forces several times. Take plenty of siege equipment, and try to take out some important defensive buildings (the gates, towers or troop-producing buildings) every time you attack. Once you've entered the town, Calais will stop defending the bridge and start defending the town center itself. When the town center falls, you win.

———— ⚬⚬⚬⚬ ————

"Calais has been conquered! We have won a great victory for England on this day!"

THE BLACK PRINCE: 1356

In the light of early morning, English transport ships glided silently through the waters of the Channel. Edward the Black Prince, son of King Edward III, was returning to France, ready to continue what would become known as the Hundred Years War. Upon reaching the French coastline, his small contingent of troops disembarked and waded ashore.

"My loyal men," he said to the band gathered before him, "though we are few in number, our mission is of the utmost importance. We are here to strike deep into the French countryside, plundering whatever we find to enrich the coffers of England! If we are successful, our actions may well determine the outcome of this war!"

Legend
F Forage
S Stone
D Dock
I Iron
G Gold
— Wall

Players

All — Middle Ages
Black Prince (you; red)
France (enemy; yellow)
Villages (neutral; blue)

Initial Resources

None

Required Objectives

Get all 4 treasures
Defeat the French in battle

English Campaign / The Black Prince

Civ Point Opportunities

10   Own 4 chests (at the same time)

15   Capture King John

Tech Opportunities

Archers   Long Sword

Pikemen   Trebuchet

You Lose If

Black Prince dies

Scenario-Specific Stats

Black Prince

HP	2,450
Attack	19 (Ms)/2
Speed	16
Armor	5 (Sh, Pr)
Heal	
Battle Cry	

France Towers

HP	3,125
Attack	60 (Ms)/4
Range	3

Boats & Citizens

HP	All HP +500

Enemy Monk

HP	800
Attack	(Ms)/180
Speed	0
Armor	4 (Sh, Pr)

Walkthrough

This is a quick, fun scenario that shouldn't be too tough.

You grab the first chest just south of where you start. The second is near a church a little west. This is probably the most dangerous treasure to grab, because it's guarded by a "priest" who'll cast a Volcano at you as you attack. Go east to the third chest, which is in a guarded tower.

The road east is blocked by men chopping wood until you collect all of the first three chests. Once you have all the treasure, the trees are felled and you can continue. The final chest is in a town on the shore of the Mediterranean. The treasure arrives by ship just as you get there; you have to fight the town guards for it. Keep the treasure with you. If you let it out of your sight for more than a few seconds, some French soldiers will appear to "steal it back" and you'll have to defeat them to regain control of the treasure.

The path you came in by has been blocked by rock slides, so you have to take a more northern route home. A "deserted" village turns out to be an ambush. Eventually, you arrive at a riverside town where a merchant needs your help fighting off bandits. When the bandits are dead, you get the use of the merchant's two transports to get you back where you started.Back on the beach, a messenger from England tells you to pick up some reinforcements across the river to go and attack the town of Voltieres to the north. The English have built a hospital for your use, if you need it.

There are several ways to go at Voltieres, but the easiest is probably to climb up the nearby hill and wait for the French to attack you. From this position you can control the choke-points leading up to the highland, and your siege engines can do a lot of good against the French troops below. Once the main body of French troops has been eliminated, you can blow the gates of the town, then destroy the castle keep. As you win the scenario, you're told that you've managed to capture the King of France, and can now ransom him for, um, a king's ransom.

"We have destroyed the Castle! Victory is ours!"

EMPIRE EARTH
THE ART OF CONQUEST

PRIMA'S OFFICIAL STRATEGY GUIDE

WE BAND OF BROTHERS: 1414 - 1415

The time has come once again to raise the sword, to reclaim the lands of William I which are England's by right. The luminous star of the Black Prince, Edward, has long since faded, but that of the present King, Henry V, is rapidly gaining in brilliance.

But alas! Treachery against the young King, both here and in France, threatens his plans. Henry's oldest and dearest friend, Sir John Oldcastle, has thrown in his lot with the heretic sect known as the Lollards, who are inciting open revolt across the countryside. They even plot to take the life of Henry himself as he sits in London!

In France, meanwhile, King Charles VI refutes Henry's righteous claims to lands there. He cites — and not without controversy — the ancient Salique rule that lands may not be passed down along the female line.

Henry must now deal with the threats at home and abroad ... and forge a legend that shall last throughout the ages.

"O for a Muse of fire, that would ascend the brightest heaven of invention, a kingdom for a stage, princes to act, and monarchs to behold the swelling scene! ... Can this cockpit hold the vasty fields of France?"

Legend

- **F** Forage
- **S** Stone
- **D** Dock
- **I** Iron
- **G** Gold
- — Wall

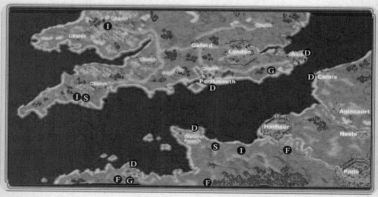

Players

All — Middle Ages
English (you; red)
First France (enemy; light blue)

Second France (enemy; dark blue)
England (ally; dark red; your troops when not under your control)
France (enemy; blue)
Lollards (enemy; yellow)

English Campaign / We Band of Brothers

Initial Resources

Food 2000   Wood 1000   Stone 500
Gold 1000   Iron 1000

Required Objectives

Find Lollards

Kill or convert Oldcastle

Kill Harfleur

Invade and defeat France

Civ Point Opportunities

10	Oldcastle killed
	or
20	Oldcastle captured (converted) and brought to Tower of London
10	Harfleur captured
20	French army defeated (16 units or fewer remain)

Tech Opportunities

Longsword   Crossbow   Halberdier

Farms   Town Center

You Lose If

Henry dies

Earl of Westmoreland dies

Scenario-Specific Stats

Henry

HP	3,270
Attack	90 (Ms)/2
Speed	16
Armor	6 (Sh, Pr)
LOS	10
Morale	

Archbishop

HP	2,800
Attack	(Ms)/180
Speed	12
Armor	4 (Sh, Pr)

Agincourt Army

| LOS | All +25% |

Earl of Westmoreland

HP	1,950
Attack	19 (Ms)/2
Speed	16
Armor	5 (Sh, Pr)
LOS	10
Heal	
Battle Cry	

Walkthrough

If the dialog in this scenario sounds a little different, it's because most of it is taken pretty much word-for-word out of Shakespeare's play *Henry the Fifth*.

You start out under fire by Lollard archers. You have to make a run for Oxford, just a short distance west. When you reach Oxford you gain control of the town — most of the buildings you need are already there, and there are plenty of resources nearby. Watch out for Lollard priests that will wander into town and try to convert your troops.

Once you're ready, you can start hunting the Lollards down. There are seven small towns with churches on the map, and four of them (randomly chosen) are under Lollard control. Whenever you find Lollards, you have to fight them off and destroy the church. At the fourth Lollard church (whichever that happens to be) you find the Lollard leader, Sir John Oldcastle. If you kill him, you get 10 Civ Points, but if you convert him and take him to the Tower of London, you earn 20. Once Oldcastle is out of the way, the Lollards are not a problem.

Now you get a really looooong cut scene of a bishop explaining the legalities of the British succession to Henry. Not one of Shakespeare's most stirring moments. Then you get to settle in and prepare for your invasion of France. When you reach your population limit, you're told to take everybody (including civilians) to the dock at Portsmouth. When everybody's loaded, you reappear in France.

EMPIRE EARTH
THE ART OF CONQUEST

PRIMA'S OFFICIAL STRATEGY GUIDE

First you have to take Harfleur, just to the east. It's not too tough of a fight. Once you're in control of Harfleur, the computer temporarily takes away your control of all units except Henry and the Earl of Westmoreland. You have to take the two of them to scout out the French army across the river at Agincourt. You're treated to an edited version of Henry's "Saint Crispin's Day" speech from the play, which *is* one of Shakespeare's most stirring moments.

Although Henry's speech seems to imply an immediate attack, you actually have all the time you need to build up your forces. You can build all the buildings you need, and there are plenty of resources available. When you're ready, move across the river and send your cavalry to take out the four bombards that guard the highlands. Now you can engage the enemy in whatever fashion you prefer. When the French are reduced to 16 or fewer units, you win the scenario and the Hundred Years War.

"Lo! We've broken their spirit — see how the dogs run from us! France is again ours!"

THE WAR AGAINST NAPOLEON: 1808 - 1814

Sir Arthur Wellesley, the future Duke of Wellington, smiled grimly as he considered the task he faced.

The brazen yet brilliant French general, Napoleon Bonaparte, had conquered most of Europe and had even crowned himself Emperor. But, by invading Spain and Portugal, he had finally overextended his forces. Iberia had become the soft underbelly of France's new empire.

And the difficult job of splitting it open had fallen upon Sir Arthur.

While the fate of Europe hung in the balance, he would cross swords with Napoleon's Grande Armee for the first time. There he would either perish ... or emerge a soldier great enough to challenge Napoleon himself.

Legend

- **F** Forage
- **S** Stone
- **D** Dock
- **I** Iron
- **G** Gold
- **—** Wall

Players

Sir Arthur Wellesley (you; red; Industrial)

London (ally; dark red; Industrial)

Salamanca (ally; yellow; Renaissance to Industrial)

French (enemy; blue; Industrial)

Spanish Rebels (ally; orange; Industrial)

Lisbon (ally; green; Imperial to Industrial)

Talavera (ally; pink; Renaissance)

Badajoz (ally; purple; Renaissance)

Toledo (ally; dark red; Industrial)

French Navy (enemy; blue; Industrial)

Portsmouth (ally; dark red; Industrial)

English Campaign / The War Against Napoleon

Initial Resources

Food 1500   Wood 1500   Stone 600

Gold 500   Iron 400

Required Objectives

Fight Junot until he surrenders

French defeated

Optional Objectives

Destroy Toledo

Resource Opportunities

Defeat Junot   1,200 gold

Liberate Toledo   200 gold, 200 iron

Civ Point Opportunities

5   Junot surrenders

5   Liberate Salamanca

5   Liberate Talavera

5   Liberate Toledo

You Lose If

Wellesley dies

Scenario-Specific Stats

Junot

HP	384
Attack	65 (Gn) / 3
Speed	16
Armor	25 (Sh)

Walkthrough

On your way to France, you'll have to take out a few French ships guarding the channel. This shouldn't be a problem for your Frigates.

Once you land in Lisbon you'll be attacked shortly by some of Junot's cavalry. Now just march north and engage Junot's force. Don't worry about tactics or anything, because 10 seconds after the fight begins, it stops and Junot wants to

EMPIRE EARTH
THE ART OF CONQUEST

talk to Wellesley. Junot surrenders and you get Civ Points plus 1,200 gold.

It's now a year later and you're told to drive the French out of the Spanish city of Talavera. You have control of all the buildings of Lisbon. What you don't have is a source of iron or gold, so be careful of your resources throughout this scenario.

You're told that Spanish Rebels in the city of Badajoz want to join your side. Once you knock down all the towers and front gates of Badajoz the Rebels come out. However, they're a hotheaded bunch and decide to attack Talavera on their own (assuming you haven't already taken Talavara — if you have, they'll choose a new target). If you just let them go they'll be cut down pretty quickly, but if you follow them and attack right behind them (take out the artillery first) you may be able to turn it into a fairly easy victory.

Once Talavera is down, you can move on to Toledo and Salamanca. Some towns may give you extra iron and gold resources to help build your forces back up. The force at Salamanca is particularly tough. Instead of taking them on head-on, considering fortifying the northern edge of Talavera with a wall and towers, then use cavalry to lure the French into attacking the wall. This should allow you to keep your casualties down to a reasonable number.

The French attack after your army crosses the slope of the Pyrenees mountains (you may find the Civ bonus for mountain fighting useful at this point). You have to reduce the French force to 15 or fewer units to win.

—————————

By the time he had defeated the French at Toulouse, Sir Arthur Wellesley had been made the Duke of Wellington — or "The Iron Duke" as his enemies came to call him. As for Napoleon Bonaparte, having surrendered at Fontainbleau three days earlier, it would be many months before he and Wellington would finally meet in battle.

THE BATTLE OF WATERLOO: 1815

Following Napoleon's defeat in 1814 and subsequent exile to the island of Elba, the corrupt Bourbon regime was restored to the throne of France. But they didn't hold on to it for long. Escaping from exile, Napoleon returned to Paris and in three short weeks raised an army that forced the Bourbons to flee to Brussels.

Stunned by the rapid turn of events, the other major powers of Europe rallied to form an alliance. Sir Arthur Wellesley, the first Duke of Wellington, was called upon to lead the main thrust of the allied forces against Napoleon. It would be the first time the two great generals were to meet on the field of battle.

The Duke of Wellington was eager to assume command, though the irony of the situation was not lost on him. Napoleon and the French believed they were fighting for liberty, fraternity and equality. The Alliance, on the other hand, were fighting ultimately to restore a dying aristocracy to power. But whatever the motives, Sir Arthur had every intention of winning the fight.

Legend

F	Forage
S	Stone
D	Dock
I	Iron
G	Gold
—	Wall

English Campaign / The Battle of Waterloo

Players

Duke of Wellington
(you; red; Industrial)

Prussians (enemy; green; Industrial)

French (enemy; blue; Industrial)

Ney's Corp (enemy; light blue;
Industrial)

Brussels (neutral; dark pink; Imperial)

Ligny (neutral; gray; Renaissance)

Quatre Bras (neutral; blue; Renaissance)

Wauvre (neutral; yellow; Renaissance)

Waterloo (neutral; pink; Renaissance)

Belgium (neutral; pink; Renaissance)

British (ally; red; Industrial)

Required Objectives

Defeat Napoleon's cavalry and cannon

Initial Resources

Food 2500   Wood 3000   Stone 600

Gold 1500   Iron 1500

Optional Objectives

Blucher defeats French

Civ Point Opportunities

5   French defeated at Wavre

10   French defeated at Quatre Bras

5   Ney killed

You Lose If

Messenger dies

Wellington dies

French take Brussels

Scenario-Specific Stats

Sir Rowland Hill

HP	480
Attack	65 (Gn) / 3
Speed	16
Armor	25 (Sh)

COPPER AGE   DARK AGE   RENAISSANCE   INDUSTRIAL AGE
0 BC   5000 BC   2000 BC   500 BC   0 AD   900 AD   1300 AD   1500 AD   1700 AD   1900 AD
STONE AGE   BRONZE AGE   MIDDLE AGES   IMPERIAL AGE   ATOMIC

PRIMA'S OFFICIAL STRATEGY GUIDE

General Blucher

HP	4,245
Attack	145 (Ms) / 2
Speed	16
Armor	10 (Sh), 8 (Pr)

Duke of Wellington

HP	4,245
Attack	145 (Ms) / 2
Speed	16
Armor	10 (Sh), 8 (Pr)
Morale	

Messenger

HP	655
Attack	60 (Sh) / 2
Speed	16
Armor	9 (Ar), 31 (Gn)

Imperial Cuirassier

HP	655
Attack	60 (Sh) / 2
Speed	16
Armor	9 (Ar), 31 (Gn)

French Sharpshooter

HP	315
Attack	30 (Gn) / 12
Speed	9

Walkthrough

This is a fast-moving, combat-intensive scenario.

Your first job is to get a messenger through the French lines to the Prussian general Blucher. Once you find him, you get control of his troops and you have to fight off a French force. The more troops that survive this battle the better — they'll be back late in the game. If fewer than 10 Prussians survive, or if Blucher is severely wounded, the Prussians won't show up at all.

Now you're back to Wellington and his troops. You're told to fortify the hill of Mt. St. Jean. You're given a force of military engineers (citizens) to do the dirty work. The French will attack after about 12 minutes, or whenever your population reaches 60. You're told to go to the city of Quatre Bras and stop the French advance into Brussels. If you reduce the French force to less than 30 units, or severely injure the French leader, Marshall Ney, the French retreat (survivors go to join up with Napoleon at Ligny). If the French make it into Brussels, the rulers of Belgium surrender and you lose.

After Quatre Bras, you have some time to recoup and prepare for Napoleon's main force. Napoleon attacks Mt. St. Jean. If your defenses hold up, Blucher's force (assuming any are left) come to your aid. You need to guard both Mt. St. Jean and the approaches to Brussels. If French troops get into the center of Brussels, you lose. You win when Napoleon's cannon and cavalry are destroyed. You don't have to kill Napoleon or Ney to win.

"Another generation of European aristocracy has been preserved, but it is only temporary. Napoleon was surely right: their privileged status cannot survive forever, though sadly neither he nor I shall live to see the change."

OPPER AGE		DARK AGE		RENAISSANCE		INDUSTRIAL AGE		INFORMATION
BC 2000 BC	500 BC	0 AD	900 AD	1300 AD	1500 AD	1700 AD	1900 AD	2000 AD
BRONZE AGE		MIDDLE AGES			IMPERIAL AGE		ATOMIC AGE	

German Campaign / Cavalry of the Sky

∾ German Campaign ∾

The early days of aviation were exciting and dangerous times. A sputtering engine, a wooden frame, and a skin of fabric were all that kept the first fliers in the air. Following the outbreak of The Great War in 1914, pilots had an additional danger to contend with ... bullets.

CAVALRY OF THE SKY

Freiherr Manfred von Richthofen has been assigned to the newly-created German Air Force as an observer. He and his pilot, Holck, have flown behind the lines of the Eastern Front to photograph the current positions of the retreating Russian army. But, near the city of Wicznice, they encounter a barrage of ground fire. With their plane full of holes and billowing smoke, they are forced to ditch. Now, deep in Russian-held territory, they must try to salvage their mission and survive their journey back to German Headquarters.

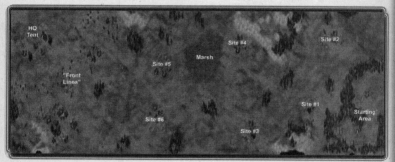

*No resources found on this map.

Players

All – Industrial

Germany (you; gray)

Polish peasants (Jozef, Stanislaw, Andrzej, Zofia, others; allies; yellow)

Russia (enemy; orange)

Initial Resources

None

Required Objectives

Save Zofia from Russians

Photograph 4 (of 6) sites

Break through Russian lines back to German HQ

Optional Objectives

Get map of area (at site #2)

Get pistols (at site #4)

Get hospital (at site #6)

EMPIRE EARTH
THE ART OF CONQUEST

PRIMA'S OFFICIAL STRATEGY GUIDE

Civ Point Opportunities

10	Get through trees with help from peasants
20	Take first 2 photos
20	Victory

Resource/Tech Opportunities

You gain units, and the opportunity to create more units, once you've taken four photos:

Cuirassier, dragoon, howitzer, artillery, grenade launcher, hand cannoneer, sniper, medic, German infantry, German MG

You Lose If

Richthofen dies

Holck dies

Scenario-Specific Stats

Jozef, Stanislaw, Andrzej and Zofia are citizens

Manfred Von Richtofen

HP	2,540
Attack	150 (only if he finds ammunition)
Speed	14
Armor	10 (Sh), 9 (Pr)
Range	10

Holck

HP	2,430
Attack	150 (only if he finds ammunition)
Speed	14
Armor	10 (Sh), 9 (Pr)

Russian Infantry, Cuirassiers and Dragoons

LOS	-3 (while taking pictures) normal (afterwards)

Russian infantry are doughboys

Walkthrough

You can't get through the forest without help, so go to the Polish farm. Since you are moved by their pleas, head west to the Russian barracks (Site #1). Use Manfred's battle cry to soften up the dastardly Russians, and they shouldn't be too hard for a fine pair of Prussians to handle. The peasants can then help you hack through the trees to the west. Select the peasants, and point them to where the trees are thinnest. You'll be through in no time.

Taking pictures of Russian installations is the next priority. After the first photos, head to Site #2, north of your crash site (on the other side of the trees). You will find a university there, and if you walk around enough, you should find a map showing you where the other installations are. Going to the next closest installation (Site #4) should provide you with some offensive power. There is also a hospital at one of the southern installations, but healing shouldn't be necessary if you're cautious.

Note that you can only take pictures of four of the six sites — you don't have film for more than that.

German Campaign / Cavalry of the Sky

When skulking about, move slowly and in short jaunts. The foolish Russians can't see as far as you can, so if you move carefully, you can avoid confrontations. Be sure to skirt the marsh; in addition to getting mud on Manfred's shiny boots, there's a good risk of malaria.

After you have taken the required four photographs, move to the northwest. The Russian city lies to the south, and you want to avoid that. When you get to the first line of Russian pillboxes, hide behind some trees. It's time to use the troops!

Take most of the troops that you are given northeast and punch holes through the barbed wire. Leave a small group of infantry and machine gunners behind to defend. Meanwhile, use your military buildings to produced a balanced group of infantry, machine gunners, grenade launchers, and light cavalry. You should also produce about five or six pieces of artillery and a like number of howitzers.

When your wire-breaking troops start encountering pillboxes and artillery, fall back. Gather these troops around the hospital to heal. Improve the speed and armor of your cavalry, and the range, attack and armor of everything else. When all of your new troops have been produced, you should be ready to roll! You may want to practice your tactics on the Russian encampment to the southeast first; this will also help cover your back.

The following tactics are highly effective once five or six artillery became available. Keep a protective force of infantry and cavalry in front of your howitzers and artillery at all times. When moving, move the troops first, then the artillery. Send a single cavalry unit towards the enemy in a roundabout fashion. When the unit spots artillery or a pillbox, turn back. The cavalry unit will get damaged, but if you've maxed out its speed, it should be able to make it back. Target all artillery on the enemy artillery or pillbox; a volley or two should do the trick. If you come under fire from enemy artillery, pull back and rely on your superior range (you did max out artillery range, right?) to carry the day. Repeat until all artillery and pillboxes are destroyed. The troops can clean up the enemy then, and artillery can take out military buildings.

Use the army to clear out most of the enemy in the north. Your two heroes can sprint around two or three pillboxes, and deal with a soldier or two, but most of the lethal obstacles should be cleared away by others. Then it's a sprint to the command tent and victory!

—————————— ⚜ ——————————

Count Holck, Freiherr von Richthofen! It's good to see you both — we believed you lost! I shall provide horses at once to return you to your Aerodrome. Your pictures will be of great value as we continue to gain ground in this sector.

EMPIRE EARTH
THE ART OF CONQUEST

PRIMA'S OFFICIAL STRATEGY GUIDE

SUPPLY AND DEMAND

Britain's naval blockade against Germany is taking its toll. Germany's High Seas Fleet is well built, but it is no match for the British fleet, especially in their home waters. To break the blockade, the High Seas Fleet opts to lure enemy vessels back to friendly waters where they can be sunk piecemeal.

In a stroke of luck for Germany, the Brits have replaced Winston Churchill as First Lord of the Admiralty. Perhaps his successor will be more susceptible to German ploys. The Kaiser and the War Office have several major offensives planned for the end of the year. But without supplies, they are doomed to failure.

Legend

- **F** Forage
- **S** Stone
- **D** Dock
- **I** Iron
- **G** Gold
- **—** Wall
- **N** Naval Yard

Players

All – WWI

Germany (you; gray)

German ports and supplies (yours; yellow)

Britain, especially the Grand Fleet (enemy; red)

Denmark (neutral trading partner; light blue)

Initial Resources

1500 Food   2000 Wood   500 Stone

500 Gold   500 Iron

Required Objectives

Dock 20 supply transports in Germany

Optional Objectives

Get spy to British capitol (stops enemy air activity for 20 minutes)

Build Coliseum (standard effect)

Build Lighthouse (gives farther vision)

Civ Point Opportunities

10   Get spy next to the British capitol

15   Victory

German Campaign / Supply and Demand

Resource Opportunities

Gold and Iron through trade with Denmark (500 Food gets 250 Gold; 500 Wood gets 250 Iron; any more at a single time loses the excess)

Tech Opportunities

Spy   Once 6 transports have safely arrived

You Lose If

Richthofen dies

Scenario-Specific Stats

British Docks	**Spy**	
All British docks have +4 range	HP	5,235
	Attack	160 (Ms) / 2
Towers	Speed	14
HP 5,875	Armor	10 (Sh), 9 (Pr)
Attack 325 (Ms) / 4		

Walkthrough

First priority is, of course, to create citizens. You have 4 town centers, so get each of them producing. One granary with 3 or 4 farms should be enough to supply all of your food needs. Put it in the north, near the border with Denmark, where it should be fairly safe from harm. Rostock should be your primary source of wood, and the capital should provide you with more than enough iron and gold. Wilhelmshaven will be able to mine as well, but it will also frequently be under attack, so don't rely on it. Work the stone quarries to the south to build towers.

Build a dock and a naval yard each at the port locations in the north and southwest. This will get the transports moving and enable you to build up a navy. Build a submarine or two soon and send them out exploring. Make an observation balloon as well and send it out to scout.

Transports from the southern supply route are headed for Wilhelmshaven or Bremerhaven. Transports from the north are headed for Kiel or Rostock.

You will probably want to focus your efforts on defending the northern supply route. The southern route is too close to England and its soon-to-be-ubiquitous planes. The British will try and choke off the northern supply route by massing a navy at the narrow strait just north of the Denmark peninsula (Jutland). That navy will consist primarily of battleships and frigates. Therefore, the fleet you build in your northern ports and naval yards should consist of submarines (to counter the battleships) and battleships (to counter the frigates). Never send out individual ships! Wait until you have a fleet of 2-3 battleships and 5-6 submarines before you go out to test the British mettle. A larger fleet would be even better, and you may need to make several sorties, but you can eventually wear down the Brits in the north. Then you can use a mixed fleet of subs and battleships to guard the supply route.

In battle, always focus your power. Have the battleships attack the frigates en masse, and likewise with the subs. Avoid having battleships fight other battleships and never have subs engage a frigate! Keep improving your subs and battleships, especially range and attack.

The lighthouse can be a great help to you. Build it in the north, and it will monitor much of the North Sea. This can give you warning when the Brits try to sneak back into the northern supply lanes!

EMPIRE EARTH
THE ART OF CONQUEST

PRIMA'S OFFICIAL STRATEGY GUIDE

Once the Brits start building planes, the southern route becomes very ... interesting. Wilhelmshaven will be under almost constant attack, first by ships, and then by ships and planes. The good news is this is the only place you will really have to worry about home defense. Build 3 or 4 towers and a like number of AA guns here. Note that AA guns can be improved too! You may also want to build a hospital, as your citizens will frequently be bombed. But towers and AA guns alone won't do the trick. You'll need the Baron.

Build an airport near the stone quarries as soon as resources allow. Von Richthofen's Flying Circus will arrive forthwith. Use the Set Rally Point feature to have the Baron and his men swarm around Wilhelmshaven. They will maintain an almost constant vigil and prevent too much damage. You should always have a citizen or two around for repair duty, just in case. Improve the speed and attack of planes, and build some fighters of your own to supplement the Baron's forces. Don't worry about the Baron getting killed while playing defense — he's seen worse than this! (Alternatively, keep the Baron near your primary air forces, to boost their morale.)

You might be able to get a few ships in along the southern route, but it will be much harder due to its proximity to England. You will need a more complex fleet to fight in the south: subs to counter battleships, battleships to counter frigates, and cruisers to knock down those planes that sink battleships with such glee. It will be a grinding battle, but you may get some transports through. Try luring ships and planes back to your coast, where your ships will heal close to a

dock, and the towers and AA guns will pound the enemy. Be sure to improve the range of your cruisers and AA guns; shoot early, shoot often!

You will definitely push the pop cap to get enough troops. Sometimes British bombers will help you with the pop cap, but there are two ways you can ease the pressure. A short-term solution is to take citizens gathering resources and use them to garrison buildings. This frees up space and increases efficiency. You can also build the stadium to get a big pop cap boost. Resources should not be a problem. You should not even have to trade with Denmark.

Getting in contact with the spy is very hard. The British coast is very well defended, and they have their own subs to boot. You could try taking a balanced fleet (subs, battleships, cruisers and frigates for the Brit subs) and punch a hole in the defenses. Alternatively, you might just build a fleet of 6-7 subs for a suicide mission. One or two will probably get through. It's worth it, because the spy can get those British planes off your back for a nice long time. Although Scotland is the least defended part of British territory, the spy has a better chance of succeeding if you trigger him closer to London in the south. Decisions, decisions!

The supplies for the coming offensives have been successfully delivered. And just in time. Intercepted messages indicate that the former British First Lord of the Admiralty, Winston Churchill, has been pushing for greater use of a new weapon in the war ... tanks. It would seem Churchill was in the wrong branch of the service!

COPPER AGE		DARK AGE		RENAISSANCE		INDUSTRIAL AGE		INFORMATIO
BC	2000 BC	500 BC	0AD	900 AD	1500 AD	1700 AD	1900 AD	2000 AD
	BRONZE AGE		MIDDLE AGES		IMPERIAL AGE		ATOMIC AGE	

German Campaign / The Red Baron

THE RED BARON

The stalemate along the Western Front has dragged on and on. The Battle of Verdun, a fight over a mere 10 square kilometers which has already lasted three months, is chewing up men like no battle ever before. Nearly 100,000 men have fallen dead or wounded so far.

Germany began the offensive hoping to wear down France's will to fight, but the attack's early momentum has since dwindled away. Now, the German High Command has detected a possible weakness in one sector, and sees an opportunity to grab new territory. The plan hinges on capturing or eliminating three French strongholds in the region. Veteran troops and fliers, including Manfred von Richthofen — now feared by the Allies as the "Red Baron" — have been dispatched to the area. Their orders: destroy the three forts by any means necessary.

Legend
- **F** Forage
- **S** Stone
- **D** Dock
- **I** Iron
- **G** Gold
- **—** Wall

Players

Germany (you; gray; WWI)

French forces (enemy; blue; WWI)

French towns (enemy; yellow; industrial)

Initial Resources

2500 Food   5000 Wood   2500 Stone

5000 Gold   5000 Iron

Required Objectives

Conquer fort at Douaumont

Conquer fort at Vaux

Conquer fort at Souville

Eliminate all 9 assassin aircraft

Civ Point Opportunities

5   Conquer first fort

5   Conquer second fort

15   Victory (when last assassin dead)

You Lose If

Richthofen dies

Scenario-Specific Stats

German Officer

HP   3,650

Attack   55 (Ms) / 2

Speed   14

Armor   10 (Sh), 9 (Pr)

EMPIRE EARTH
THE ART OF CONQUEST

PRIMA'S OFFICIAL STRATEGY GUIDE

Observation Balloon

HP	1,500
Speed	16

German Towers

HP	4,875
Attack	225 (Ms) / 4
LOS	12

Walkthrough

Iron is *the* most important resource in this scenario. You're going to need a lot of it, so get the citizens crackin' on the iron deposits in the north central section of your territory. Build a settlement nearby to facilitate gathering. Food will also be quite important, so get a citizen working on the chickens just west of the capitol, and build a granary in the far north with 4-5 farms. Wood and gold will be somewhat important, but you should have just about all the stone you need without working the available quarries.

While you're getting the citizens started, decide whether you want to tackle this scenario with air or ground units. Choose one or the other; don't try to hedge your bets with some of both.

By Air. This walkthrough describes a ground approach, but air units will be a lot more fun for some players. The basic steps described here (like taking out your first fortress with the balloon) apply to either approach. If you go through the air, it'd be a good idea to plant an airfield just north of Vaux (after you've taken it, of course). Build

French Walls

HP	17,000

French Gates

HP	34,000

French AA Guns

HP	600
Attack	150 (Ms) / 3
Armor	7 (Gn)

towers near your airbases; build a town center (giving a morale bonus to towers) and the base, then build one or more towers. And remember the morale boost the Red Baron gives nearby units — it's a good idea to keep him in the middle of the action.

By Ground. The balloon lets you take out one of the French forts early, but you must use it wisely. Use the Baron's planes to find a route to one of the cities (probably Vaux) that is free of AA fire. Send the balloon in, and when it's over the fort, click on a building and watch the fun! Don't stay around too long, however, because that will attract a lot of attention! Can you say, "hornet's nest"? (Remember that you don't have to take down the walls, towers and AA to conquer a fort — just the interior structures.)

The French have a lot of planes, and you will need the Baron and his boys just to protect your troops. Use the rally points to keep Jasta 11 either over your troops or just ahead to clear a path. The Baron will be fine as long as you heed his warnings and get him back to the Aerodrome when he's hurting. When returning to base, try to lure enemies near your capital, where 6 AA guns await. If only your citizens could build them .... You will have to build new planes every now and then. Be sure to improve the planes' stats, especially attack and speed. Don't waste resources improving the AA guns.

Partisans will also be valuable in keeping planes away from your units in the field, so make sure plenty are with any attack group. Improve their range and attack values; hit those planes hard and often.

As always, any attack group should be balanced, with a nice mix of infantry,

German Campaign / The Red Baron

machine guns, grenade launchers, howitzers and a couple of mortars and AT guns. A serious attack group should also have 4-5 artillery, with range, attack and area effect all maxed out. Cavalry might occasionally be good for charging enemy artillery, but their time has largely passed, and they're not very useful. You may want to build an officer or two at the capitol, as the Battlecry ability may come in handy. You are limited to 10 total tanks (although you can see what happens when you queue up tanks at multiple factories after you get your ninth), so you might want to save them up for one big push at the end. Meanwhile, be sure to improve their armor (duh!), attack and speed.

You needn't worry much about home defense, as the pillboxes and towers you have should be up to the task of repelling the French counterattack. Use a citizen and an engineer to lay wire and build towers and pillboxes. You should only need a few infantry and a machine gunner and an AT gun to defend the NW part of your territory from the occasional foray. The Baron may need to divert from the main battle to kill some planes as well. Remember to try and lure the French flyers into the AA guns.

Build a hospital or two for your men to visit between battles, because the battle to take the second fort (usually Douaumont) may be touch and go. First attack the village between the two closest forts and destroy the French buildings there. Then use a plane or the balloon to get the lay of the land. In addition, use the plane or balloon as a "spotter" to find structures for your artillery to eliminate. Target AA guns first, then towers. Always take time to deal with enemy artillery when you see it. After a few rounds of improvement, your artillery range should be superior,

and the improved area effect should show the French why it's a bad idea to bunch artillery together.... As always, concentrate fire on single targets. Always keep a screen of troops between the enemy and artillery. Be aware of attacks from the flank, the rear and above; the French are sneaky like that.

There's no need to destroy all the towers and AA guns — just enough to clear a path for your troops to attack the gates and break into the fort. Beware: while you're in the fort breaking things, the computer will have troops and artillery firing into the fort at you! Use the artillery to take them out, and keep your troops moving inside as they destroy buildings. Target the artillery factories first.

A word to the wise — the tank factories at Bras are the source of those irritations.

In the far west are the enemy's airports. After you've reduced the second city, take them out. By now, your panzer battalion should be ready, so roll 'em out. A squad of artillery, howitzers and tanks should destroy the airfields in no time. Be sure to keep reinforcing them with troops, however!

Once the airports are gone and the skies are clear, you can turn back east to the final fort, Souville. There is a hill to the west of the fort that is perfect for an assault. As before, eliminate towers and AA guns first. Eliminating the towers will enable your troops to assault the gate, and eliminating AA guns will allow you to send in bombers. Again, no need to eliminate them all — just clear a path. Howitzers with maxed-out range and attack are great for attacking towers and AA guns, while you again use spotters to take out enemy artillery and siege factories with your own big guns. Then knock the gates down and cry havoc!

EMPIRE EARTH
THE ART OF CONQUEST

PRIMA'S OFFICIAL STRATEGY GUIDE

Once the final fort is taken, a message comes that the Baron is being targeted by a squadron of assassins. No problem! Build nothing but fighters and partisans, and have them rally 'round the capitol. When the Baron comes under attack, quickly fly him towards the capitol. Remember the 6 AA guns? Hardly chivalrous, but if they're going to be that stupid, c'est la guerre. And say good-bye.

～◆◇◆～

Well done, Manfred! Once again we rule the skies as well as the land in Verdun. And there is greater news as well. I have been informed that the Kaiser himself has approved the Orden Pour le Merite for you. The "Blue Max" you desired for so long is finally yours.

THE SOMME

Following the withdrawal of Russia from the war, Germany's troops on the Eastern Front have been transferred to the west for a final, all-out assault. The main offensive, code-named "Michael," is to be centered on the Somme River Valley near Saint-Quentin. With luck, the Allies can be thrashed before fresh troops arrive from the United States, who has just entered the war.

Freiherr Richthofen, suffering constantly from a head wound that refuses to heal, has grown bitter and weary. Nonetheless, he cannot bear to abandon the courageous men on the ground. He and his squadron, Jasta 11, will help hide German preparations for the assault from enemy eyes.

Legend

F Forage
S Stone
D Dock
I Iron
G Gold
— Wall

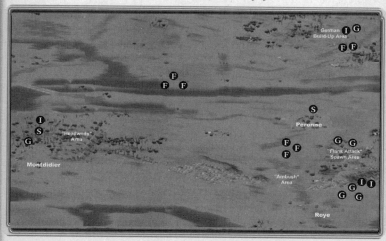

German Campaign / The Somme

Players

All – WWI

Germany (you; gray)

Great Britain (enemy; red)

French towns (enemy; yellow)

French forces (enemy; blue)

Empty buildings (neutral; light yellow)

Initial Resources

15,000 Food   15,000 Wood
15,000 Stone   15,000 Gold
15,000 Iron

Required Objectives

Destroy Peronne's town center and build barracks

Destroy Roye's town center and build barracks

Destroy Montdidier's town center and build barracks

Civ Point Opportunities

10   Complete entire buildup without being detected

10   Victory

Resource Opportunities

1000 Food   When you begin offensive (all other resources disappear)

1000 of each   When you build the barracks at Peronne

500 of each   When you build the barracks at Roye

You Lose If

None (Richthofen doesn't have to survive)

Scenario-Specific Stats

British Doughboy

HP	370
Attack	44 (Gn) / 2
Speed	12
LOS	4 (during first phase) 7 (after that)

British Artillery

HP	225
Attack	175 (Gn) / 12
Speed	10
Armor	20 (Gn), 8 (Ms)
Range	22

Sopwith Fighter

HP	425
Attack	17 (Ms) / 0.5
Speed	14

Walkthrough

There is a different element of strategy at the start of this scenario, because you have so many civ points to play with. Spend 'em! You may want to buy build-time decreases for most of your units at the start, since time will be of the essence. You will also want to get the Pop Cap increase, if you haven't done so yet. The more units, the better. Increasing the yield of gold and iron would probably be a good idea as well.

EMPIRE EARTH
THE ART OF CONQUEST

PRIMA'S OFFICIAL STRATEGY GUIDE

It's a real spending spree at the start, so do a lot of queueing while paused. Put the 6 citizens to work building extra production facilities (tank, artillery, air), and send one south to the river to build a port for a troop transport. Don't explore too much, since you don't want to be found out. No need to gather resources yet; it's an embarrassment of riches. Build a well-balanced army, with a few of everything, and more than a few tanks and Fokkers. You will need a lot of planes. Create a few extra citizens, to erect fortifications during the "build-up" phase. Get a medic as well.

You can queue unit improvements, so buy all unit improvements at once. (You won't be able to buy any more once the first phase is over.) Remember the function of each unit (range and area effect for artillery, defense for tanks, flight time and range for planes, etc.) and give most units a little extra speed. Don't forget to improve your AA guns! Build pillboxes and towers (a few) and AA guns (a lot) to defend your turf while supplies are plentiful.

There's a British airfield to the west, and one to the south. Have your planes patrol from two airports, one group guarding each direction. The British will probably come in from the west first — they won't report you to HQ (go figure), but get rid of them, anyway. If you are discovered, quickly hunt down the enemy scouts before they can report back to HQ. Try to stay close to home in the initial phase, so that spies have to go farther to get back to base.

When you reach the Pop Cap (or the Tommies discover you), the gravy train derails, and you'll have to get your citizens to work gathering resources. Stone is not all that important, but everything else is. You should be able to stay at the Pop Cap long enough to build up resources for reinforcements.

Send most of your troops (about two-thirds) east to deal with the British there. Use one airport's planes (including the Baron) to fly over and protect your troops. Reducing the airfield should be easy, as should be taking the French town a bit to the south. The Brits have infantry and tanks, but they also have the courtesy to attack in a line if you are cautious. So nice of them to parade for the artillery, eh? Send a tank or two to draw them out, and then bombard them from a distance.

The French town by the western bridge has resources, so build a settlement there and send a few citizens over. Keep a tank or two in the village to protect it and to keep the settlement functioning.

The second bridge is a major choke-point, and the key to protecting everything north of the river from ground assault. Build a tower or two and some pillboxes and AA guns at the entrance to the bridge. Leave behind a tank, a machine gunner, and an AT gun to hold the line, and move the rest of your troops along the south bank of the river.

Use a transport to ferry tanks across the river while your other troops are doing this. Get behind the barbed wire and, in a series of lightning strikes, take out the AA guns along the river. You will get

German Campaign / The Somme

pounded by airplanes, but the more AA guns you destroy, the more your planes can help. Have planes from both airports swarm over the city when all the AA guns are gone. By this time, your other troops should have skirmished along the river, and can hook up to lay waste to Peronne.

You may want to avoid building the barracks at Peronne yet, since that will cost you the Baron. You should ferry some citizens across, however, and build lots and lots of AA guns. You will not be attacked by land at first, but the skies will be dark with British planes. Once that is done, build production facilities, especially a new airport. Lastly build some towers in case a sneak attack comes while you're attacking the other towns. You may want to use a cargo truck to get citizens to Peronne. Remember to leave a unit in Peronne to keep the buildings active (a partisan is probably good, to complement the AA guns). Lastly, a hospital might be a good idea, because of what is to come.

Next, attack the southeastern town, Roye. There are two reasons for this. First, Montdidier is heavily fortified and protected by cliffs from the north. Also, contrary winds will absolutely prevent your planes from going over or past the western forest. Roye is definitely easier, but it will still be very difficult, largely because of all the planes the British will send against you. Always keep planes above you to defend as you advance, or you could be bombed into oblivion. Have citizens build AA gun "safe zones" along the invasion route.

The road to Roye is guarded by artillery on the high ground to the east. However, if you use lesser units as spotters, and have improved the range of your artillery to the maximum, you should take out that artillery with minimal losses. Roye is defended by a choke point filled with barbed wire. Send in tanks to knock down the wire, howitzers to take out the tank traps, and machine gunners to mow the infantry-heavy forces down. Once you break through, destroy the airfields first, then everything else. Send your aircraft west to guard the approach to Roye from Montdidier.

At this point, you may want to simultaneously build barracks at Roye and Peronne. Build on the blue spot where the town center was. You will lose the Baron, and the ability to build Fokkers, but you will get an influx of needed resources for your final assault.

Montdidier is best approached from the south. You may want to build an airport in Roye to fly planes in from the east and avoid the "headwinds." There is once again artillery on the high ground in the northeast, but it can be dealt with as before. The defenders of Montdidier have many tanks, so bring the AT guns and grenade launchers to the fore!

You should leave a few defenders in Peronne, and have a lot of defenses in town — those Allies are sneaky.

Be sure to check out the casualty numbers when you finish the scenario. If this is victory ...

———————— ✂ ————————

Montdidier has been captured, but our men are tired and underfed. I fear that Richthofen witnessed the last rattle of Germany's might.

EMPIRE EARTH
THE ART OF CONQUEST

PRIMA'S OFFICIAL STRATEGY GUIDE

LIGHTNING WARFARE

German military planners have learned much from the Spanish Civil War. They found that the key to conquering an enemy is to apply overwhelming force with maximum speed. Called the Blitzkrieg, it is now time for German forces to make full use of that lesson ... and their first victim will be Poland.

Great Britain and France have each announced their intention to fight, but their forces are unproven. The English have repudiated their weak leader, Prime Minister Chamberlain. Perhaps his replacement, Churchill, is made of harder stuff. The French have full confidence in their fortifications. But they will sokon understand their folly. The Luftwaffe is ready. The Panzers are ready. The Wehrmacht is ready. Where Germany failed in 1914, it will succeed in 1939.

Legend

- **F** Forage
- **S** Stone
- **D** Dock
- **I** Iron
- **G** Gold
- — Wall
- **N** Naval Yard

Players

Germany (you; gray; WWII)

France/Benelux (allies; potential enemies; blue; WWII)

Denmark/Norway (allies; potential enemies; light blue; WWII)

Poland (ally; potential enemy; light yellow; WWI)

Britain (potential enemy; red; WWII)

U.S.S.R. (steadfastly neutral; dark red; WWII)

Initial Resources

5000 Food   5000 Wood   2500 Stone
6000 Gold   6000 Iron

Required Objectives

Destroy French capitol and build your own town center there

Destroy Norwegian capitol and build your own town center there

Destroy Polish capitol and build your own town center there

German Campaign / Lightning Warfare

Optional Objectives

You can build a capitol instead of a town center in each country

Civ Point

Opportunities

5   Building your first capitol

15   Victory

Resource Opportunities

Each time you conquer a country:

3000 Food, 2500 Wood, 2500 Stone, 3000 Gold, 3000 Iron

You Lose If

Reichstag is destroyed

Time expires (one year, a.k.a. 80 minutes)

Scenario-Specific Stats

Reichstag

HP   5,000

LOS   2

French Monument

HP   3,500

LOS   5

Walkthrough

The game time is broken down into 4 seasons, each lasting approximately 20 minutes of game time: Fall 1939, Winter 1939-1940, Spring 1940 and Summer 1940. If you have not won by the end of the Summer 1940 season, you are defeated. Total game time is then approximately 1hour and 20 minutes.

"Blitzkrieg" means "lightning war," so you've gotta move fast, but move smart. In the civ point spending phase at the start, increase the speed of just about all of your units. Decreasing build time

would also be good, and upping iron and gold production never hurts. Don't forget the Pop Cap Increase!

Get the peasants cracking building AA guns for defense and another tank and airplane production facility. Build a granary as well. If you practice a "scorched earth" policy, you should not need defenses for the Reichstag beyond AA and maybe a tower or two. There are no resources to gather so far except wood and food, so build, build, build! Use the hospital to increase citizen speed. Produce a few extra citizens at the start.

Assemble a balanced force of machine gunners, bazooka, AT guns, artillery, and howitzers. Build at least one of the other ground units as well. Infantry uses up iron, which will be precious at times, so you may want to build very few of them. Build a pair of medics and at least one engineer. And tanks. Lots of tanks. Also build 4-5 flakpanzers (mobile AA). Bombers and fighters will be essential. Remember to queue up unit improvements as soon as a unit of that type appears. Improve according to the units function, as always: range for artillery, armor for tanks, flight time for planes, etc. As you are building up, build an observation balloon to scout out future enemy territory.

Once you have a maxed-out force, it's time to get busy. Hmmm ... where to go? Poland has a lot of the resources you need, and will be a pushover. Cavalry? Please. When you declare war on Poland, Britain will declare war on you, although France does not. Place your fighters and flakpanzers near the French border to shoot down British planes. Keep building lots of AA west of your city. Send everyone else into Poland, attacking north of the forest.

EMPIRE EARTH
THE ART OF CONQUEST

PRIMA'S OFFICIAL STRATEGY GUIDE

Note that although you can't send ground troops into future enemy territory until you declare war, there's nothing stopping you from circling other capitols with aircraft and floating a battleship in as close to shore as possible, before everything becomes official.

The basic attack strategy is this: Send in tanks, machine gunners and AT guns to deal with Polish forces. There are a lot of tanks near Warsaw, so be careful. Once the Polish defenders have been eliminated, move the tanks, MG and AT guns beyond the city and put the artillery, howitzers and bazookas to work. When one city is almost reduced, move the tanks forward until resistance is encountered, then repeat. It is important to keep moving, as time is of the essence. Use the bombers to hit more distant targets which the balloon has hopefully spotted. The Polish air force is a myth, so after you destroy the airport in the city closest to you, your bombers can operate at leisure. Poland is pretty big, so make sure you've rooted out every pocket of resistance, or you could find Polish tanks hitting the Reichstag later.

As soon as Warsaw is reduced, send 5 citizens in to build a settlement on the blue square. Once the settlement is built, populate it up to a town center. As soon as your town center is up, the natives stop fighting. There might be one or two units in the queue that appear, but they don't move. Gifts will flow into your coffers. There is gold and iron in Warsaw, and in the extreme southeastern corner.

Build another settlement down there to keep materials going. Don't worry about the Soviets; their time will come later.

Take all troops back to Germany. Use the new riches to upgrade them further and max out the army again. You may want to do a few extra planes, since you will soon have to deal with those French planes you see circling overhead. Army not big enough? Build a stadium with this new wealth! Heal up near the hospital and use the balloon to scout out French territory. Watch out for British planes! Did we mention to build AA guns?

See the Maginot Line? Avoid it! You can go around it after you declare war, and attack Belgium first. It is very important that you reduce Belgium to rubble, to guard your back as you invade France. Attack first with troop destroyers (tanks, MG, AT guns), then once the defenders are dead, use the structure destroying units (artillery, howitzers, bazookas) to lay waste. While that is happening, move the tanks across the far north side of the fords and engage the French troops. Watch your artillery, as it tends to want to attack the Maginot line. Be sure to have flakpanzer units on hand, as well as fighters and bombers overhead. In Paris, destroy the Arc D'Triomphe and capitol as soon as possible — they both strengthen the natives.

Once over the river, destroy the tank and siege facilities NW of Paris. Remember to send troop destroyers ahead while the artillery is doing its job.

German Campaign / Preparations For Invasion

Take down the monuments and town center as soon as the factories are down. Once the town center is destroyed, move in five settlers as before to build a settlement and town center. Troops will attack from the west, so use the engineer to build pillboxes at the crossing of the Seine and leave the troop destroyers there while the structure destroyers move south around the forest to destroy the buildings in the west. Take a tank or two with the artillery. Then it's a push to the sea.

As you are reducing the west of France, a new threat appears: British ships. They are vulnerable to artillery, submarines and bombers, however, so get a little practice in for the next phase.

Meanwhile, back home, build a coliseum and hospital to pump up your pop cap. Send the balloon to scout out Scanda-navia. Note the big navy in the North Sea. Build a few extra bombers and artillery to deal with them until the time comes.

Denmark and Norway are well defended with towers and ships, so a different strategy is needed. Advance slowly across the peninsula, with assault troops guarding artillery, while bombers and artillery take out towers and ships. You might even send a special force to eliminate the capitol as early as possible. The Scandinavian air force is very weak, so use your fighters to protect the invasion force. Have five citizens ready. Once you're in Norway, the previous strategy can be employed: use assault forces to kill troops while artillery attacks buildings. Send in the settlers to rebuild Oslo, and the Blitzkrieg will come to a satisfactory conclusion.

───────── ⌀⌀⌀ ─────────

German authorities were pleased to announce today their total hegemony over Continental Europe. Parades were arranged in many European capitals, while in Great Britain, Prime Minister Churchill reaffirmed that German victory on the Continent would not weaken his nation's resolve to continue the struggle, with or without direct support from the United States.

PREPARATIONS FOR INVASION

With Continental Europe largely under the control of the Axis, Great Britain finds itself isolated and relying increasingly on supplies from America. Knowing this, Germany has dispatched additional U-boats to blockade the island nation, seeking to destroy all convoys bound for its shores.

But a weakened Britain is not a defeated Britain. To achieve absolute victory, a German invasion will be necessary. But an invasion can never succeed so long as the British Home Fleet protects her coast. Prior to launching an amphibious landing, Germany must build up its naval strength. Then, they must send the Home Fleet to the bottom.

Legend

F	Forage
S	Stone
D	Dock
I	Iron
G	Gold
—	Wall
N	Naval Yard

EMPIRE EARTH
THE ART OF CONQUEST

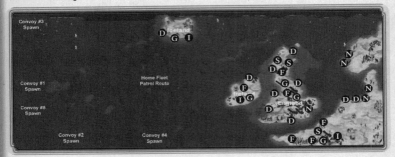

Players

All – WWII

Germany (you; gray)

Great Britain (including convoys; enemy; red)

British Home Fleet (enemy; dark red)

Iceland and Ireland (neutral; light yellow)

Initial Resources

1000 Food	2000 Wood
1000 Gold	1000 Iron

Required Objectives

Destroy all British docks (including new ones that are built)

Sink the British Home Fleet (1 or 2 ships can survive)

Optional Objectives

Block supply transports from the U.S. (gives you resources, rather than Britain)

Civ Point Opportunities

5   Bismarck joins the action

10   Sink 8 transports (only awarded once)

5   Sink the Home Fleet (1 or 2 can survive)

5   Victory

Resource Opportunities

Each successful transport delivers 1000 of each resource to Great Britain (but Britain can have no more than 3000 of any resource at one time)

Each transport sunk rewards Germany with 250 of each resource

Tech Opportunities

Lighthouse

Great Britain can build docks between the time that any transport successfully arrives and the time that you sink another transport

Scenario-Specific Stats

Bismarck (completed)

HP	6,625
Attack	800 (Ms) / 4
Speed	12
Armor	20 (Ar, Pr, Ls), 30 (Gn)

German Campaign / Preparations For Invasion

HMS Arbiter

HP   16,000

Speed   10

Armor 20 (Ar, Pr, Gn, Ls)

Convoys

Transport, battleship, cruiser
(in first 30 min.)

Transport, battleship, frigate (Good Hope), two frigates (Warrington)
(after 30 minutes)

British Airbase

HP   31,000   LOS   3

Walkthrough

In this scenario, you rely on your ships and planes, so improve those in the point-spending phase. Improve the flight time and speed of planes, and the toughness and build time of ships. Make sure you have your gold and iron gathering improved and your pop cap raised. You might also want to make your citizens tougher, because they'll need it.

And remember, Ireland is neutral, so their docks will heal your ships.

You will get bombed in this scenario. Build lots of AA guns at the start. Your people will need to gather all resources except stone and food. No ground forces are needed in this scenario, just sea and air. Go to the university to up your ship repair times, and improve your wood gathering ability at the capitol. Don't forget to make more citizens to mine.

You will need an air force of 6-7 bombers and a like number of fighters or fighter bombers. Do not use rally points to attack! Have all planes rally in the vicinity of your airport. Never send your planes in piecemeal; mass air assaults not only look pretty, they're much more likely to survive. Never send a bomber without escort! Be sure to improve your planes from time to time, especially flight time.

You need to build a balanced navy to complement and protect the Bismarck. Get 5-6 battleships, 7-8 cruisers, and about twice that number of subs. Use the "wolfpack" you already have to patrol the western waters and interdict convoys. You get resources for this, so it's worth doing, but don't add more than 3 other subs to the pack. You will need to amass a huge fleet at home. Don't bother with frigates, since the Brits don't build subs. When you run up against the pop Cap, be sure to use resources to improve your units.

When the time comes to attack, use the fleet first to take out coastal defenses, such as the AA guns and the radar installation. Use the planes to bomb the useless Home Guard troops, but make sure there are plenty of fighters around. Once most of the AA guns on the southern coast have been cleared out, send two-thirds of the fleet around to clear out the other AA defenses and to bombard the northern airports and docks. With the Bismarck's big guns, they should crumble.

Don't underestimate the importance of cruisers. Send about half the cruisers north with the main fleet to scour the coastline, and place the other half in the Channel with a battleship or two and some subs to protect them. They can shoot planes down before they can cross the Channel, or get to the Bismarck. You may need to shuffle ships from time to time over to the docks for repairs. The far northern docks may get destroyed, but that's not a big deal. You're on offense, not defense.

EMPIRE EARTH
THE ART OF CONQUEST

PRIMA'S OFFICIAL STRATEGY GUIDE

At a certain point, the Brits will start to reinforce their convoys with frigates. Withdraw the wolfpack to the main fleet, and then use a variety of ships to interdict convoys and destroy facilities along the west coast of England.

Bomb targets in this order: AA guns, town centers and capitols, and airports. If the fleet has done its job, AA guns should be few in number and easily handled. It takes about 6-7 bombers to take out a capitol in one sortie. Why the capitols? Because that keeps the British citizens from repairing things — like docks and airports. You may want to take out the two airports nearest you first, just to clear the skies a little.

Remember that fighter escort is essential to a successful bombing raid. Once you have decimated the citizenry and taken out most of the airports, you may bomb docks at leisure while your fleet seeks out the Brits.

The lighthouse might be useful in helping you find them, but remember, only a well-balanced (and large) navy can succeed. Bombers might be helpful if they're in range of the fleet. Take cruisers with you; you never know what tricks the Brits may have.

England's fleet and naval bases are smashed! The path to invasion is now clear.

OPERATION SEA LION

Despite years of war and enmity, Goering admires the English nation and its people. But they foolishly refuse to surrender, so his Luftwaffe is ready to initiate what will become their demise. Heinkel bombers will melt the barbed wire and guns that stand between the beaches and London. Messerschmitt fighters will blur through the skies, sending the Royal Air Force down in flames.

Once London is conquered, a new German town center will serve as the heart of the occupation. This center will be built upon the embers of Buckingham Palace, breaking the spirit of the entire British Empire in one symbolic act.

The ground troops of the invasion force are already en route to France by train from all across Europe. Additional resources have been made available to provide for sea transports and any emergencies, which are sure to arise. By the time the troops are ready, their landing site on the shore of Britain should be prepared.

Against the roar of the Luftwaffe's engines, the dawn of a Greater Germany begins!

Legend

F	Forage
S	Stone
D	Dock
I	Iron
G	Gold
—	Wall
N	Naval Yard
R	Radar Center

German Campaign / Operation Sea Lion

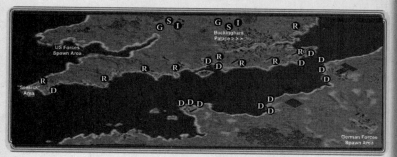

Players

All – WWII

Germany (you; gray)

Great Britain (enemy; red)

United States (enemy; green)

Free French (enemy; blue)

Vichy France (possession; light yellow)

Initial Resources

10,000 Food   10,000 Wood

2000 Gold   2000 Iron

Required Objectives

Destroy Buckingham Palace

Build your own town center or capitol there

Eliminate all U.S. buildings in Britain

Optional Objectives

Destroy British RADAR sites

Civ Point

Opportunities

10   Sink U.S. carrier

10   Get a land unit into Britain

10   Reduce Britain's RADAR sites to fewer than 5

Resource Opportunities

Six task forces arrive to assist you:

1) After 4 minutes: Infantry, medic, 57mm AT guns

2) After 6 minutes: Infantry, bazooka(s), panzer(s)

3) After 8 minutes: Infantry, machine gun(s), trench mortar(s), panzer(s)

4) After 10 minutes: Infantry, flame thrower(s), flak halftrack(s)

5) After 12 minutes: Infantry, machine gun(s), artillery

6) After 14 minutes: Panzers, flak half-track(s), Rommel

Tech Opportunities

(Anytime a spy succeeds, that spy is no longer available)

If spy gets next to a town center or capitol, the center or capitol collapses, and you get 250 Gold and Iron

If spy gets next to a British barracks, tank factory, siege factory, airport, dock or hospital, you gain possession of the building

If spy captures a British dock, you get Bismarck, Warrington and Dardo (cruiser) techs

If spy captures a British airport, you get ME-110, Heinkel, ME-262, ME-109 and FW-190 techs

EMPIRE EARTH
THE ART OF CONQUEST

Scenario-Specific Stats

Rommel

HP	8,650
Attack	55 (Ms)/2
Speed	14
Armor	10 (Sh), 9(Pr)

Recon Plane

HP	425
Attack	17 (Ms)/0.5
Speed	20
LOS	10
Fuel	400

Drop Plane

You get up to three drop planes, each with 4–6 paratroopers

HP	600
Speed	22

Paratrooper

HP	405
Attack	60 (Gn)/12
Speed	9

Spy

HP	5,235
Attack	160 (Ms)/2
Speed	14
Armor	10 (Sh), 9 (Pr)

British Bomber

HP	940
Attack	135 (Ms)/0.5
Speed	19

Free French Infantry

HP	350
Attack	35 (Gn) / 1.5
Speed	12
Armor	10 (Gn)

Free French Mortar

HP	375
Attack	90 (Gn) / 8
Speed	12

U.S. Subs (two types)

HP	1,350
Attack	200 (Ms)/6
Speed	13
HP	1000
Attack	130 (Ms)/6
Speed	13

U.S. Carrier

HP	6,000
Speed	10
Armor	20 (Ar, Pr, Gn, Ls)

Walkthrough

The Battle of Britain will be won or lost in the skies, so before beginning, spend Civ Points to improve bombers (flight time, hit points and punch) and fighters (flight time, hit points and speed). Also up the hit points and armor of tanks and infantry units; they'll need to be tough. You will not be gathering resources or building many units, and Pop Cap won't matter, so don't worry about those.

Your first thought should be organizing the Luftwaffe. Use rally points over the channel to organize the planes into three groups: north, central, and south. Make sure there are both bombers and fighters in each group. Since you will not be building much, use resources to improve planes. Send reconnaissance planes out to scout the coastline. Hold back the drop planes by having them rally somewhere separate.

Build four transports immediately; as troops arrive, the Pop Cap will keep you from gathering more (unless you store them in fortresses). Before the invasion force masses, use the fleet to attack coastal defenses, especially AA guns and radar stations. You may have to hunt diligently, as many installations are too far inland to attack from the sea. You may want to use the drop planes to attack those with paratroops. When that is done, assemble the fleet with the transports where the channel is narrowest. Keep the subs on the lookout for ships in the Channel.

Use the planes to take out facilities in this order: AA guns, radar installations and airports. Group North will also want to destroy towers and barbed wire along the coast where the invasion will take place. Always attack en masse, with a mixed group of bombers and fighter escort. Use the fighters to take out RAF planes and those annoying balloons, and then send them home with the bombers; no need to hang about. Also bomb any ships that get into the Channel.

German Campaign / Operation Sea Lion

As the troops arrive, send them straight-away to the Channel. A group of Frenchies will attack, but they can be quickly dispatched. Make sure that the bombers have punched holes in barbed wire and knocked down towers at the landing sites. Keep the fleet, especially the cruisers, with the transports. Try to get everyone over in one or two trips. Shock troops should go first (panzers, MG, and AT guns, along with Rommel), then infantry and flakpanzers, and finally medics and artillery. Devote a group of fighters to fly over the troops, and send bombers to take out British troops and facilities. While the ground troops take out AA guns, bombers should take down towers and production facilities.

Once a beachhead has been established, turn your attention to the leveling of Buckingham Palace. Send the north and central bomber groups to destroy the very southern tip of the wall. You will be exposed to AA fire, but it will be worth it. Keep the ground troops focused on the wall; left to their own, they may destroy valuable buildings that can be taken by spies later. Once the wall is down, send tanks in to destroy the remaining AA while the other troops guard the artillery. Pound the palace with bombers and artillery until it comes down. During the bombardment, get those lazy citizens over on a transport. Don't forget troop escorts! Build a settlement in the ruins of the Palace, and shuffle the new citizens you get over to make it a capitol.

You should move your army west as soon as the capitol is completed. Otherwise, the idle soldiers will attack buildings that you can now take over with spies. The hospital is an obvious target, and you will want to take the production facilities north of the palace and crush a city center or two to get

resources. Once you take the production facilities over, you can build much needed reinforcements! Bomb the towers around to make sure these reinforcements don't come under fire. Again, watch your units carefully, otherwise these buildings could get knocked down.

Move the fleet west, because a new threat has appeared: the Americans! They have a carrier, some frigates, and some subs, so send the whole navy together, healing up a bit if need be. Something for Bomber Group South to do, eh? The carrier will produce planes soon, so you will get in maybe one or two bombing runs before the corsairs will be a threat. Do not take the Americans lightly; corsairs can sink a battleship!

Bring the army west with haste, as the flakpanzers will be needed to combat the American corsairs. You will have to deal with stiff British resistance and American reinforcements, so keep the army together. Travis Shackelford will be in the central regions, so take him down when you can. Speaking of heroes, remember to use Field Marshall Rommel's battlecry liberally! Use bombers and artillery to soften up pockets of British troops. The Allies will mostly have tanks, so keep the AT guns healed!

Once the 8th Fleet has been dealt with by your ships and bombers, move the troops around into Wales to attack the American buildings. Be careful of an American attack from behind! They only have a few buildings, so it should be relatively easy for a force of tanks, AT guns, and infantry to win the day.

The British throne has retreated to Canada! England is now a province in the far greater German empire.

EMPIRE EARTH
THE ART OF CONQUEST

∞ Russian Campaign ∞

The life of Grigor Illyanich Stoyanovich had largely comprised dark corners and back alleyways: the run-down tenements of his birthplace, the shadowy meeting rooms of the Russian Mafia, the political rallies held in abandoned warehouses. He had struggled against adversity since the day of his birth, just as so many other Russians had. Just as so many continued to do.

Now, following his failed election campaign and an abortive coup in Moscow, Grigor's future seems no less grim than his past. Hounded by the Russian Government's security forces, who seek to try him as a criminal and a traitor, Grigor has taken refuge in the city of Voronezh. But true safety lies further south in Volgograd, where faithful supporters stand ready to deliver him the city upon his arrival.

It is time for this heretofore unsuccessful yet supremely confident political agitator to step out of the shadows and into the limelight.

THE CROCODILE

Grigor, Grigor! Your life is in danger!

It has been for months, if not years, Pyotr. What is it now?

The authorities in Moscow know you are here in Voronezh — they have alerted the local security forces. We must leave before they find you!

My only surprise is that the so-called "authorities" did not try to seize me sooner. It is just as well; colleagues in Volgograd have sent word that the whole city is prepared to rise up in support of me if I join them there.

Legend

F	Forage
S	Stone
D	Dock
I	Iron
G	Gold
—	Wall

Players

All – Modern Age
Ushi Party (you; red; Modern ➔ Digital)
Voronezh (enemy; light blue)
Volgograd (potential ally; light blue)
Saratov (potential ally; yellow)
Rostov (potential ally; purple)
Ukraine (potential ally; orange)

Initial Resources

None

Required Objectives

Escape Voronezh
Ally with Volgograd
Destroy Voronezh's capitol

Optional Objectives

Ally with Saratov
Ally with Rostov
Ally with Ukraine

Russian Campaign / The Crocodile

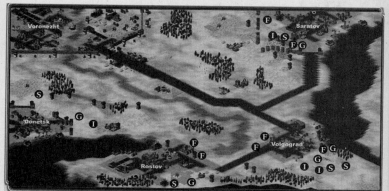

Civ Point Opportunities

10   Ally with all three optional allies

15   Victory

Tech Opportunities

All normal techs become available when you ally with Volgograd

You Lose If

Grigor Stoyanovich is captured or dies

Scenario-Specific Stats

Grigor's car is a staff car

The potato truck is a cargo truck

Pyotr is a citizen

In early-dawn Voronezh, enemy troop LOS is reduced to 3 tiles.

Vassili

HP	3,600
Attack	90 (Ms)/2
Speed	14
Armor	10 (Sh)

Veronezh Capitol

HP	10,000
LOS	5

Veronezh AA

HP	2,400
Attack	100 (Ms)/3
LOS	8
Armor	7 (Gn)

Diplomat (envoy to other cities)

HP	2,540
Attack	3 (Ar) / 2
Speed	12

Walkthrough

Your first task is to get Grigor safely out of Voronezh. You start in control of Grigor Stoyanovich and are informed the local authorities are pursuing you. Your immediate goal is to find a way to escape the city. The use of a car is suggested; however, this is not the correct strategy. If Pyotr tries to tuck Grigor in the trunk of his car and toodle right out the front gate, the guards will get wise. Cruise around town for awhile until you get to the agricultural district. You'll find a potato truck that Grigor can successfully hide in. Make sure Grigor isn't seen by enemy troops while you're loading and unloading him. If Grigor is seen, you lose.

When you get to Volgograd, you're given control of the city. The first thing to do is build diplomats and send them off to bring the neighboring cities over to your side. Saratov and Rostov are easy, if you give them the tribute they want (you have it when you take control of Volgograd, if you don't spend it). They don't give change, however. Any surplus given will be lost to you.

The Ukraine requires a little bit of stealth going in, so your diplomat isn't killed by city defenses before he reaches the fortress. Nothing fancy, just make sure he keeps moving and avoids the towers and troops until he has a straight shot at the fortress.

Voronezh will harass you, but with all three neighbors on your side they'll have a hard time even getting troops to you.

Now you have to build up your forces and take Voronezh. Air superiority will be a huge help. Don't hesitate to go nuclear. Helicopters are good at taking out the local AA defenses to clear the way for your bombers. When the town center goes down, you win.

――――――― ⌘ ―――――――

It is done! With the fall of Voronezh, the Moscow government can't possibly stop me from controlling the region. Novaya Russia is a reality at last! Now those fools in Moscow who counted me out shall pay dearly.

NOVAYA RUSSIA

It took many years, but the dual humiliations of a lost election and failed coup had finally been avenged. Deep inside the Kremlin, as Grigor Stoyanovich settled into his new residence, vodka flowed freely in celebration of the victory. But maps and battle plans were already being prepared for the next phase of expansion. Grigor wanted more territory, and he knew just from where to take it.

In the years of consolidation that followed the capture of Moscow, a problem had surfaced. Grigor's propaganda machine could not gloss over the violence being committed by his Black Robes. Commoners and dissidents were fleeing Novaya Russia in droves and spreading tales of "atrocities" and "terror." Ukraine, sensing the danger, had already begun forging alliances with the major powers of Europe. And those powers, mindful of the lessons of the previous century, were not going to ignore the perceived threat growing to the East. The Ukraine had to be brought under Novaya Russia's banner, and Grigor confidently predicted his former Ally would be easy prey.

But the European powers were another matter. If they were to be neutralized, he had to move swiftly and decisively against them ... or risk losing all he had accomplished.

Legend

F Forage
S Stone
D Dock
I Iron
G Gold
N Naval Yard

Players

Novaya Russia (you; red; Digital)

United Kingdom (enemy; yellow; Digital)

Norway (Oslo; enemy; yellow; Digital)

Poland (Copenhagen; enemy; purple; Digital)

Ukraine (Kiev; enemy; orange; Digital)

Rebel forces (enemy; green; Modern)

St. Petersburg (potential ally; red; Digital)

Arkhangelsk (potential ally; red; Digital)

Other European towns (enemy; pink; Digital ➔ Nano)

Allied air force (enemy; purple; Digital)

Russian Campaign / Novaya Russia

Initial Resources

2000 Food 2000 Wood 500 Stone
2500 Gold 2500 Iron

Required Objectives

Destroy two of the three nearby capitols
(Oslo, Copenhagen, Kiev)

Defeat rebel forces

Optional Objectives

Control St. Petersburg
(adds 10 to Pop Cap)

Control Arkhangelsk
(adds 10 to Pop Cap)

Civ Point Opportunities

15   Defeat rebels

15   Victory

Tech Opportunities

Cyber Factory   When you meet
Septimus (after
conquering first
capitol)

You Lose If

Grigor Stoyanovich dies(the cyber can be
destroyed)

Scenario-Specific Stats

Medical Center is identical to Temple of
Zeus (in both cost and effect)

Monument to Grigor is identical to
Ishtar Gates (in both cost and effect)

Enemy towers have +3 range

Each stone mine has only 1500 stone in it

Walkthrough

This is a much tougher scenario than
anything you've faced before, in any of
the campaigns. You're under pretty
much constant fire, but you have to
not only defend your home base, but
also build up and effectively use an
offensive force.

EMPIRE EARTH
THE ART OF CONQUEST

The first thing to do is to take out the rebels *fast*. If you don't, they'll spread all over the map, like kudzu, and you'll be under attack literally from all directions. If you do get the Rebels taken care of quick, you have a direction to expand into with relative safety.

While you're mopping up the rebels, try to get some kind of resource collection system organized at the same time. Your iron mine is particularly exposed, and the nearest trees are far enough from town to be risky. Stone is a severely limited resource in this scenario: quarries only give a little stone before they run out. Between wonders and defenses, you're going to need more than one quarry's worth of stone.

Pretty soon the raids start. The Western Alliance of your enemies sends in strike forces from all directions (they're good at sneaking around your city to come at you from unexpected directions). Build up your air defenses right away, because a nuclear strike (probably directed against your siege factory) is coming early on. Plus, Great Britain is sending stronger, more advanced forces against you. These attacks almost always come from the northwest (as do a significant proportion of the alliance forces) so concentrate your defenses in that direction.

Once you've stabilized your defensive situation you have several options, none of them good. You have two allied cities to the north, Arkhangelsk and St. Petersburg. Taking over these cities will provide you with more offensive options (largely naval), and increase your Population Cap, but before you grab them be perfectly sure you can defend them. (On a related note, the Espionage Center wonder can be extremely useful in this scenario, but building it will reveal Arkhangelsk and St. Petersburg, so don't build it before you're ready.)

You can take Britain out of the picture by destroying all the British docks and naval yards on the map, but this will require a major sea and air campaign, and you might be better off just continuing to soak up the attacks.

It's not until you actually take (by whatever means you can come up with) the first of the two enemy capitals that you get your first real break. You get the ability to build cybers, plus a crazy old scientist presents you with a unique and very powerful cyber called (for now) the Rostov JK 1. Don't worry if the Rostov is destroyed in the line of duty. It can be repaired in time for the next scenario.

Once you've managed to take both enemy capitals and have eliminated all Rebel buildings from the map, you win.

With the rebellion crushed and our Western borders secure, I feel I can finally rest my weary bones for a time. But Novaya Russia has not reached her zenith yet!

COPPER AGE | DARK AGE | RENAISSANCE | INDUSTRIAL AGE | INFORMATIO
BC | 2000 BC | 500 BC | 0 AD | 900 AD | 1800 AD | 1500 AD | 1700 AD | 1900 AD | 2000 AD
BRONZE AGE | MIDDLE AGES | IMPERIAL AGE | ATOMIC AGE

Russian Campaign / Changing of the Guard

CHANGING OF THE GUARD

Years have passed and Grigor has grown old. He is in command of a strong, unified Russia. He has conquered most of Europe, the Middle East and Northern Africa. His empire ranks as one of the largest the world has ever known. But, despite his accomplishments, his life's work remains unfinished. He wants more, but knows he won't have time to obtain it.

Grigor had hoped to pass his legacy on to an heir, but, despite utilizing the most advanced medical techniques available, that goal has eluded him. Now, with time growing short and his mistrust of others growing stronger, he has made a decision that he knows some will view with skepticism. But it may also serve to root out the very people he mistrusts.

Just before his foray into Eastern and Central Europe, Grigor was presented with a mechanical bodyguard – an early "cyber". Since then, the field of Artificial Intelligence matured to a point where sentience became possible. Dr. Septimus, the machine's creator, updated the cyber with the latest AI technology, bestowing upon it true consciousness. He additionally set up facilities to produce other types of intelligent cybers, but Grigor's bodyguard was his greatest single achievement.

The aging leader of Novaya Russia eventually came to regard the cyber as his successor, naming "him" Grigor II. After spending many months preparing him, Grigor was ready to announce his heir to his people.

Legend

B Barracks Garrison

C Cyber Factory Garrison

F Rebel Fortress

H Hospital

S Siege Factory Garrison

T Tank Factory Garrison

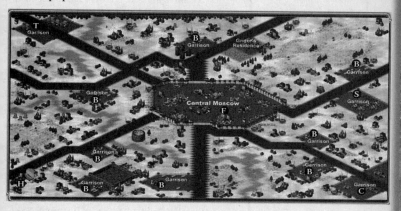

Players

All – Digital

Novaya Russia (you; red)

Rebel Russians (enemies; blue)

Yukov, Kulenka, Kolchov, Palutkin (traitors; yellow and pink)

Initial Resources

None

EMPIRE EARTH
THE ART OF CONQUEST

PRIMA'S OFFICIAL STRATEGY GUIDE

Required Objectives

Travel to all 11 garrisons
(to raise troops)

Destroy rebel fortress

Defeat 4 traitors

Optional Objectives

Get Grigor to hospital to repair his heart

Civ Point Opportunities

10   Visit all 11 garrisons

20   Victory

Resource Opportunities

Three Thor AT guns, paladin cannon
   At siege factory garrison

Apollo, two Hyperions
   At cyber factory garrison

Three gladiator tanks
   At tank factory garrison

Five to eight black robes, random chance
of black robe officers
   At each loyal barracks

You Lose If

Grigor Stoyanovich dies before the end
of the scenario

Grigor II dies

Molotov dies

Scenario-Specific Stats

Yukov	
HP	7,650
Attack	55 (Ms)/2
Speed	14
Armor	10 (Sh), 9 (Pr)

Kulenka	
HP	4,040
Attack	3 (Ar) / 2
Speed	12

Kolchov	
HP	9,235
Attack	160 (Ms)/2
Speed	14
Armor	10 (Sh), 9 (Pr)

Palutkin	
HP	7,600
Attack	90 (Ms)/2
Speed	14
Armor	10 (Sh)

Grigor II	
HP	6,000
Attack	200 (Ms)/2
Speed	12
Armor	50 (Ar, Pr, Gn), 75 (Ls)

Walkthrough

This is by far the easiest scenario in the campaign. Think of it as a sort of vacation, because from here on out things get hairy.

An aging and ill Grigor has just named his heir — his personal bodyguard — the Rostov JK 1, hereafter known as Grigor II. His generals are not pleased to be passed over for promotion in favor of a piece of hardware. They've taken over the town center of Moscow and dug in until they can mount a devastating attack on both Grigors. Warned by a young man named Lt. Molotov, Grigor has to tour the garrisons around town, gathering those troops that are still loyal to him. However, those troops that aren't still loyal to him are in the way.

Four (randomly chosen) infantry garrisons in the city are still loyal to Grigor. Plus, he can pick up a few cybers and tanks along the way as well. About halfway around the map, Grigor has a small heart attack, leaving him at half hit points. Get him to the city hospital (in the lower western section of the map) to fix him up (temporarily).

Russian Campaign / Jewel in the East

Once you've gathered all your forces, you can attack the central city. There's a building spitting out fresh troops at a rapid rate; if you destroy it your job will be that much easier. Once you've destroyed rebel headquarters and killed the four traitorous generals, you win.

Molotov and both Grigors have to survive to the end of the scenario. Once you've won, however, Grigor's ticker gives out and he dies, leaving the Tin Man in charge.

Sir!?! Are you all right?

No, my devoted young Lieutenant. My age and the strain of dealing with these traitors has simply been ... too much, even with the Doctor's medical device. Remember, Novaya Russia above all ... do not let the dream ...

Rest easy, my master. I will ensure your dreams do not die here with you.

JEWEL IN THE EAST

With his power base firmly established, Grigor II began a lightning campaign to defeat the last remaining power on the continent that still posed a major threat to Novaya Russia: mighty China.

The slaughter was terrible. Wave after wave of Chinese defenders were met by matching waves of Black Robes and Russian-produced cybers – the legacy of Dr. Septimus. The stalemate was finally broken in the highlands of Mongolia, which had the misfortune of being caught between the two clashing superpowers. The Russians achieved a major breakthrough, but at a terrible price.

Legend

- **F** Forage
- **S** Stone
- **D** Dock
- **I** Iron
- **G** Gold
- — Wall

Now, the spearhead of the Russian forces has moved far beyond their lines of supply. The bitter fighting and equally bitter Mongolian Winter, in an ironic twist on Russian history, has begun to take its toll on Novaya Russia's flesh-and-blood troops. If total victory is not achieved soon, it may never be.

But Grigor II and his personally led forces have nearly reached their ultimate goal: Beijing, the Chinese capital. While the massive armies on both sides continue to fight, a secret mission has been launched to capture the Factories that are producing the bulk of the Chinese cybers. If this daring raid succeeds, the Chinese forces will surely crumble. Victory is close, but timing will be everything.

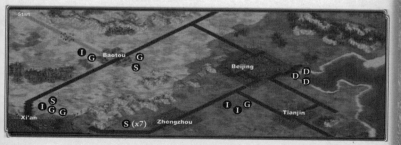

EMPIRE EARTH
THE ART OF CONQUEST

PRIMA'S OFFICIAL STRATEGY GUIDE

Players

Novaya Russia (you; red; Digital ➔ Nano)

Beijing (enemy; yellow; Nano)

Baotou and Xi'an (enemy; purple; Nano)

Other Chinese cities (enemy; light yellow; Nano)

Science Complex (enemy; blue; Nano)

Chinese Air Force (enemy; yellow; Nano)

Initial Resources

2500 Food   2500 Wood   1500 Stone

5000 Gold   1500 Iron

Required Objectives

Convert 8 cyber factories and/or labs

Destroy time machine

Optional Objectives

Get near Xi'an's advanced science facility (see Tech Opportunities)

Civ Point Opportunities

15   Epoch up to Nano Age

10   Victory

Tech Opportunities

By getting near Xi'an's advanced science facility, epoch up to Nano Age (including Apollo, Furies, Hades, Poseidon and Tempest cybers).

You Lose If

Grigor II dies

Molotov dies before dealing with time machine

There aren't enough cyber factories/labs left to convert

You don't have enough citizens, priests and gold (in combination) to win

Scenario-Specific Stats

Molotov
HP   8,100
Attack   380 (Ms) / 2
Speed   14
Armor   10 (Sh)

Baotou and Xi'an Cyber Factories
HP   11,000
LOS   3
Armor   50 (Ar, Pr)

Hyperion
HP   3,200
Attack   80 (Ls) / 2
Speed   16
Armor   50 (Ar, Pr), 35 (Gn), 46 (Ls), 19 (Ms)

Towers
HP   5,250
Attack   350 (Ms) / 4
Range   11
LOS   9

Walkthrough

On campaign in China, Grigor II and Molotov have led a force of cybers on a mission deep behind enemy lines. When you get to the town near your starting point, you take control of the temple. (Remember, to gain control of temples, you must keep them in the line of sight of your units. The temples must be out of the line of sight of enemy units.) The

Russian Campaign / Jewel in the East

temple can be used to create priests which can convert the town to your side. Remember, you have to destroy all the universities in the town before you can convert anything or anyone. Do not let your cybers destroy the whole town before your priests can convert it. Grab the three cyber factories first, and then start converting citizens. Once you have a solid core of workers, convert the rest of the town. Even after you build a town center you won't be able to build your own citizens, and of course you'll be under pretty constant attack from the Chinese. You want to defend your town well enough to fight off enemy troops, but not so well that new citizens can't get through. If you run out of potential converts in town, try the forest to the west.

Be aware that if you lose your priests and cannot make more, you can't win the mission. That means if you have no citizens, no priests and less than 125 gold, you'll lose.

Shortly after you convert your first cyber factory, you get a new mission. Molotov has to break into Xi'an, in the far southwest corner of the map. You can either break into Xi'an with a medium-sized force of cybers, or you can (with a bit of luck) sneak Molotov in (time his passage through the gates so he enters or leaves with a civilian). This will reveal important intelligence (the Chinese are building a time machine) and allow your civilization to proceed to the Nano Epoch (using the button at the town center you should have built by now).

There are 11 total cyber factories — 6 in Tianjin, 3 in Baotou and 2 in Zhengzhou. There are 4 total cyber labs — 2 each in Tianjin and Zhengzhou.

When you go Nano, you get lots of nifty tech upgrades, but unfortunately there's a catch — once you either epoch up or complete your initial objective (eight cyber labs or cyber factories in your control), you get a message that the Chinese are preparing to use their new time machine in Beijing. You have to get Molotov into town to stop it – and there's literally a time clock running. Beijing is very well defended. Lots of Ares flying cybers will be useful in taking it. They're vulnerable to AA, but invulnerable to pretty much everything else, including towers and most ground cybers. Your Apollo has a shield power that will protect Molotov on his way into the factory. Once Molotov gets into the factory, he destroys the Time Machine and is out of the game.

To win, you must both destroy the Time Machine and have eight cyber facilities in your control. Grigor II must survive, and Molotov must survive long enough to take out the Time Machine.

———————— ⌘ ————————

With the Chinese cyber factories under our control and the Black Robes at the front lines poised for victory, the supremacy of Novaya Russia on this continent is assured. The plans of my predecessor and master continue to fall into place … these time travel experiments were too little, too late.

| COPPER AGE | DARK AGE | RENAISSANCE | INDUSTRIAL AGE |
| STONE AGE | BRONZE AGE | MIDDLE AGES | IMPERIAL AGE | ATOMIC AC |

BC 5000 BC 2000 BC 500 BC 0 AD 900 AD 1800 AD 1500 AD 1700 AD 1900 AD 9

PRIMA'S OFFICIAL STRATEGY GUIDE

EMPIRE EARTH
THE ART OF CONQUEST

A CHANGE OF HEART

Grigor II has subdued all of Europe and Asia, but there is one world power with which he must still contend: the United States. Beyond a few skirmishes, little military or diplomatic interaction had taken place between the Americans and Novaya Russians during this time. The US prepared for the presumed invasion, but refrained from launching offensives for fear of harming Grigor's captive population. Instead, they waited for him to come to them.

And now Grigor is doing just that. His troops under newly-promoted General Molotov have been sent to set up operations in the Caribbean. The Americans have responded by sending forces to bolster the defenses of their ally, Cuba. The final showdown has begun.

Legend
F Forage
S Stone
D Dock
I Iron
G Gold
N Naval Yard

Players

Molotov's Expedition (you; red; Nano)

United States (enemy; green; Nano)

Novaya Russia (purple; Nano)

Caribbean League (enemy; orange; Digital)

Cuba (enemy; light blue; Nano)

Initial Resources

2500 Food   2500 Wood   2500 Stone

3500 Gold   3500 Iron

Required Objectives

Destroy Havana capitol

Build Havana facilities (town center, 3 cyber factories and/or labs, 2 docks, navy yard)

Build and defend time machine

Get Ryan and Molotov near fully charged time machine

Optional Objectives

Eliminate Hispaniola outpost

Civ Point Opportunities

15   Havana facilities built

10   Victory

Resource Opportunities

1500 Stone, 2000 Iron, 1500 Wood, 1500 Food, 2000 Gold, citizens shortly after you build Havana facilities

Tech Opportunities

Sentinel trooper, temple and time machine when Havana rebuilt (lose black robe, prophet)

Russian Campaign / A Change of Heart

You Lose If

Molotov dies

Molly Ryan dies

Scenario-Specific Stats

Hyperion

HP   3,200

Attack   80 (Ls) / 2

Speed   16

Armor   50 (Ar, Pr), 35 (Gn), 46 (Ls), 19 (Ms)

Walkthrough

After his injuries in China, Molotov gets "repaired" into a cyborg. He also gets promoted to general. This scenario sees him spearheading the invasion of Cuba. As soon as Molotov's forces land, Grigor II destroys all the transports. It's now do-or-die time.

You begin on the island of Hispaniola. There's an enemy garrison on the island. You don't have to take it out, but you should, to give yourself room to develop your invasion force. (Building a few more tanks and some artillery before you make your move is advised.) There are plenty of resources on the island. Watch out for building too near the coast, particularly to the north and east, as American warships will sail up and bomb your facilities.

Take your time and build up your infrastructure on Hispaniola. When your forces are good and ready, take over Cuba. Destroy the capitol and build a town center on the site. Do not build more facilities on Cuba than you absolutely have to to stay alive. (You'll see why in a second.) Once Cuba is secure, Grigor orders the invasion of Florida to begin. Once again, do not destroy anything in Florida unless you absolutely have to.

Once you establish a beachhead on Florida, Grigor makes a rare miscalculation. He orders Molotov to exterminate several million Cubans! Molotov refuses, and when Grigor insists, Molotov defects to the Americans, surrendering to a plucky American agent named Molly. To prove his sincerity, Molotov presents the Americans with a present, the plans for a time machine that he stole from the Chinese.

Now all of Grigor's forces on Cuba become the enemy, and all the American forces on Florida come under your control. (See why you didn't want to wipe them out?) When the Americans have time to look over the Time Machine plans, there's good news and there's bad news. The good news is the machine can be built; the bad news is that it has to be built on Cuba. So now you have to re-invade Cuba, build a time machine, and successfully defend it until it's ready to be used. If you do that, you win.

――――――― ⌘ ―――――――

Who do we send back? No offense, but you may not blend in very well in the past. I propose that I make the trip. My Russian is pretty fluent and I'm well trained for special operations, although they don't exactly cover these kinds of situations in the manuals.

Very well, Molly. But I know to when we should travel, and my intimate knowledge of that time period could prove essential. We shall go back together.

We are about to perform the most improbable feat ever conceived by Humankind. May the world forgive us if we make a mistake.

I hope I'm still around in the new world we are about to create. And I hope our forged credentials keep us from being shot in the past.

EMPIRE EARTH
THE ART OF CONQUEST

A BAD CASE OF DÉJÀ VU

*A blinding light ... an agonizing pain ... and General Molotov with his
American ally, Molly Ryan, have gone back in an attempt to alter what
cannot be undone. Or can it?*

*Molotov has chosen his target carefully. He hopes to confront the original
Grigor just before his escape from Voronezh, when he has not yet attained
power. But he may also have to confront an age-old riddle: is it right to
murder a man for crimes he has yet to commit? Molotov is troubled by
that question. His recollection of the strong leader he met near the end of
his life so long ago is difficult to reconcile with the legacy left by his metal-
lic successor.*

*Written history and even memories are sometimes romanticized to such a degree that they no
longer match up with the actual events of the time. And so Molotov wonders, when he and
Molly arrive, will they meet Grigor the hero ... or Grigor the villain?*

Legend
F Forage
S Stone
D Dock
I Iron
G Gold
N Naval Yard

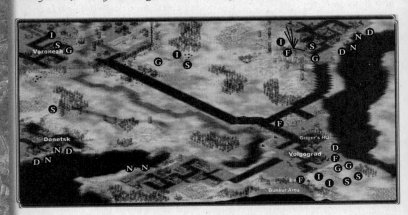

Players

Molotov's Expedition (you; green; Modern)

Voronezh (ally; light blue; Modern)

Ushi Party (enemy; red; Nano)

Ukraine (potential ally; orange; Modern)

Initial Resources

2500 Food   2500 Wood   500 Stone

1500 Gold   1500 Iron

Required Objectives

Kill Grigor II

Russian Campaign / A Bad Case of Déjà Vu

Optional Objectives

Ally with Ukraine

Deploy spies to gain Grigor's tech (see list)

Civ Point Opportunities

5   Each time a spy succeeds in acquiring Nano (XIV) tech

Resource Opportunities

Ukraine resupplies you about every five minutes (if it's an ally). If you have less than 1000 of any resource, Ukraine will give you 500 of that resource. This holds true for each resource, every five minutes.

Tech Opportunities

Spy (initial tech)

When you get a spy to a	You get
Cyber factory	Cyber Factory, plus nearly all the cyber techs
Cyber lab	Specialized Cyber Factory tech
Nano airport	You lose your Modern aircraft techs, and gain the corresponding Digital and Nano techs
Nano tank factory	You get centurion and skywatcher AA tech (but lose your Modern tank techs)
Nano siege factory	You switch out Modern tank techs for Future techs
Nano dock	You switch out Modern techs for Future techs
Nano naval yard	Nano carrier, sub and Avenger tech (while losing your Modern techs)
Barracks	Guardian and medic-info replace medic-atomic and marine for the player

You Lose If

Voronezh capitol is destroyed

Both Ryan and Molotov die

Grigor's HQ is destroyed before Grigor II is eliminated

Walkthrough

This scenario takes up immediately after the events in the previous one, and a hundred years before. Molotov and Molly have just jumped back in time ... to the first scenario in this campaign. Molly wants to kill Grigor (the original), Molotov wants to talk to him and try to warn him about Grigor II. Unfortunately, they arrive just a few minutes too late to stop Grigor's escape to Volgograd.

More bad news. Shortly thereafter Molotov is contacted by Grigor II, who's now in Volgograd. His army took the time machine back, and he arrived earlier than our heroes (even though he left later ... time travel is annoying that way) and has been building up Grigor's forces with future technology.

As soon as you talk to Grigor II, start building up defensive units as fast as you can. At the same time, send either Molotov or Molly to the Ukraine, to get them on your side. This will not only defend your flank, it will also provide a continuous flow of resources, in the form of tribute from the Ukrainians.

EMPIRE EARTH
THE ART OF CONQUEST

PRIMA'S OFFICIAL STRATEGY GUIDE

When Grigor II's future forces attack, your only defense is sheer numbers. This will not work for long against a two epoch technology deficit. Now you need to build the Espionage Center. Use it to build spies and sneak them behind enemy lines to enemy buildings (conveniently revealed by the building of the Espionage Center) to steal technology. You can only have one spy at a time, but you can build a new one when the old one is killed. In this way, you'll be able to close the technology gap, but you'd better hurry. In the meantime, build up lots of AA.

Once you're on equal technological footing, all that's left is for you to build up an invasion force, enter Volgograd, kill Grigor II and destroy the city.

That's all. Massive bomber blitzes combined with a large ground force is about the only way to go here.

Now get Molotov (or Molly, if Molotov is dead – either one can die during the course of the scenario, but at least one has to survive) to Grigor's bunker (the real Grigor – head spinning yet?). Don't destroy the building before you talk to Grigor. If you do, you lose. Whether Molly or Molotov actually reaches Grigor, the result is the same. He's been too propagandized by the cyber, and he has to be assassinated for the good of the future. Do this and you win.

I feel the tug of the time vortex ... pulling ... me ... back. But what future will I return to? One that is better, or worse?

Roman Campaign / Soldiers for Rome

∾∾ Roman Campaign ∾∾

The Roman Republic was born sometime in the 6th Century BC, when the growing village of Rome rebelled against its Etruscan leaders. The local Roman aristocrats set up a Senate and delegated executive action to a pair of annually elected Consuls. Over the next few centuries the village grew into a prosperous city and united much of Italy under its rule by conquest and diplomacy. It eventually expanded its influence into the Mediterranean by challenging and defeating the established power of Carthage. It would be in the 1st Century BC, however, that the Roman Republic would face a series of its most difficult challenges from both within and without its borders — confrontations that would inevitably dissolve a republic, establish an empire and dramatically change the course of Western European history.

SOLDIERS FOR ROME

Gaius Marius, newly elected consúl, having recently won fame in the Jugurthian Wars, had been summoned back to Rome from his conquests in Numidia to defend the Republic from barbarian migrations.

The Senate was worried that two prominent Germanic tribes on its borders, the Teutons and the Cimbri, would soon cross the Alps and take control of all of Northern Italy. These barbarians had been making their way through the mountains, burning and pillaging as they went ... They had to be stopped before they grew bold enough to sack Rome herself!

Legend

F	Forage
S	Stone
I	Iron
G	Gold

The new reforms that Marius had demanded upon his ascension to Consul, namely the new idea of "conscription" has given Rome the manpower she needs to fight the coming battles, ... but just barely. What Rome's army needed now was for the man himself to train these raw troops into the cohesive well-oiled machine that is a Roman Legion.

Rome's new armies would not only consist of its landed citizens, as it did in the past, but also slave and landless freemen classes. Many in the Senate doubted the loyalty and morale of such troops, but Marius had assured them that they would perform their duties as true Romans, especially with the promise of money and land awaiting them at the end of their terms.

Players

Republic of Rome (you; red; Dark Age)

Republic of Rome (ally; blue; Bronze Age)

Republic of Rome (ally; yellow; Bronze Age)

Republic of Rome (ally; purple; Bronze Age)

Republic of Rome (ally; orange; Bronze Age)

Ambrones (enemy; light blue; Copper Age to Bronze Age)

Cimbri (enemy; green; Copper Age to Dark Age)

Teutons (enemy; black; Copper Age to Dark Age)

Initial Resources

Food 200   Wood 200   Gold 175

Required Objectives

Build an army.

Build a defensive fortification.

Slay the leader of the Cimbri.

PRIMA'S OFFICIAL STRATEGY GUIDE

EMPIRE EARTH
THE ART OF CONQUEST

Resource Opportunities

Rescue Mutania from the Teutonic invasion and receive gold.

Civ/Tech Opportunities

None

You Lose If

Gaius Marius dies.

Scenario-Specific Stats

AMBRONES
Gretunix

HP 1,275
Speed 16
LOS 6
Attack 41 (Ms)/2
Range 0.6
Armor 2 (Sh, Pr)
Morale

AMBRONES FORCES INCLUDE

Barbarians
Celtic Warriors
Chariot Archers
Polearms

HP 155
Speed 12
LOS 4
Attack 24 (Pr) / 2
Range 0.5
Armor 3 (Sh)

Javelin

TEUTONS
Thederic

HP 1,800
Speed 12
LOS 6
Attack 52 (Ms)/2
Range 0.5
Armor 3 (Sh, Pr)
Morale

Teuton Messenger

HP 275
Speed 16
LOS 6
Attack 23 (Ar) / 2
Range 5
Armor 6(Sh), 4(Pr)

TEUTON FORCES INCLUDE

Barbarians
Bronze Cavalry

Celtic Warriors
Cavalry Archers
Simple Bowmen (Fire)
Horsemen
Huskarls
Light Spearmen

HP 155
Speed 12
LOS 4
Attack 24 (Pr) / 2
Range 0.5
Armor 3 (Sh)

Pilum
Vikings
War Hounds

HP 16
Speed 14
LOS 3
Attack 10 (Sh) / 2
Range 0.5

Roman Campaign / Soldiers for Rome

CIMBRI

King Ulfir

HP   1,800
Speed   16
LOS   6
Attack   46 (Ms)/2
Range   0.6
Armor   3 (Sh, Pr)
Morale

CIMBRI FORCES INCLUDE

Barbarians Cavalry

HP   290
Speed   16
LOS   4
Attack   23 (Pr) / 2
Range   0.6
Armor   5(Sh), 2(Pr)

Celtic Warriors

Chariot Archers

Composite Bow (Fire)

Horsemen

Polearms

HP   155
Speed   12
LOS   4
Attack   24 (Pr) / 2
Range   0.5
Armor   3 (Sh)

Javelin

Macemen

War Engines (Catapults, Rams, Stone Throwers)

HEATHENS

Heathens from Hell #1

HP   180
Speed   16
LOS   5
Attack   17 (Ar) / 2
Range   4
Armor   1(Ar), 4(Pr)

Heathens from Hell #2

HP   350
Speed   14
LOS   6
Attack   18 (Sh) / 2
Range   0.5
Armor   2 (Ar, Pr)

Heathens from Hell #3

HP   300
Speed   12
LOS   6
Attack   16 (Sh) / 2
Range   0.5
Armor   3 (Sh), 5 (Ar), 2 (Pr)

MUTANIA

Elder

HP   40
Speed   12
LOS   2
Attack   3 (Ar) / 2
Range   2

ROMANS

Quintus Flavius

HP   40
Speed   12
LOS   2
Attack   3 (Ar) / 2
Range   2

Quintus on Foot

HP   1,300
Speed   12
LOS   6
Attack   19 (Sh) / 2
Range   0.5
Armor   5 (Sh, Pr)
Heal, Battle Cry

Sulla

HP   1,800
Speed   12
LOS   6
Attack   52 (Ms)/2
Range   0.5
Armor   3 (Sh, Pr)
Morale

Walkthrough

In this first scenario for the Roman campaign, you must stave off a barbarian invasion through clever use of troop deployment and unit conscription. Conscription is the concept of recruiting soldiers from the local populous, much like a militia. To learn how to conscript troops, use the hero Marius. Then, select the Conscript button and click on any citizen to conscript him. This action deducts 25 gold from your stockpile and replaces the citizen with a Pilum unit.

Once you build up a decent force, you must journey to a nearby town and save it from a barbarian raid. If you accomplish this, then the town falls under your control and you can either conscript the citizens there or use them for resource gathering.

TIP: Before journeying into the countryside to wipe out the barbarian threat, visit all three towns and conscript additional citizens!

Conscript the citizens in your first base to give your army more military might. Unload the three fortresses to further supplement your military force. Then, move west and rescue the town of Mutania. Once you have a defensive perimeter set up there, you can visit each of the nearby towns to recruit more troops.

| COPPER AGE | | DARK AGE | | | RENAISSANCE | | INDUSTRIAL AGE |
| STONE AGE | | BRONZE AGE | | MIDDLE AGES | | IMPERIAL AGE | ATOMIC A |

0 BC   5000 BC   2000 BC   800 BC   0AD   900 AD   1500 AD   1600 AD   1700 AD   1900 AD

EMPIRE EARTH
THE ART OF CONQUEST

After you build up your army, you'll have enough forces to move west and eliminate the Teutons and their leader.

To close out the scenario, move to the north and battle your way into the camp of the Cimbri. Slaying the leader wins the scenario.

> *Marius: "King Ulfir is dead! These cursed barbarians are finally and utterly defeated. Now will I head back to Rome to enjoy my victory and receive the laurels that I so richly deserve!"*

RESTORING THE REPUBLIC

Legend

D Dock
I Iron
G Gold

And so it was that after his successes against the German tribes, Marius returned to Rome and was showered with rose petals and well wishes from the citizens of Rome. In the following years Marius would rise to the Consulship again and again, but the life of a peaceful administrator did not come easily to the great battle leader, as his skills on the battlefield far outweighed his skills in politics and law giving. Marius was quickly becoming a forgotten man, while his one time lieutenant, Sulla, was proving himself a talented general and ambitious competitor in Roman politics. Marius then took it upon himself to travel to Asia Minor and there attempt to confront Mithridates, king of Pontus, a growing power in the region. Perhaps Gaius Marius was desperate to once again prove his worth on the battlefield, for he insulted and bullied Mithridates, who played an excellent host to the visiting Roman dignitaries, and eventually returned to Rome with nothing but a loss of prestige. Sulla, however, found incredible fame and popularity as he helped Rome put down uprisings in Italia and eventually was made a Consul and asked to lead Rome's legions against Mithridates, who was becoming more and more hostile to Rome. Although at first it seemed Marius would disappear from public service, but the Senate changed its mind and overturned Sulla's appointment and instead asked Marius to lead Rome against Mithridates.

Sulla quickly joined with his legions and found his troops all would support him if he defied Rome. Most of his troops were from the poor and slave classes, and owed whatever they had, or would have, to their leader's success. Sulla immediately marched on Rome and took the city by surprise. Marius, the only man anyone could potentially look to for resistance to such audacity, was outlawed from Rome, and his political supporters were speedily executed and replaced with Sulla's own partisan politicians. Marius fled the city and took ship for Carthage, where he hoped to hide until he could make new plans. Many of Marius' former soldiers, veterans of the Jugurthine Wars, lived in Carthage and upon hearing of Marius' plight, took it upon themselves to aid and protect their patron and hero. Upon hearing the news of Sulla marching to Asia Minor, Marius knew the time was right to plot revenge...

Roman Campaign / Restoring the Republic

Players

Marius (you; red; Dark Age)

Carthaginians (enemy; blue; Dark Age)

Etrurians (enemy; purple; Dark Age)

Sardinians (enemy; black; Dark Age)

Sulla (enemy; orange; Dark Age)

Jugurthians (enemy; yellow; Dark Age)

Required Objectives

Gather aid for Marius in Carthage.

Kill the 4 Roman Senators.

Force the surrender of Rome.

Civ Point/Tech Opportunities

None

Resource Opportunities

Aid the Carthaginians against the Jugurthian raids and receive a ship and supplies (300 Iron, 300 Food, 250 Gold).

Ally with Etruria and receive 350 Food, 250 Gold, 250 Iron and 450 Wood.

Wound Carales on Sardinia, and he'll lead you to his treasure, 1000 gold.

You Lose If

Gaius Marius dies.

Sulla's senators retake Rome after you seize it.

Scenario-Specific Stats

Carales the Mad

HP	1,275
Speed	16
LOS	6
Attack	41 (Ms)/2
Range	0.6
Armor	2 (Sh, Pr)

Etrurian Governor

HP	40 (I), 68(IV)
Speed	12
LOS	3
Attack	3 (Ar) / 2
Range	2

Gallic Reinforcements (version 1; 2)

HP	400; 130
Speed	12; 11
LOS	4
Attack	29 (Sh)/2; 11 (Pr)/2
Range	0 .5; 3
Armor	6(Ar);4(Sh)

EMPIRE EARTH
THE ART OF CONQUEST

Italia Reinforcements (version 1; 2)

HP	215; 155
Speed	12; 11
LOS	4; 5
Attack	15 (Sh)/2; 13 (Pr)/2
Range	0.5; 4
Armor	6(Ar);5(Sh)

Lackey

HP	100
Speed	9
LOS	6

Marius' Transports

HP	360
Speed	13
Capacity	24
LOS	4
Armor	7 (Ar, Pr)

Macedonian Reinforcements (version 1; 2)

HP	155; 95
Speed	12; 11
LOS	4; 5
Attack	24 (Pr) / 2; 9 (Ar) / 2
Range	0.5; 4
Armor	3 (Sh), 1 (Ar), 3 (Pr)

Sulla's Sicilian Legion (Roman Legionnaires)

Sulla's Sicilian Legion (version 2)

HP	155
Speed	11
LOS	5
Attack	13 (Pr) / 2
Range	4
Armor	5 (Sh)

Sulla's Sicilian Tower

HP	1,750
LOS	6
A/D	Tower
Attack	75 (Ms)/4
Range	5 (AE 0.3)

Sulla's Battleships

HP	1,560
Speed	10
LOS	7
Attack	90 (Ms)/4
Range	7 (AE 1)
Armor	8 (Ar, Pr)

Sulla's Harassment 1, 2

See Sulla's Sicilian Legion (version 1)

See Italia Reinforcements (version 2)

Sulla's Harassment 3

HP	440
Speed	16
LOS	4
Attack	24 (Sh) / 2
Range	0.6
Armor	2 (Sh), 6 (Ar), 20 (Gn)

Walkthrough

Your first objective is to defeat the Jugurthians, who as of late have been raiding Carthage's overland trade routes. Be sure to use Marius' Battle cry attack and the Legionnaire's Pilum attack to avoid losing too many units. Eventually, you must land on Sardinia and fight Carales the Mad. You have to convince him to join you, but you help persuade him by wounding him to below half of his original hit points.

Once on Sardinia, you can conscript the citizens or use them to gather resources – be sure to save most of your foot power for resource gathering, since you now can construct some of your own units at the barracks there. To fund them, find the pile of gold on Sicily when you go there to free the ship yards.

Once in Italy, quickly escort Marius to the Town Center in Etruria to avoid a prolonged battle with its defenders. Once again, you can gain citizens, which you can subsequently use for conscription or resource gathering. You can also build Scorpions now, which you should build in quantity for the assault on Rome. Finally, block all exits from Rome, break into the city, slow down the game speed and kill those Senators as soon as you see them!

Rome has been recaptured and Sulla's dictatorship is ended. Marius cannot rest easy, however. His former lieutenant still has a formidable force in the east, and once he hears of Marius' actions, Sulla will no doubt return to Italy as soon as he can. But Marius is aging, he is uncertain how much longer he can carry the burden of fighting for Rome. Perhaps soon it will be time for another man to guide the Republic.

UPPER AGE		DARK AGE		RENAISSANCE		INDUSTRIAL AGE		INFORMATION
2000 BC	500 BC	0 AD	900 AD	1300 AD	1500 AD	1700 AD	1900 AD	2000 AD
BRONZE AGE			MIDDLE AGES		IMPERIAL AGE		ATOMIC AGE	N

Roman Campaign / A Conqueror Learns His Trade

A CONQUEROR LEARNS HIS TRADE

Soon after Marius' triumphal return to Rome and the restoration of the Republic, preparations were begun to defend the city from Sulla's inevitable counterstrike. Envoys and legions were sent east to confront the treacherous general and attempt to convince his soldiers to swear allegiance to the true Roman army of the Republic. These efforts failed, however, and Sulla made a hasty peace with his enemies in Asia Minor in order to return to Rome to settle accounts. Marius fell ill during this time and died before he was able to finish preparing an adequate defense, leaving behind a weakened and leaderless army to protect an inexperienced and frightened Senate.

Sulla's eventual return was contested but briefly at the gates of Rome and his legions soon secured the capitol and made possible his reinstallment as dictator. Sulla, infuriated by the destruction Marius had wrecked on his estates and followers, demanded that all former associates of Marius be exiled from Italy, or even executed if they would not willingly leave. One such person was a young man named Gaius Julius Caesar, an eloquent politician and brilliant soldier. Sulla took exception to his marriage to the daughter of a close friend of Marius and ordered Caesar to divorce if he wished to stay in Rome. Caesar, already developing the trait of stalwart defiance, refused and instead fled the peninsula in search of an opportunity to make a name for himself and eventually take vengeance upon Sulla.

Legend

F Forage
D Dock
I Iron
G Gold

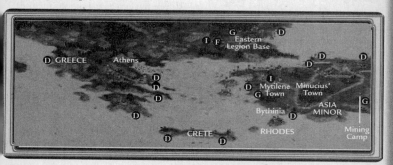

Players

Julius Caesar (you; red; Dark Age)
Bithynia (enemy; blue; Dark Age)
Greeks (enemy; orange; Dark Age)
Mytilene (enemy; purple; Dark Age)
Pirates (enemy; yellow; Dark Age)
Eastern Legions (enemy; black; Dark Age)

Initial Resources

100 Gold

Required Objectives

Find Minicius Thermus and bring Caesar to him.

East Legion Base destroyed.

Civ Point/Tech Opportunities

None

PRIMA'S OFFICIAL STRATEGY GUIDE

EMPIRE EARTH
THE ART OF CONQUEST

Resource Opportunities

Agree to help King Nicomedes of Bithynia recover a gold mine from the Mytilene rebels, and receive 250 Iron and 250 Food.

You Lose If

Caesar dies.

Sulla captures Bithynia.

You can't deliver gold to Nicomedes on time.

Scenario-Specific Stats

Appollonius Molon

HP	240
Speed	9
LOS	8
Attack	Calamity (Sh) / 180
Range	6
Armor	6 (Ar, Pr), 10 (Gn)

Caesar's Transport

HP	360
Speed	13 (24)
LOS	4
Armor	7 (Ar, Pr)

King Nicomedes

HP	40 (I), 68 (IV)
Speed	12
LOS	3
Attack	3 (Ar) / 2
Range	2

Legion Commander

HP	1,235
Speed	16
LOS	6
Attack	14 (Ms)/2
Range	0.6
Armor	3 (Sh, Pr)

Minucius Thermus

HP	215
Speed	12
LOS	4
Attack	15 (Sh) / 2
Range	0.5
Armor	6 (Ar)

Mytilene Island Tower

HP	1,750
LOS	6
A/D	Tower
Attack	75 (Ms)/4
Range	5 (AE 0.3)

Pirate King

HP	825
Speed	12
LOS	6
Attack	14 (Ms)/2
Range	0.6
Armor	3 (Sh, Pr)

Walkthrough

In the third scenario, the first objective is to get Caesar safely to Bithynia. You have two basic choices — the west dock makes for a longer ocean voyage, where pirates and Greek patrols will chase you if they spot you. The east dock will reveal your final destination, but the Greek land forces might overwhelm you before you can board the ship. Either way, you must move quickly and deliberately to succeed.

Once you make it out into open seas, there are two secondary objectives that you can find if you're brave enough to sail around a little. Your transport is the fastest thing afloat at this point in the game, so it's worth exploring the aquatic map for a while. Track down the Pirate King, who gives you ships in exchange for future gold. Also, seek out Appollonius to add some powerful prophetic punch to your endeavors.

At your destination of Bithynia, you can easily rescue the gold mine from the Myteline/Greek forces, but you must be sure to protect the miners at ALL times. You can't get more of them, and both the Pirate King and Nicomedes expect payment within a certain time limit. (If you don't pay up in time, you'll get warnings.)

Roman Campaign / The Gallic Wars

The assault on Myteline should go quickly with Appollonius' Volcano or Earthquake attacks and the Standard Bearer's morale bonus. But even without these, Myteline's walls should come down without too much fuss. Destroy the Town Center quickly to have all the citizens — and more importantly, the towers — convert to your side. Then, bring your navy around and take out Lesbos.

The final two steps are to assault the Eastern Legion's base and protect Bithynia from Sulla's wrath. The Greek invasion of Asia Minor is significant, but not overwhelming. The assault on the Eastern Legion is bloody, but might prove easier if you charge the palisades in the back of the base and make a bee-line for its military structures.

━━━━━━━━ ∘◦∘ ━━━━━━━━

The news of the defeat of Sulla's eastern legions and the victorious exploits of Julius Caesar eventually reach the ears of the Roman populace. Caesar's name becomes well known, and interested parties in Rome begin to consider how to use Caesar's rising star once Sulla passes from power...

THE GALLIC WARS

Two years after Caesar's victory over Myteline, Sulla died and Rome began to rebuild its Republican form of government. In the years that followed, Caesar involved himself in the politics of Rome and began a friendly partnership with Marcus Licinius Crassus, a wealthy and influential politician. Together they formed a talented and ambitious political team and eventually Crassus was able to secure an appointment to the governorship of Spain for Caesar. This was the opportunity Gaius Julius Caesar had been waiting for - the chance to showcase his organizational and military genius in an official capacity for Rome.

Caesar's performance in Spain brought the attention of the Roman people and Senate as he won honor and fame by defeating the native hill tribes again and again and insuring the profitability of the Roman colonies there. Crassus realized his investment in his friend had paid off and he now began to pull the necessary political strings to arrange more prominent roles in the Republic for the both of them. Entering into his first Consulship, Caesar's greatest opportunity for fortune and prestige would soon be discovered in the mysterious and dangerous lands north of Italia - in Germania and Gaul.

Legend

F Forage
S Stone
D Dock
I Iron
G Gold
— Wall

Players

Roman Republic (you; red; Dark Age)

Helveti (enemy; yellow; Copper Age)

Suebi (enemy, possible ally; black; Copper Age)

Belgae (enemy, possible ally; purple; Copper Age)

Celts (enemy; orange; Copper Age)

Hill Tribes (enemy; light blue; Copper Age)

Ambrones (enemy; blue; Copper Age)

Initial Resources

None

Required Objectives

Get Caesar to Rome to give resources to Crassus

Defeat all hostile tribes in Gaul.

Destroy all Celt buildings

EMPIRE EARTH
THE ART OF CONQUEST

PRIMA'S OFFICIAL STRATEGY GUIDE

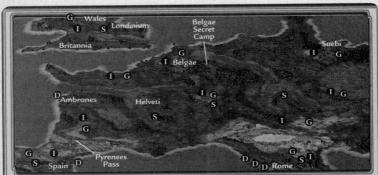

Optional Objectives

Build a temple, university in captured cities (brings peace and gives you Gallic and Celtic Warriors)

Building a temple and university in Helveti and Belgae gives you a skilled laborer and a noble, respectively

Civ Point Opportunities

None

Resource Opportunities

If you collect 50 Stone and 100 Gold, 100 Food, 100 Wood, and 100 Iron, then send Caesar to Rome, he gives those resources to Crassus, and you get Titus Labenius.

Tech Opportunities

Celtic Warrior   Gallic Warrior

You Lose If

Caesar dies

Titus Labenius dies

Town Center is destroyed in Spain and Rome

Scenario-Specific Stats

AMBRONE FORCES
Barbarians
Simple Bowmen

Ariovistus
HP	825
Speed	12
LOS	6
Attack	14 (Ms)/2
Range	0.6
Armor	3 (Sh, Pr)

Heal, Battle Cry

Belgae/Helveti/ Suebi Cavalry
HP	290
Speed	16
LOS	4
Attack	23 (Pr) / 2
Range	0.6
Armor	5(Sh),2(Pr)

Belgae/Helveti/ Suebi Archer
HP	95
Speed	11
LOS	5
Attack	9 (Ar) / 2
Range	4
Armor	1(Ar),3(Pr)

Belgae/Helveti/ Suebi Infantry
HP	300
Speed	12
LOS	6
Attack	16 (Sh) / 2
Range	0.5
Armor	3(Sh),5(Ar), 2(Pr)

Roman Campaign / The Gallic Wars

Caesar's forces in Spain

HP	155
Speed	11
LOS	5
Attack	13 (Pr) / 2
Range	4
Armor	5 (Sh)

Celtic Elite Guard

HP	180
Speed	16
LOS	5
Attack	17 (Ar) / 2
Range	4
Armor	1(Ar),4(Pr)

Celtic Force

HP	350
Speed	14
LOS	6
Attack	18 (Sh) / 2
Range	0.5
Armor	2 (Ar, Pr)

Celtic Cavalry

HP	240
Speed	16
LOS	4
Attack	17 (Sh) / 2
Range	0.6
Armor	6 (Ar)

Celtic Noble

HP	215
Speed	12
LOS	4
Attack	15 (Sh) / 2
Range	0.5
Armor	6 (Ar)

Crassus

HP	1,300
Speed	12
LOS	6
Attack	19 (Sh) / 2
Range	0.5
Armor	5 (Sh, Pr)

Crassus' Cavalry

HP	440
Speed	16
LOS	4
Attack	24 (Sh) / 2
Range	0.6
Armor	2(Sh),6(Ar), 20 (Gn)

Crassus' Legionnaires

HP	215
Speed	12
LOS	4
Attack	20 (Sh) / 2
Range	0.5
Armor	2(Sh),6(Ar)

Helveti Diplomat (Diplomat)

Londinium Guard

HP	95
Speed	11
LOS	5
Attack	9 (Ar) / 2
Range	4
Armor	1(Ar),3(Pr)

Spanish Raiders

HP	325
Speed	14
LOS	6
Attack	16 (Sh) / 2
Range	0.5
Armor	2 (Sh, Pr), 4 (Ar)

Walks through forests

Suebi Lieutenant

HP	400
Speed	12
LOS	4
Attack	29 (Sh) / 2
Range	0.5
Armor	6 (Ar)

Walkthrough

Get a comfortable chair. This is one long scenario ...

It took Caesar many years to "tame" Gaul, and the feel of that epic conquest shows through here. First of all, take the time to get the extra resources to pay Crassus back and explore Spanish Gaul. You'll find the Hill Tribe base in the lower left corner, behind a stand of trees. This is not a problem for the Hill Tribe's barbarians, but it's definitely a problem for you.

After you finish collecting enough of one of the resources (stone, probably) send those citizens to fell two weakened trees. They're not hard to find — just look for a small gap in the line of trees. While they're chopping away and immediately after you have your main resources gathered, send Caesar off to Rome – but ONLY Caesar. Keep your forces local and handy, as the barbarians could appear at any time. Once the loggers are finished removing the trees, charge in and demolish the barracks. You may need to solicit some troops from Rome for assistance, but that's okay because Crassus gives you some of his units as soon as you pay him what you owe.

EMPIRE EARTH
THE ART OF CONQUEST

As you gather resources and build up an army, produce some cavalry in Rome and explore Gaul. Don't be shy about spending some big bucks on the Centurion. You'll be very happy you did so after his Battle cry helps the Romans cut through waves of Gallic troops like a hot knife through a stick of butter.

After you've discovered all the tribes in Gaul, the Helveti begin an offensive towards Spain. Find the pass in the mountains connecting Spain and Gaul and immediately concentrate your troops there. Once you've defeated the Helveti force, march on their barracks and destroy it. Immediately build a temple and university there to start producing some much-needed citizens and build up a fortified town in or around the Helveti.

The Suebi are next, and you'll need everything you can possibly build to take them out on the first try. To be honest, that's not likely to happen very easily. Also, note that they may have sent "explorers" to Rome while you were at peace — and these tourists turn very nasty very quickly. Defend Rome and Spain with Palisades and a few Palisade Towers, and you should be fine.

When the Suebi die, go after the Belgae. You should be feeling a little more established in Gaul by now, but watch out for nasty Belgae ambushes. The two units you can build by "civilizing" the

Belgae and Suebi are pretty rewarding, but you're truly better off staying Roman. The volunteers they send, however, are some tough hombres. Be sure to load them up when you invade England and be on the lookout for Celtic amphibious raids.

Other hints:

- There's a time limit of 960 seconds, or 16 minutes, in which you must unite Caesar and Crassus in Rome. Get your resources first, then send Caesar to Rome to deliver resources to Crassus. This

- If you destroy the Helveti barracks but leave the other buildings intact, they sign a treaty with the Romans. (This makes the Suebi even more hostile.)

- Destroying all Belgae buildings makes the Romans hostile to the Celts, but makes peace between the Ambrones and Belgaens.

Caesar's conquest of Gaul is complete! Rome now controls nearly all of Western Europe and the people of Rome hail Julius Caesar as the conqueror of Europe, the savior of Rome....

BC	2000 BC	500 BC	0AD	900 AD	1300 AD	1500 AD	1700 AD	1900 AD	2000 AD
	COPPER AGE		DARK AGE		RENAISSANCE		INDUSTRIAL AGE		INFORMATION
	BRONZE AGE			MIDDLE AGES		IMPERIAL AGE		ATOMIC AGE	

Roman Campaign / Crossing the Rubicon

CROSSING THE RUBICON

For nearly ten years, Caesar was sole master of Gaul and its riches swelled his coffers to bursting. Unfortunately, there was a growing faction in Rome that was jealous of his success and fearful of his power. His enemies were eventually able to get control of the Senate after Crassus died in the Parthian war, and soon they made it clear that by the end of the following year, Caesar would have to step down from public office, surrender Gaul, and disband his legions. Considering the brutality of the power politics in Rome's recent history, Caesar saw obeying this declaration as simple suicide. With no legions to protect him, he would be an easy target for any assassin charged with making sure he never rose to power again.

Legend

F Forage
S Stone
D Dock
I Iron
G Gold
— Wall

Thus, on January 11th, 49 B.C., Gaius Julius Caesar crossed the Rubicon River into Roman Italy and uttered the immortal words "the die is cast." Pompey, Caesar's political ally during the days that Crassus was alive, decided to support the Senate and agreed to lead Rome's armies against the would-be dictator.

Players

Julius Caesar (you; Dark)

Gnaeus Pompey (enemy; blue; Dark)

Egypt (ally; yellow; Dark)

Pirates (enemy; gray; Dark)

Greeks (enemy; orange; Dark)

Italia (ally; blue; red; Dark)

Initial Resources

500 Food 450 Wood 150 Stone

250 Gold 250 Iron

Required Objectives

Kill enemy units

Protect grain shipments from Egypt to Rome

Drive Pompey out of Italy

Optional Objectives

Destroy Greek docks to stop naval attacks

Civ Point Opportunities

None

PRIMA'S OFFICIAL STRATEGY GUIDE

Resource Opportunities

Give Pisae 200 Gold, 100 Food and 50 Stone to get them to ally with you.

Put Caesar next to the Ravenna Senator to bribe him. Destroy the fortress in Pisae to drop the bribe to 100 Food, 100 Wood and 100 Iron.

Destroy Mediolanum to receive 100 Stone, 150 Gold, 170 Wood, 240 Food, 170 Iron

Destroy Ravenna to receive 135 Stone, 300 Gold, 125 Wood, 320 Food, 150 Iron

Destroy Pisae to receive 70 Stone, 125 Gold, 225 Wood, 180 Food, 280 Iron

Destroy Asculum to receive 100 Stone, 175 Gold, 210 Iron, 225 Wood, 75 Food

Destroy Neapolis to receive 300 Stone, 110 Gold, 135 Wood, 175 Food, 135 Iron

... or, bribe Senators in each city:

Bribe Pisae with 100 Food, 200 Gold, 50 Stone

Bribe Asculum with 750 Food, 250 Gold, 250 Wood

Bribe Neapolis with 500 Food, 300 Iron, 300 Gold, 500 Wood

Bribe Ravenna (second offer) with 100 Food, 200 Gold, 100 Iron, 100 Wood

Destroy Segestica fortress to get Macedonian Mine

Destory Phillippopolis fortress to get the Temple of Zeus

Tech Opportunities

None

You Lose If

Julius Caesar dies

More than 3 grain transports are lost

Scenario-Specific Stats

Assassins

HP	215
Speed	12
LOS	4
Attack	15 (Sh) / 2
Range	0:5
Armor	6 (Ar)

Discontent Rebels (three units)

HP	85;150;325
Speed	12; 12; 14
LOS	4; 4; 6
Attack	15 (Pr)/2; 13 (Sh)/2; 16 (Sh)/2
Range	0.5 (AE)
Armor	2(Sh);4(Ar); 2(Sh, Pr), 4(Ar)

Unit 3 walks through forests

Egyptian Transport

HP	360
Speed	13 (24)
LOS	4
Armor	7 (Ar, Pr)

Greek Bowmen (two units)

HP	95; 145
Speed	11
LOS	5; 6
Attack	9 (Ar) / 2; 13 (Ar) / 2
Range	4; 5
Armor	1(Ar),3(Pr); 2(Ar),7(Pr)

Greek Cavalry

HP	290
Speed	16
LOS	4
Attack	23 (Pr) / 2
Range	0.6 (AE)
Armor	5(Sh),2(Pr)

Greek Frigate

HP	400
Speed	16
LOS	9
Attack	21 (Ms)/2
Range	6
Armor	8 (Ar, Pr)

Greek Galley

HP	440
Speed	14
LOS	7
Attack	9 (Ms) / 2
Range	6

Roman Campaign / Crossing the Rubicon

Greek Raider/ Battleship

HP	1,560
Speed	10
LOS	7
Attack	90 (Ms)/4
Range	7 (1)
Armor	8 (Ar, Pr)

Pompey's Transports

HP	360
Speed	13
Capacity	24
LOS	4
Armor	7 (Ar, Pr)

Senators

HP	100
Speed	9
LOS	6

Walls/Gates

HP	7,750(Wall); 16,000(Gate)
LOS	1 (Wall); 2 (Gate)

Walkthrough

As you make your way down Italy's boot, remember that there's always more than one way to approach a city. There are a few patrols of Pompey's soldiers, but nothing too tough in your way. Concentrate on methodically getting each city under your belt. None of the cities' challenges are very hard, so don't expect that you always have to pay the bribe price.

If you decide to sack any of the cities, all we can offer is good luck. The populace of Italy becomes a little unruly once you start burning their homes. You'll have your hands full trying to deal with revolts while also chasing Pompey around the landscape. The easiest way to drive Pompey out of Italy is to target Titus when you meet his forces outside of Brundisium. Once he falls to half health, his soldiers all flee to Brundisium to board a ship for Greece.

At this point, you can build a navy and sail after him, or go north over land and circle through Macedonia and Thrace to hit Pompey from behind. Both ways are equal drains on your resources, but keep in mind that even if you do go overland, you'll need at least a small fleet to protect Egypt's grain shipments.

An amphibious landing on Greece means destroying two Greek naval bases – one in southern Greece, and the other on Crete. Although you don't have to destroy these bases, they'll keep sending ships at you until you do. Upgrade your battleships and destroy the base's towers and catapults, then load up and land in southern Greece.

Pharsalus is just a little way off to the north, but make sure your troops are upgraded before beginning the battle. Once you've destroyed enough of them, they'll usually try to flee north to the Greek city of Philippopolis. There, you'll have another monumental battle on your hands. If you go overland, remember that even though you destroy a fortress in a Greek city, the army there keeps on fighting. So, keep those Standard Bearers mixed in with your troops so you don't get hurt too badly.

Once you get to Serdica, build some structures to re-establish supply lines. Not a big deal, but don't try to press forward without doing this. Once the supply line is re-established, Philippopolis launches an attack to retake Serdica. By this time, you should have more than enough troops produced and waiting to protect the city from the attack. It's a good idea to take out Philippopolis before marching south to Pharsalus, because taking that city deprives Pompey of his haven and also earns you the Temple of Zeus!

PRIMA'S OFFICIAL STRATEGY GUIDE

Other Notes:

- ⊕ After you claim Rome or Pompey retreats, Egypt sends grain to Rome. Protect the shipments and ensure they arrive safely to get Egypt to ally with you
- ⊕ Kill pirates to earn Neapolis' allegiance
- ⊕ Send citizens to Asculum's farm.
- ⊕ Brundisium gates lock when you engage Pompey

Greek Fleet: 2 Battleships, 4 Galleys, 2 Frigates

Pirate Fleet: 1 Battleship, 2 Galleys, 2 Frigates

―――――――

Titus is dead and Pompey's forces have been annihilated. The Roman Republic belongs to Caesar! All that remains is to follow Pompey to Egypt, execute him and secure Egypt's allegiance.

ROME'S PHARAOH

Although Pompey had been defeated, Caesar knew that while he still lived, he would remain a threat to the new dictator's power in Rome. So, Caesar quickly embarked as many troops as possible and sailed off in pursuit of his enemy to Egypt. Disembarking at Alexandria, Caesar found a city in turmoil. The people were starving and close to rioting. Two ruling factions, Ptolemy and his sister Cleopatra, were locked in a bitter dispute over rightful rule of Egypt. Cleopatra controlled the city itself, while Ptolemy held sway over most of the countryside. Caesar and his legions were about to find themselves in the middle of a civil war. Forming up his men, Caesar decided to immediately march on the Royal Palace and seize both rulers and force them to surrender Pompey. Only then would he look to the issue of helping to solve Egypt's troubles.

Legend

D Dock

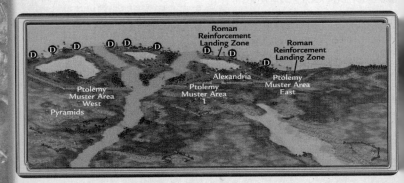

Roman Campaign / Rome's Pharaoh

Players

Julius Caesar (you; red; Dark Age)

Ptolemy (ally; yellow; Dark Age)

Cleopatra (ally; purple; Dark Age)

Alexandria (ally; blue; Dark Age)

Initial Resources

None

Required Objectives

Force Cleopatra or Ptolemy to surrender Pompey.

Destroy either all of Ptolemy's bases, or Cleopatra's capitol and town center at Alexandria.

Civ/Resource/Tech Opportunities

None

You Lose If

Caesar dies.

Scenario-Specific Stats

All Transports
HP	360
Speed	13
Capacity	24
LOS	4
Armor	7 (Ar, Pr)

Center Reserve Spears
HP	125
Speed	12
LOS	4
Attack	16 (Pr) / 2
Range	0.5
Armor	2 (Sh)

Cleo Relief (two units)
HP	130; 125
Speed	11; 12
LOS	4
Attack	11 (Pr) / 2; 16 (Pr) / 2
Range	3; 0.5
Armor	4(Sh);2(Sh)

Pyramid
HP	3500
LOS	5

Cleo Relief Archer
HP	180
Speed	16
LOS	5
Attack	17 (Ar) /. 2
Range	4
Armor	1(Ar),4(Pr)

Cleo Spear, Guard
HP	125
Speed	12
LOS	4
Attack	16 (Pr) / 2
Range	0.5
Armor	2 (Sh)

Ptol's Bows
HP	95
Speed	11
LOS	5
Attack	9 (Ar) / 2
Range	4
Armor	1(Ar),3(Pr)

Ptol's Spears
HP	125
Speed	12
LOS	4
Attack	16 (Pr) / 2
Range	0.5
Armor	2 (Sh)

Royal Elephants
HP	600
Speed	10
LOS	5
Attack	25 (Ar) / 2
Range	4
Armor	3(Ar),5(Pr)

Siege Guard
HP	180
Speed	8
LOS	6
Attack	65(Ms)/10
Range	2 - 5 (AE 1.2)
Armor	5(Ar),4(Pr)

Ptol Lieutenant
HP	290
Speed	16
LOS	4
Attack	23 (Pr) / 2
Range	0.6
Armor	5(Sh),2(Pr)

EMPIRE EARTH
THE ART OF CONQUEST

Walkthrough

Although the Tigers may seem like unstoppable killing machines, they can't be healed by Alexandria's hospitals. (In other words, don't be too concerned about trying to keep them alive.) The more important units are the Centurions and Standard Bearers, since their bonuses work wonders in evening the odds against Cleopatra or Ptolemy.

This particular scenario is very difficult, no matter which side you decide to support. (Siding with Cleopatra is perhaps a little easier than siding with Ptolemy.) Both sides have timed reinforcements, but the side you oppose will always get reinforcements more quickly and in greater numbers than you. A helpful tip is to remember that even if your side loses a Town Center or the Capitol, your ally gets a reinforcement dump if you can retake it.

Be patient and look for opportunities to increase your odds of survival, since this is the most important objective for the first hour of the scenario. If you made it this far by playing conservatively, you should be able to handle protecting the pyramids, as well as launching counter offensives once you've built some Scorpions.

If you're siding with Cleopatra, it's generally a good idea to immediately take your forces out and crush one of the Ptolemy's attacking forces, then retreat to lick your wounds and harass Ptolemy if he breaks into another part of the city.

Siding with Ptolemy, it is absolutely essential that you make quick tracks to a city gate and join with him as soon as your Tigers finish off Cleopatra's diplomat. Make a stand at the gate you choose, however. Simply running all the way to one of Ptolemy's bases will just annihilate your ally's attacking forces and hand Cleopatra many more initial defenders than she needs. That means you'll see a lot of these units later when she launches her own counterattack.

Remember, press the advantage when you have it. Always use the morale bonus, Pilum Attack, Battle Cry and the hospitals. There isn't a moment's rest in this scenario, but then again, who said being the first Roman Emperor was going to be easy?

———————— ∞ ————————

(If allied with Ptolemy) Alexandria has fallen to Caesar and Ptolemy's forces. Cleopatra has been brought before the boy Pharaoh and Caesar is content to let him decide his sister's fate. Julius now makes ready to return to Rome to solidify his power over his new empire....

(If allied with Cleopatra) Caesar has destroyed the last of Ptolemy's support bases and brought the young would-be Pharaoh to Cleopatra to let her decide her brother's fate. Egypt is now firmly under Roman influence and Caesar makes ready to return to Rome to solidify his power over his new Empire....

UPPER AGE		DARK AGE		RENAISSANCE		INDUSTRIAL AGE		INFORMATION
2000 BC	500 BC	0 AD	900 AD	1300 AD	1500 AD	1700 AD	1900 AD	2000 AD
BRONZE AGE			MIDDLE AGES		IMPERIAL AGE		ATOMIC AGE	

Pacific Campaign / Carrier Strike

∼∼∼ Pacific Campaign ∼∼∼

The devastating attack at Pearl Harbor left the United States struggling to re-establish a military presence in the Pacific. America faced battle-hardened Japanese forces that had been operating with relative impunity. But the "sleeping giant" soon awoke. The United States — along with British, Australians and New Zealanders — began a relentless effort to push the Japanese back to their home shores. Lead the Allied forces all the way from the Battle of Midway to the brutal sands of Iwo Jima.

CARRIER STRIKE

Intelligence has intercepted a Japanese transmission about an impending invasion. The message is vague, and a lot of my officers think it refers to an invasion of the Aleutians. But I think any activity there would be a feint. My gut tells me that the Japanese are going to try to take Midway.

Yamamoto is one shrewd customer. He knows Midway is our westernmost outpost in the Pacific. And without it, there ain't a thing standing between Tokyo and Hawaii. We have reports that a large naval force has already left Japan, which means we have to act now.

I'm sending you out there with everything we got, which unfortunately isn't much. The Hornet, the Enterprise, and some escort ships. Task Force 16 will join you as soon as we get the Yorktown patched up.

Find those enemy carriers, those are the backbone of the Japanese Imperial Navy. Hit 'em fast and hard. Without air support, their invasion plans will fold. You're heavily outnumbered, but you also have the element of surprise. Best of luck out there.

Players

United States (you; blue; WWII)

Empire of Japan (enemy; red; WWII)

Unites States (ally; gray; WWII)

Initial Resources

None

No resources are found on this map.

Required Objectives

Sink four Japanese carriers

Prevent the Japanese from reaching Midway

Civ Point/Resource Opportunities

None

Tech Opportunities

None

You Lose If

All your planes or carriers are destroyed

Japanese transports deposit infantry on Midway

Any Japanese carriers retreat

EMPIRE EARTH
THE ART OF CONQUEST

Events and Groups

TF02: 2 Transports, Troops

TF03: 5 Frigates, 2 Cruisers

TF16: 1 Carriers, 3 Frigates, 2 Cruisers, Shark

TF17: 2 Carriers, 4 Frigates, 2 Cruisers

JIN air squadrons: large (5 to 15), small (4 to 8)

JIN1: 1 Battleship, 5 Frigates, 2 Cruisers

JIN2: 2 carriers, 4 Frigates, 2 Cruisers

JIN3: 2 Battleships, 5 Frigates, 1 Cruiser

JIN4: 5 Submarines

JIN5: 7 Transports, 1 Frigate

JIN6: 1 Battleship, 5 Frigates, 2 Cruisers

Losing radar center, Midway trucks calls TF02

Landing in the lagoon calls TF17, JIN1, TF03

Sinking the Soryu and Kaga makes JIN1 retreat; TF03 is dispatched to intercept it.

3 minutes later, JIN5 transports land on islands

Sinking the Akagi and Hiryu makes JIN1 retreat, calls JIN4 (submarine group)

Destroying all JIN5 transports calls TF16

Sinking all JIN5 transports brings TF16

Losing two U.S. carriers brings in TF16

Sinking 1 enemy carrier calls in JIN3

Sinking 3 enemy carriers calls in JIN2

Zero Squadrons: 6 waves of 2-5 Zeros each

Scenario-Specific Stats

Radar Center

HP	2,500

Airfield

HP	2,000

Zero

HP	496
Speed	22
LOS	7
Attack	12(Ms)/0.5
Range	6

Japanese Carrier

(Akagi/Hiryu/ Hosho/Kaga/ Soryu/Zuiho)

HP	6,000
Speed	17
LOS	4
Armor	20 (Ar, Pr, Gn, Ls)

Japanese Submarine

HP	1,000
Speed	13
LOS	8
Attack	130(Ms)/6
Range	7

Yamato

HP	6,625
Speed	17
LOS	9
Attack	276(Ms)/4
Range	8 (AE 1)
Armor	20 (Ar, Pr, Ls), 30(Gn)

Japanese Transport

HP	750
Speed	19 (28)
LOS	5
Armor	20 (Ar, Pr), 25 (Gn)

Japanese Destroyer

HP	1,600
Speed	17
LOS	10
Attack	68(Ms)/2
Armor	20(Ar, Pr, Ls),30(Gn)
Range	8

Japanese Cruiser

HP	2,300
Speed	17
LOS	9
Attack	70 (Ms)/2
Armor	20(Ar, Pr), 25 (Gn)
Range	8

Pacific Campaign / Carrier Strike

Japanese Frigate

HP	1,600
Speed	20
LOS	10
Attack	68 (Ms)/2
Armor	20 (Ar, Pr, Ls), 30 (Gn)
Range	8

Japanese Battleship

HP	5,750
Speed	17
LOS	9
Attack	230(Ms)/4
Armor	20 (Ar, Pr), 25 (Gn)
Range	8 (AE 1)

Dauntless

HP	496
Speed	25
LOS	7
Attack	12(Ms)/0.5
Range	6

Walkthrough

This is essentially a seek-and-destroy mission, but you must also play defensively. Once you fend off the first attack, you should land and deploy reinforcements on the western island. When the first task force arrives, bring it into the atoll harbor. There, you will soon receive reports indicating the approximate location of the enemy carrier fleet. Use carrier planes to explore the area and spot the enemy ships, then dive in for the kill.

Once you destroy two carriers, an enemy invasion force will approach from the southwest. Take your destroyers and spread them out in a battle line on the southwest side of Midway, far enough out to give them a chance to catch and sink enemy transports in case

one gets past your initial blockade.

If enemy troops reach the island, the mission is over. You can also deploy ground troops along the shoreline to try to sink any transports that might have slipped past the destroyer screen. Once the transports are deep-sixed, hunt down and sink the two remaining carriers. A second task force will arrive to help you accomplish this.

Use a divide-and-conquer method to help you split the destroyers, cruisers and carriers into separate groups. The carrier group can hunt down enemy flattops. The destroyers, in turn, can sink the enemy invasion force and provide protection for the carriers. The cruisers can help to shoot down enemy planes attacking the airport or to attack the carriers as needed. If any of the planes at the Midway airport survive, they can be used to help locate enemy ships.

That's pretty much the goal here — don't let the enemy units make landfall on the island. Use whatever means necessary to make sure it doesn't happen.

———— ∽∾∾ ————

The Battle of Midway could prove to be one of the most decisive battles of this war. The loss of four heavy aircraft carriers deprives Japan of crucial strategic advantages. Also, the loss of so many veteran pilots will force them to spend months equipping and training replacements.

At last we have a little breathing room. It is absolutely crucial that we take advantage of this opportunity to push forward before Japan can recover from this defeat.

EMPIRE EARTH
THE ART OF CONQUEST

PRIMA'S OFFICIAL STRATEGY GUIDE

OPERATION WATCHTOWER

We've had to step up our plans to recapture Guadalcanal. There are reports that the Japanese are building an airfield on the island.

It is crucial to take Guadalcanal before the base can be completed, otherwise we'll be facing an enemy with the advantage of significant air support. Just to the North lies Florida Island, which has an ideal protected harbor. We will need to secure this as well. With these two strategic locations in our hands, we'll have a strong foothold in the Solomons from which we can launch further operations.

I know you need more time to prepare and equip your men. I've heard some of the grunts have even nick-named it 'Operation Shoestring.' But time and materials are luxuries we don't have. We have to press on.

With our victory at Midway, the momentum of the war is starting to shift away from the Japanese. It is essential that our forces take advantage of the situation before that momentum swings back in favor of the enemy.

Legend
- **F** Forage
- **N** Naval Yard
- **I** Iron

Players

1st Marine Division (you; blue; Atomic WWII)

Empire of Japan (enemy; red; Copper ☮ Atomic WWII)

Coast Watcher (neutral; gray; Atomic WWII)

United States (ally; blue; Copper ☮ Atomic WWII)

Required Objectives

Destroy enemies at Florida Island to capture it

Destroy enemies at Lunga to capture Guadalcanal

Build an airport at Lunga

Pacific Campaign / Operation Watchtower

Initial Resources

480 Food   750 Wood   1000 Stone
400 Gold   500 Iron

Optional Objectives

Capture western base, find
Coastwatcher for maps

Destroy 4 "snitch" patrols to prevent
Japanese alert forces

Seek out a medical crate in S. base to
heal 10 to 200 troops

Civ Point /Tech Opportunities

None

Resource Opportunities

Build airstrip to bring in squadron
of P-38s

Complete capitol to get "Bulldog"
Ramsey

You Lose If

75% of your Marines are destroyed

All friendly transports are destroyed

Scenario-Specific Stats

"Bulldog" Ramsey

HP	5,235
Speed	14
LOS	9
Attack	160(Ms)/2
Armor	10 (Sh), 9 (Pr)
Range	8

P-38 Lightning

HP	1000
Speed	25
LOS	7
Attack	24(Ms)/0.5
Range	6

Japanese Frigate

HP	1,600
Speed	17
LOS	10
Attack	68 (Ms)/2
Armor	20 (Ar, Pr, Ls), 30(Gn)
Range	8

Japanese Cruiser

HP	2,300
Speed	17
LOS	9
Attack	70 (Ms)/2
Armor	20 (Ar, Pr), 25 (Gn)
Range	8

Bamboo Tower

HP	1000
LOS	6
Attack	40 (Ms)/4
Range	5 (AE 0.3)

Japanese Battleship

HP	5,750
Speed	17
LOS	9
Attack	230(Ms)/4
Armor	20 (Ar, Pr), 25 (Gn)
Range	8 (AE 1)

Walkthrough

Shortly after landing your marines, you
receive a message that reinforcements
are unavailable. Lucky you. The safest
route is to avoid detection on the east
side of the island, making sure to kill
any enemy patrols that try to head for
their home base.

If you takes your forces south and
move west, you can proceed north
over the island's peak and enter the
enemy base through a breach in its
defenses. Once the island is captured,
you receives a squadron of fighter
planes that you should use to destroy
enemy units on the base on the northern island. At the same time, you
should also use citizens and engineers
to rebuild the defenses in case the
enemy makes a counterattack. Once
enough units are destroyed in the
base on Florida island, you can load
up transports and finish off what's
left. Once this base is captured, the
mission is won.

Here are a few other hints that can help
you win this scenario.

EMPIRE EARTH
THE ART OF CONQUEST

Once troops have been unloaded, move your transports to the lagoon at the east end of the island. There, they will be safe from enemy destroyers.

It's easy for troops to get separated in the jungle terrain. Try to keep your troops together so they can attack in force. Splitting the different unit types (mortars, snipers, bazookas, etc.) into subgroups enables you to make well-coordinated attacks that deliver maximum damage.

It pays to explore the island. On the southeast side, there's a friendly coast-watcher who provides a map to the back entrance of the base and joins your marines in the fight.

On the south face of Guadalcanal is a small base. Once it's captured, you can use the crate of medical supplies there to heal your troops at any time. This is a timely item for your attack on the

main base: you'll b able to heal your troops in mid-battle, reducing the number of losses you take.

On the southwest side of Guadalcanal, you can receive a small group of reinforcements. If you destroy the two towers guarding the shoreline there, you can beach long enough to pick up extra marines dropped off by a submarine.

Finally, capturing the west base provide another map, which shows you how to reach the weakest spot of the main base.

The fighter planes can also be used to sink enemy ships that might pose a threat to the transports trying to land troops on Florida island. The Japanese Navy has 2 Battleships, 3 Frigates and 2 Cruisers in the area.

———————— ∽∼∽ ————————

We've done it! Florida Island and Guadalcanal are ours!

TOOTH AND NAIL

We are aware that our country's 'Europe First' policy is having significant repercussions in the Pacific Theater. Men and materials are at a premium, and we have to economize. Without the manpower in the Pacific to retake every position held by the Japanese, we have come up with an "island hopping" strategy whereby only some targets will be recaptured.

Instead of getting bogged down in protracted island sieges, the plan is to leapfrog some of the Japanese positions. Men and resources could then be applied to acquiring more strategic targets. This will leave the remaining Japanese strongholds isolated and left to 'die on the vine.' Then the Third Fleet can make the push up through the Philippines and force the Japanese back to their own soil.

Legend

N	Naval Yard
S	Stone
D	Dock
I	Iron
G	Gold

Players

United States (you; blue; Atomic WWII)

Empire of Japan (enemy; red; Atomic WWII)

Natives (ally; orange; Copper)

Initial Resources

1000 Food	500 Wood	500 Stone
500 Gold	500 Iron	

Pacific Campaign / Tooth and Nail

Dashes indicate enemy patrol routes; numbers indicate islands referenced in text.

Required Objectives

Rescue pilot east of island 18 with a transport

Rescue Major, paratroopers on 13

Shoot down Yamamoto's plane

Protect your friendly base

Optional Objectives

Secure islands 9, 10, and 11 and build radars to bring in friendly planes to protect home base

Skip islands 3-5, 16 and capture the rest, building docks and naval yards (capturing more islands makes destroyers retreat)

Build airfields and P-38s to help hunt Yamamoto

Construct Catalinas to help fend off submarines

Talk to Native at outpost east of island 8

Give native 70 Food and follow raft to avoid two destroyers

Destroy pillboxes on island 18

Civ/Resource/Tech Opportunities

None

You Lose If

Downed pilot is captured before you rescue him

Scenario-Specific Stats

Espionage HQ		Shark	
HP	8,000	HP	300
LOS	13	Speed	10
		LOS	6
Native Boat		Attack	30 (Pr) / 2
HP	120	Range	0.6
Speed	10	Armor	3(Sh),6(Ar)
LOS	4		
Attack	1 (Ms)		
Range	0.5		

EMPIRE EARTH
THE ART OF CONQUEST

Major		*Yamamoto's plane*	
HP	5,235	HP	1,300
Speed	14	Speed	19
LOS	9	LOS	8
Attack	160(Ms)/2	Attack	135 (Ms) /
Armor	10 (Sh),		0.5
	9 (Pr)	Range	5 (AE 1.5)
Range	0.5		
Morale			

Walkthrough

This scenario poses another island-based adventure — we're sensing a theme here. You can take many routes to reach an island, the ultimate goal being that you must construct an airport. Certain areas will trigger certain objectives, so if you don't take the time to explore the whole map, you might not have to accomplish all that's possible in this mission.

This maneuver requires some caution. There are many subs and destroyers lurking in the waters that will sink your transports if you're not careful. You have no warships with which to defend the transports, so you must rely on Catalina sea planes to provide reconnaissance as you proceed. Catalinas can also be used to sink subs.

You have a few citizens that you have to keep alive, or the mission will fail. Gather them together and task them with collecting resources right away so that you can build more troops, transports and Catalinas on an as-needed basis.

As each island is captured, build more naval yards and Catalinas, ever-expanding your observation area. Affix your RADAR center on a flat island — really, the only suitable location is on a small island approximately in the center of the map. The RADAR can detect incoming planes, at which point you'll get some

fighters on loan. Immediately direct them to shoot down all enemy planes before they can reach the home base and start killing citizens.

Rescuing the paratroopers (another mission objective) may be a little tricky. You must extract them quickly, while at the same time avoiding destroyers in the area.

If you're told to rescue a downed pilot, hastily dispatch Catalinas to explore the southwest corner of the map. Send a transport that way, too, in order to pick up the pilot as soon as he as located. (If an enemy destroyer reaches him first, the mission fails.)

You will eventually be told to build a forward airbase. The only island with enough flat ground is in the northwest corner, which also happens to be where a large enemy force resides. Once you take over that island, build an airport and fighters. After Yamamoto enters the scene, scramble the fighters and send them on a wide search pattern to locate him and shoot him down. Transports and Catalinas can also be used to help spot Yamamoto's plane.

- ⊕ If there is a destroyer patrol between two islands, capturing both islands makes the destroyer leave.

- ⊕ Toward the west end of the map is a small island that is home to native villagers. If you bribe them with a few small morsels of food, one of them will happily lead you to the undefended side of the enemy base on the northwestern island.

———— ❧ ————

With the death of Admiral Yamamoto, you have dealt a crushing blow to the morale of Japan and her armed forces.

Pacific Campaign / Merrill's Marauders

MERRILL'S MARAUDERS

Your first mission will be to cut the Kamaing Road in the vicinity of Walawbum and to attack a forward command post believed to be near there. I want you Marauders to move from Ningbyen to Tanja Ga and await my instructions, which will be given at the moment the Chinese operations along the road to the north of Maingkwan and give you men the best shot at a surprise attack.

No resources are found on this map. Black dots indicate pillbox locations.

Players

Merrill's Marauders (you; blue; Atomic WWII)

Japanese 18th Infantry (enemy; red; Atomic WWII)

China (ally; dark green; Middle —> Industrial)

Japanese 32nd Armored (enemy; light green; Atomic WWII)

Empire of Japan (enemy; gray; Atomic WWII)

Initial Resources

None

Required Objectives

Bring Lt. Stock's and Cmdr. Merrill's troops to Walawbum

Use Engineers to knock down Walawbum Gates and capture city

Destroy six pillboxes in the swamp.

Capture Shadazup

Destroy Radar Center at Myitikina and secure airfields

Optional Objectives

Eliminate patrols, snipers near Walawbum

Destroy truck convoy before it reaches Walawbum to prevent alert

Use Engineers to diffuse 30 landmines

Keep Radio Men alive (important!)

Civ/Resource/Tech Opportunities

None

EMPIRE EARTH
THE ART OF CONQUEST

You Lose If

Lt. Stock or Cmdr. Merrill dies

Scenario-Specific Stats

Commander Merrill

HP	5,235
Speed	14
LOS	9
Attack	160(Ms)/2
Armor	10 (Sh), 9 (Pr)
Range	0.5
Morale	

Walawbum Gates

HP	14,000

Japanese Sniper

HP	325
Speed	12
LOS	7
Attack	20 (Gn)/3
Armor	10 (Pr)

Japanese Spy Plane (Zero - Strafe)

Japanese Sharpshooter

HP	470
Speed	12
LOS	7
Attack	52 (Gn)/2
Range	6

Japanese Officer

HP	2,430
Speed	14
LOS	9
Attack	55 (Ms)/2
Range	8
Armor	10 (Sh), 9 (Pr)
	Heal, Battle Cry

Events

Destroying the convoy activates snipers

Destroying the Walawbum Radar Center calls in ground troops and fighter attack waves (2 Zeros, 1 ME110 Bomber each)

Destroying the Walawbum gates activates the 18th Infantry ground force (grenadiers, heavy machine guns, infantry)

Destroying swamp pillboxes aggravates partisans

Taking over Shadazup aggravates partisans and Myitikina Town Patrols and calls in Heinkels

Walkthrough

Your troops are separated at the beginning of the scenario. One group is located at the northern end of the map, the other at the southern end. In order to reunite them, you must make your way to the village of Walawbum and eliminate the enemy presence there.

Deploy one team at a time. The northern team must eliminate the outer base defenses before moving into the village. The southern team must eliminate a convoy truck and its escort troops, then move up the road to the village. It really doesn't matter which group you work with first, as long as they both accomplish their objectives.

Once both troops are outside the city walls, use Engineer units can to destroy the gates with explosives. The units can battle their way in to secure the village. After this is accomplished, reinforcements will arrive (snipers and radio men). You'll need to use them to help out with the next phase of your operation as you blast your way toward the airfield.

First, move through the swamp and eliminate the six pillboxes scattered around there. Then, move to the southwest and secure the town of Shadazup. Finally, secure the airfield at Myitikina. Once this is accomplished, you've won the mission.

Watch out for mosquitoes and one tiger on the loose!

The climax of the Marauders' operations was the capture of the Myitikina airfield, the only all-weather strip in northern Burma. This was the final victory of the 5307th Composite Unit, which was disbanded in August 1944.

THE RETURN

Your primary objective is to liberate the Island of Leyte. Air support for the landing will be provided by planes from the Escort Carriers of the Seventh Fleet. Your first objective should be capture of the Airfields near Tacloban.

Your final objective is the Naval base at Ormoc. Destroying it will end any chance of the enemy resupplying the island. Reach and destroy Ormoc by any means necessary.

Be on alert for the Japanese battleship Yamato. It has escaped from US forces engaging it to the North.

Japanese defenses on the island are expected to be entrenched. Good Luck.

Legend

N Naval Yard
S Stone
D Dock
I Iron
G Gold

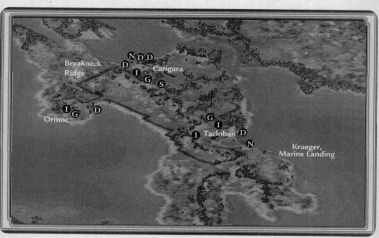

Players

United States (you; blue; Atomic WW II)

Empire of Japan (enemy; red; Atomic WW II)

Empire of Japan (enemy; red; Atomic WW II)

Empire of Japan (enemy; red; Atomic WW II)

United States Navy (ally; blue; Atomic WW II)

Initial Resources

1000 Food   1000 Wood   1000 Stone
1000 Gold   1000 Iron

Required Objectives

Capture Tacloban

Repair the airfields

Build fighters for defense

Defeat the Yamato or force it to retreat

Capture Carigara

Take the roadblock

PRIMA'S OFFICIAL STRATEGY GUIDE

EMPIRE EARTH
THE ART OF CONQUEST

Clear the Southern Road

Clear Breakneck Pass (destroy 8 pillboxes)

Capture Ormoc

Civ/Resource/Tech Opportunities

None

You Lose If

General Krueger dies

You lose either airport

Scenario-Specific Stats

Krueger

HP	5,235
Speed	14
LOS	9
Attack	160(Ms)/2
Armor	10 (Sh), 9 (Pr)
Range	0.5

Carigara Fighter Bomber (Zero Strafe)

Betty Bomber

HP	1,300
Speed	19
LOS	8
Attack	135 (Ms) / 0.5
Range	5 (AE 1.5)

Tank (Sherman)

HP	400
Speed	16
LOS	7
Attack	100(Gn)/4
Armor	60 (Sh, Pr, Gn), 50 (Ar, Ls)
Range	6

Yamato

HP	20,000
Speed	12
LOS	9
Attack	276(Ms)/4
Armor	20 (Ar, Pr, Ls),30(Gn)
Range	8 (AE 1)

Japanese Frigate

HP	1,600
Speed	17
LOS	10
Attack	68 (Ms)/2
Armor	20 (Ar, Pr, Ls),30(Gn)
Range	8

Japanese Battleship

HP	6,625
Speed	12
LOS	9
Attack	276(Ms)/4
Armor	20 (Ar, Pr, Ls),30(Gn)
Range	8 (AE 1)

Japanese Dreadnought

HP	5,750
Speed	12
LOS	9
Attack	230(Ms)/4
Armor	20 (Ar, Pr), 25 (Gn)
Range	8 (AE 1)

P-51

HP	550
Speed	21
LOS	7
Attack	52(Ms)/0.5
Range	6

Composition

Roadblock: 1 Artillery, 4 Pillboxes, 3 Howitzers, 2 Concrete Towers

Yamato Group: 3 Frigates, 1 Battleship, 1 Dreadnought).

Walkthrough

Capturing Tacloban is quite easy, in the grand scheme of things. All you need to do is repair the airports and build citizens and fighters as fast as you can. You need to then rally your fighters to the north-west end of the northern airport and the west end of the southern airport. Got it?

Fighter Bombers from Carigara continue to attack until you take that city, and Bombers persistently attack you until the end of the mission. You can't build Anti-aircraft or Flak guns, so the fighters are your only hope.

Pacific Campaign / The Meat Grinder

Build Howitzers like mad — it's the only effective way of fighting the Yamato. You'll lose a fair number of them, but by damaging the ship and forcing it to retreat, you essentially buy some time to rebuild.

Once you have built a large enough force, begin to expand northward. You'll find troops immediately north of the city, followed by a large, well-defended roadblock. Trying to take out this roadblock by a straightforward attack will cost you dearly. Don't even try it — you need to resort to more subtle means.

Here's how to do it. Once you hit the roadblock, build LSTs to transport your troops north to Carigara. (The Yamato will return to attack your LSTs, so beware.) Once you have taken over Carigara, the troops will abandon their weapons at the roadblock, and you can march right through it unopposed.

Then, clear the southern road by sending citizens to cut down trees. The last stretch involves slugging your way through Heartbreak Ridge from the north and also the southern road to attack Ormoc.

Other hints:

⊕ The ridge has 8 pillboxes.

⊕ Capturing Tacloban creates Tacloban citizens, and causes Japanese Bombers to attack the Tacloban South Airport and Carigara Fighter/Bombers to attack Tacloban

⊕ Repairing both airfields creates P51s, activates the Yamato attack, and gives the objective to attack Carigara

⊕ Attacking the roadblock adds LSTs, then causes the Yamato to attack the transports

⊕ Destroying the Carigara Military Buildings captures Carigara, destroys the airport, and causes the LSTs to go away

⊕ Attacking the Breakneck Ridge pillboxes causes the Northern Reinforcement Marines to attack

⊕ Clearing the southern road causes the southern road exit to be attacked by Southern Reinforcement Tanks

---

Well done, men. It's been a long battle. I know that you are tired and will soon be relieved. The battle for Luzon lies ahead. And after that, Japan.

THE MEAT GRINDER

"It has become clear we need a base for escort fighters to protect bombing raids on Japan. Iwo Jima lies only 650 miles from Tokyo and two airfields are under construction. The capture of these airfields is the preliminary objective, with the elimination of the enemy forces on the island being the final objective.

The island has been subjected to days of intense naval and air bombardment to soften up the defenses, but the Japanese have had time to entrench their positions, so results are uncertain.

The Japanese have long regarded Iwo Jima as part of the Japanese Islands, so expect stiff resistance."

EMPIRE EARTH
THE ART OF CONQUEST

PRIMA'S OFFICIAL STRATEGY GUIDE

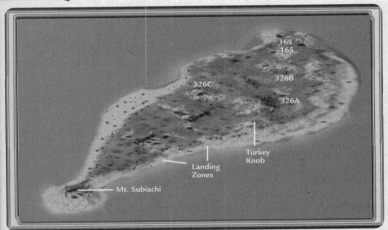

Players

United States (you; blue; Atomic WW II)

Empire of Japan (enemy; red; Atomic WW II)

United States Air Force (ally; blue; Atomic WW II)

Initial Resources

None

Required Objectives

Capture and defend both airfields.

Clear the island of Japanese forces.

Civ/Resource Opportunities

None

Tech Opportunities

Iwo Jima Statue

You Lose If

Either airfield is destroyed.

Scenario-Specific Stats

Japanese Battleship

HP	6,625
Speed	12
LOS	9
Attack	276(Ms)/4
Armor	20 (Ar, Pr, Ls),60(Gn)
Range	8 (AE 1)

Japanese Howitzer

HP	500
Speed	10
LOS	10
Attack	50 (Gn)/8
Armor	13 (Gn), 15 (Ms)

Friendly Transport

HP	750
Speed	17
Capacity	28
LOS	5
Armor	20(Ar, Pr), 25 (Gn)

Pacific Campaign / The Meat Grinder

Composition

Beach Defenses:
12 Howitzers, 3 Pillboxes, 3 Marines

Transport (Atomic)

Friendly Reinforcement Groups:
1 Marine, 2 Machine Guns, 3 Medics,
4 Sherman Flamethrowers, 5 Howitzer
Cannon, 6 Flame Throwers

Tank (Sherman Flamethrower)

Japanese Reinforcements:
165, 326A, 326B, 326C, Turkey Knob
(each location—5 Marine,
2 Snipers, 1 57mm AT Gun)

B29 Bomber

B17 Bomber

Suribachi Pillboxes (Artillery)

Events

Destroying Japanese defenses near the
beaches on the East side of the Island
activates fire reinforcement and creates
troop transport.

Tasking the transports to the landing
zones (player normal condition) creates
Tanks and some reinforcement groups.
Player weak, creates some reinforcement
groups.

Capture the airfields. Destroy the
Japanese defenses near the airfields. Do
not destroy the airfields.

Create a field hospital.

Move North and destroy the pillboxes
and defenders (Turkey Knob, Hills
362A-C).

Clear the pillboxes from the North end
of the Island. (Hill 165)

Capture Mt. Suribachi by moving 5
Marines to the summit.

Walkthrough

This is a very short, very straightforward mission. Once again, you start out
on the water. Your first goal is to clear
out the beach defenses, make an
amphibious landing, and put your
troops on dry sand. Let them slug it out
with the Japanese forces.

In this scenario, you will quickly discover that you've got far more many
Marines than any other unit.
Unfortunately, they're disposable and
you also soon discover that you have to
expend many of them to take each
group of pillboxes.

Taking out a group of pillboxes pre-
vents additional units from spawning
there, but it doesn't do much to slow
down the roving snipers on the island.
They're going to constantly harass your
men and attack precious airports. Deal
with them as you can and continue
driving north. Once you take Mt.
Suribachi, you've accomplished the
final objective and can declare victory.

EMPIRE EARTH
THE ART OF CONQUEST

⮜⮜⮜ Asian Campaign ⮞⮞⮞

After a long period of turmoil, both economic and military, the newly established nation known as the United Federation of Asiatic Republics, UFAR, now finds itself on divided ground. Enemies from within are threatening to destroy the country's economic infrastructure. And hostile nations are making rumbling threats about invasion, eager to see the UFAR government lose control of its power base due to the numerous rebel attacks it has suffered.

If circumstances are not taken into hand, and quickly, then this new national power will fade from the world stage. Do you have what it takes to lead this new nation to glory?

A NEW DYNASTY

After a turbulent political election, a new figurehead has risen to take the leadership of China. This man, Hu Kwan Do, head of the Kwan Do electronics and communications conglomerate, now finds himself on the brink of a civil war unequaled in his nations — and perhaps all the world's — history'.

Several radical groups wholly opposed to Kwan Do's policies fled the capitol after the election and set up or joined existing camps of outlaws and terrorists. Through coercion of the local populous, these groups have gathered enough support to wage open war against the new Dynasty.

The last three weeks have been one of intense struggle for the newly formed UFAR government. Rebel attacks and acts of terrorism have almost crippled the economic and military production of the entire country. The rebels have succeeded in stealing technologies and military hardware and are using this to their advantage.

The loss of life has been horrendous. Emperor Kwan Do has been pushed to his limits and has come to a decision:

"For the good of the nation, this civil war must end. Violently, as violence seems to be the only language these terrorist groups understand."

Using the enormous resources of his communications empire and the many Global Satellites it has constructed or owns, the New Dynasty now awaits its Emperor's command to unleash the power of its might upon the rebels.

Legend

N Naval Yard
S Stone
D Dock
I Iron
G Gold
— Wall

Asian Campaign / A New Dynasty

Players

UFAR (you; light green; Digital Age)

Rebel Forces (enemy; light gray; Atomic Modern)

Rebel Forces (enemy; light blue; Digital Age)

Rebel Forces (enemy; blue; Atomic Modern)

Rebel Forces (enemy; light yellow; Atomic Modern)

Rebel Forces (enemy; green; Digital Age)

Rebel Forces (enemy; maroon; Digital Age)

Initial Resources

500 Food   500 Wood   300 Stone
100 Gold   100 Iron

Civ Point/Resource Opportunities

None

Required Objectives

Research and develop new technology: The Extrasensory Stimulus Signal.

Eliminate four rebel strongholds.

Optional Objectives

Defend UFAR Capitol City.

Tech Opportunities

Rescue Dr. Sung and receive the ESS technology.

You Lose If

Dr. Sung dies before you get ESS.

Emperor Hu Kwan Do, Chancellor Ming or Dr. Kwai Sung die.

Scenario-Specific Stats

Assassin Gunship, Rebel Strafe Forces 1, 3

HP	450
Attack	25 (Gn)
Speed	21
Range	5
Armor	15 (Gn,Ls)

Chancellor Ming

HP	5600
Attack	230 (Ms)
Speed	14
Range	8
Armor	10 (Sh)
Morale	

Chinese Mech #1, Huey, Dewey, Louie Mechs

HP	1500
Attack	72 (Ms)
Speed	16
Range	7
Armor	50 (Ar,Pr), 30 (Gn), 40 (Ls), 10 (Ms)

Dr. Kwai Sung

HP	3600
Attack	90 (Ms)
Speed	14
Range	8
Armor	10 (Sh)

Heal, Battle cry

EMPIRE EARTH
THE ART OF CONQUEST

Hu Kwan Do

HP	2500
Attack	10 (Ms)
Speed	14
Range	6
Armor	10 (Sh), 9 (Pr)

Heal, Battle cry

Rebel Fighters

HP	500
Attack	26 (Ms)
Speed	21
Range	6

Rebel Land Forces 1, 3; Response Force

HP	600
Attack	62 (Ls)
Speed	12
Range	6

Rebel Land Forces 2, 4

HP	800
Attack	74 (Ls)
Speed	12
Range	6

Rebel Strafe Force 2

HP	850
Attack	75 (Ms)
Speed	21
Range	5
Armor	13 (Gn,Ls)

Rebel Transport (Atomic)

HP	750
Speed	14
Capacity	28
Armor	20 (Ar,Pr), 25 (Gn)

Secret Police

HP	800
Attack	74 (Ls)
Speed	12
Range	6

Spy Satellite 503

| HP | 1000 |
| Speed | 20 |

Rebel Marine

HP	470
Attack	52 (Gn)
Speed	12
Range	6

United Federation of Asian Republics, and rebel groups are staging an uprising.

When the game begins, your city is under attack and most of its technology and military production units have been disabled by rebel sabotage. You must eliminate two of the four rebel encampments threatening to destroy your city and economy. On top of this, you must also effect the rescue of an eminent scientist who is working on a secret project — a project that could spell certain doom for the rebels.

You begin with the scientist trapped on one of the northeastern islands. That's a pretty black-and-white situation, but the kicker is that you have no way to transport him by air or sea. Rebels have blocked the overland route, and trying to bring the scientist to the base by that route is suicide.

However, there's a remedy. Once the scientist has been rescued, he can restore the functionality of the military buildings. He'll also have discovered the ESS (extrasensory Stimulus Signal), which is a rudimentary form of Mind Control. With this research, you can then build Riot Policemen who can pacify enemy infantry units.

Reducing the fighting capacity of the enemy infantry makes it much easier to penetrate two of the four bases. Once you've done that, you've achieved victory.

Walkthrough

Welcome to the age of technology, and to the first scenario in the new Space epoch! The first mission in this campaign may have new technology, but the problems you'll face aren't all that different from previous scenarios. In this case, the Kwan Do family has assumed power in the new Far East nation of UFAR, the

---

Emperor Hu Kwan Do: "At last! The rebel forces are defeated! Now we can concentrate on more important matters — our economy and our technological research — it is "now our goal to be the first to colonize Mars. It is our destiny!

EMPIRE EARTH™

Hot Key Quick Reference Card

Key	Action
BUILDINGS	
I	Set Rally Point
Town Center/Capitol (H)	
C	Create Citizen
E	Train Strategist Hero
R	Train Warrior Hero
B	Produce Spotting Balloon
D	Train Canine Scout (Dog)
A	Research Epoch Advance
G	Research Gold Mining Technologies
N	Research Hunting / Foraging Technologies
S	Research Iron Mining Technologies
T	Research Stone Mining Technologies
U	Research Wall and Tower Upgrades
W	Research Wood Cutting Technologies
Archery Range (Ctrl-A)	
A	Train Foot Archers
C	Train Chariot and Cavalry Archers
E	Train Ranged Spear Throwers
F	Train Elephant Archer
X	Train Crossbow Man
Barracks (Ctrl-B)	
A	Train Ranged Shock (Gun) Units and Sampson
B	Train Grenade Launcher and Bazooka
C	Train Medics
D	Train Elite Guard
E	Train Pierce (Spear) Units and Flame Thrower
F	Train Hand Cannoneer and Mortars
G	Train Machine Gunner
N	Train Barbarian
R	Train Sharp-shooters and Snipers
S	Train Melee Shock (Sword) Units and Stinger Soldier
T	Train Partisan
V	Train Viking
W	Train Rock Thrower
Dock (Ctrl-D)	
B	Build Battleships
C	Build Cruisers (Anti-Air)
D	Build Frigates
F	Build Fishing Boats
G	Build Galley/Galleons
T	Build Transports

Key	Action
Stable (Ctrl-S)	
C	Train Shock (Melee) Cavalry
E	Train Pierce (Spear) Cavalry
F	Train War Elephant
G	Train Gun Cavalry
S	Train Persian Cavalry
Siege Factory (Ctrl-C)	
A	Build Anti-Tank (AT) Guns
B	Build Artillery
C	Build Siege Weapons
E	Build Field Cannon
G	Build Siege Cannon
R	Build Rams
S	Build Field Weapons (pre-gunpowder)
T	Build Siege Towers
Navy Yard (Ctrl-V)	
C	Build Aircraft Carriers
G	Build Sea Kings (Anti-Sub)
S	Build Attack Submarines
T	Build Nuclear-Powered Missile Submarines
Tank Factory (Ctrl-F)	
F	Build Mobile AA Units
S	Build Armor-Piercing (AP) Tanks
T	Build High-Explosive (HE) Tanks
Airport (Ctrl-Q)	
V	Set Atomic Bomber Rally Point
X	Set Bomber/Helicopter Rally Point
Z	Set Fighter Rally Point
A	Build Atomic Bombers
B	Build Bomber s
C	Build Anti-Tank (AT) Helicopters
E	Build Gunship Helicopters
F	Build Fighter/Bombers
G	Build Sea Kings (Anti-Sub)
R	Build Transport Helicopters
S	Build Fighters
T	Build Anti-Tank (AT) Airplanes
Aircraft Carrier (Ctrl-Q)	
F	Build Fighter/Bombers
Cyber Factory (Ctrl-R)	
A	Build Ares Cybers
C	Build Pandora Cybers
R	Build Hyperion Cybers
T	Build Minotaur Cybers
Z	Build Zeus Cyber
Cyber Lab (Ctrl-X)	
A	Build Apollo Cyber
D	Build Hades Cyber
E	Build Poseidon Cyber
F	Build Furies Cyber
T	Build Tempest Cyber

Key	Action
Temple (Ctrl-Y)	
E	Train Priest
R	Train Prophet
A	Research Tech to Increase Temple Range
B	Research Tech to Allow Conversion of Buildings
C	Research Tech to Allow Conversion of Priests
D	Research Techs to Increase Prophet Speed
F	Research Techs to Increase Priest Hit Points
M	Research Tech to Increase Priest Recharge Rate
N	Research Techs to Increase Prophet Range
P	Research Techs to Increase Prophet Hit Points
S	Research Techs to Increase Priest Speed
T	Research Techs to Increase Priest Range
University	
B	Research Techs to Increase Building Line of Sight
F	Research Techs to Increase Building Hit Points
R	Research Techs to Increase University Range
S	Research Techs to Increase Rate of Repair at Dock
T	Research Tech to Decrease Cost of Tributes
Hospital	
A	Research Techs to Increase Citizen Attack and Hit Points
C	Research Techs to Increase Your Pop Cap
R	Research Techs to Increase Hospital Healing Rate
S	Research Techs to Increase Citizen Speed
Granary	
F	Research Techs to Increase Farming Rate
R	Replant Farms
Wall	
G	Make Gate

7109721

EMPIRE EARTH™

Hot Key Quick Reference Card

Key	Action
VIEW KEYS	
Up Arrow	Scroll Up
Down Arrow	Scroll Down
Left Arrow	Scroll Left
Right Arrow	Scroll Right
Right Bracket	Zoom in
Left Bracket	Zoom out
Period	Follow Unit
F2	Toggle through perspective Zoom modes
F5	Toggle through 3 Show Hidden Units modes
F9	Take a Screen Shot with UI
Shift – F9	Take a Screen Shot without UI
Ctrl – F9	Take a Low Resolution Screen Shot of Entire Map
Alt – F9	Take a High Resolution Screen Shot of Entire Map
Space	Move to location of last player event (keep pressing to review the queue of recent events)
SELECTION KEYS	
Tab	Idle Citizen
Comma	Idle Military Unit
A	Idle Atomic Bomber
B	Idle Bomber
D	Idle Fighter/Bomber
F	Idle Fighter
Ctrl - #	Create group #
Shift - #	Add selection to group #
Alt - #	Select and center group #
#	Select group # (Press the group's number)
##	Select and center group # (Press number twice)
H	Select and center Town Center
Ctrl – A	Select and center Archery Range
Ctrl – B	Select and center Barracks
Ctrl – C	Select and center Siege Factory
Ctrl – D	Select and center Dock
Ctrl – F	Select and center Tank Factory
Ctrl – G	Select and center Granary
Ctrl – I	Select and center Missile Base (Campaigns Only)
Ctrl – N	Select and center Settlement
Ctrl – Q	Select and center Airport

Key	Action
Ctrl – R	Select and center Cyber Factory
Ctrl – S	Select and center Stable
Ctrl – V	Select and center Naval Yard
Ctrl – X	Select and center Cyber Lab
Ctrl – Y	Select and center Temple
GAME COMMANDS	
Numpad +	Increase Game Speed
Numpad -	Decrease Game Speed
Esc	Cancels Current Input or Action Mode (exits cinematics in scenarios)
Enter	Chat
F1	Return to Scenario Editor (When in Test Mode)
F3	Pause
F4	Quick Save
Shift – F4	Quick Load
Ctrl – F4	Auto Save Load
F10	In-Game Options
F11	Toggle Display of Game Clock/Speed and Frame Rate
Alt – F	Enter Flare Mode
Page Up	Previous Messages
Ctrl – Shift - Z	All out "Banzai" computer player attack - allied computer players will assist you (single player only)
Ctrl - Alt - Z	All out "Banzai" computer player attack - allied computer players will not assist you (single player only)
UNIT COMMANDS	
Shift	Show Goal
Queue/Add	Goal to Queue (with other key)
B	Unit Behaviors
G	Garrison/Populate a Building
L	Explore
M	Formations
P	Stop
D	Unload Transport/Fortress
Z	Patrol (Land Military Units Only)
Del	Kill First Selected Unit
Shift – Del	Kill All Selected Units

Key	Action
Unit Behaviors	
Alt – A	Aggressive
Alt – D	Defend (Stand Ground)
Alt – G	Guard (Guards a location)
Alt – S	Scout
Citizens	
A	Build Archery Range or Gun
AA	Build Barracks
B	Build Barracks
C	Build Siege Factory
D	Build Dock
E	Build House
F	Build Tank Factory
J	Build Granary/Farms
N	Build Settlement
O	Build Fortress
Q	Build Airport
R	Build Cyber Factory
S	Build Stable
T	Build Tower
U	Build University
V	Build Naval Yard
W	Build Wall
X	Build Cyber Lab
Y	Build Temple
Z	Build Hospital
Priests	
C	Convert
Prophets	
A	Plague
C	Hurricane
E	Earthquake
F	Firestorm
R	Malaria
V	Volcano
Tempest	
A	Anti-Matter Storm
R	Resonator
Hades	
E	Teleport
T	Time Warp
V	Nano-Virus
Apollo	
C	Ion Pulse
R	Repair
S	Diffraction Shield
Furies	
D	Self-Destruct
Poseidon	
C	Assimilate
Transports	
D	Unload
Strategist Heroes	
C	Battle Cry

COPPER AGE		DARK AGE		RENAISSANCE		INDUSTRIAL AGE		INFORMATIO
BC	2000 BC	500 BC	0 AD	900 AD	1500 AD	1500 AD	1700 AD	1900 AD	2000 AD
	BRONZE AGE		MIDDLE AGES			IMPERIAL AGE		ATOMIC AGE	

Asian Campaign / The Breaking Point

THE BREAKING POINT

With the colonization of other worlds now an actuality, a worldwide race has begun to explore, colonize, and exploit the mineral riches of other planets.

With an exploding population, UFAR realizes it cannot sustain itself with its dwindling natural resources. The Federation has committed huge amounts of resources to its space program, including terraforming and Faster-Than-Light (FTL) technology that can ferry resource-laden cargo ships from Mars to Earth.

This economic burden has placed enormous strain on the quality of living conditions in Southeast Asia. Several opposing factions have arisen out of the disapproval of the government. Even some religious groups have dissented, believing that Man's place is on Earth and only on Earth.

Acts of sabotage and terrorism hamper the space effort, and the weakened UFAR military is having trouble protecting its key research and production facilities. Faced with the possibility of total collapse in the Southeast Province, UFAR is running out of options to stabilize its economy and diffuse the political climate.

Legend

 I Iron

 G Gold

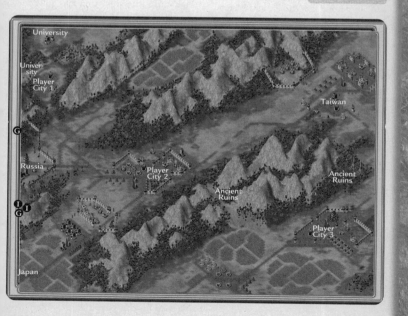

PRIMA'S OFFICIAL STRATEGY GUIDE

Players

UFAR (you; light green; Digital Age)

Russia (ally; maroon; Digital Age)

Japan (ally; light blue; Digital Age)

Taiwan (ally; orange; Digital Age)

Rebel Forces (enemy; blue; Atomic Modern to Digital Age)

UFAR (ally; green; Digital Age)

Initial Resources

3000 Food   5000 Wood   1000 Stone

2000 Gold   2000 Iron

Required Objectives

Get 60 troops from Taiwan, 5000 Gold and 5000 Iron from Russia, and Faster-Than-Light travel technology from Japan.

End the revolt.

Destroy the rebels and Hyperion.

Civ Point Opportunities

None

Resource Opportunities

Send Food to Taiwan for troops.

Send troops to Russia for Gold and Iron.

Send Iron to Japan for research assistance.

Tech Opportunities

With assistance from Japan, build the Faster-Than-Light travel technology.

You Lose If

All universities are destroyed.

Scenario-Specific Stats

Leader

HP	2430	
Attack	55 (Ms)	
Speed	14	
Range	8	
Armor	10 (Sh),	
	9 (Pr)	

Heal, Battle cry

Troops

HP	450
Attack	60 (Gn)
Speed	9
Range	9

Walkthrough

This mission is more trade-oriented than battle-oriented. You must harvest food and exchange it for troops from Taiwan. These troops can consequently be sent to Russia for iron and gold. Lastly, iron can be given to Japan in exchange fore Faster-Than-Light data technology.

Your first step should be to immediately set all citizens to harvesting rice from the fields. The more food you can harvest, the more citizens you can create, and in turn, the more food you can harvested. There's a definite circular pattern involved in winning this mission.

Once you have food and iron, you must deliver them to their respective countries using Cargo Trucks. When the rebels see Cargo Trucks en route, they will of course attack. You must protect the Cargo Truck and ensure that your resources are delivered as scheduled.

Meanwhile, Rebel forces will try to disrupt trade by attacking buildings, citizens and sometimes even universities. So, you should set up defensive perimeters around all of these places. Any excess troops acquired from Taiwan can be used for this purpose.

Asian Campaign / Look to the Stars

Once you have delivered five iron shipments to Japan, you can build the Faster-Than-Light research center. However, by this point the economic crisis has become so unstable that your citizens start a revolt. You have to eliminate a good amount of your military (no more than 10 units of each type) in order to appease the public. Once the conflict is resolved, however, you can begin rebuilding your forces. You'll have to do so quickly, because the rebels will launch one final assault on the research center.

Once the final attack is rebuffed (mostly by destroying enemy Cybers), the research center quickly finishes its project, and the mission is complete.

Other hints:

⊕ Taiwan, Japan, and Russia are no friends of the rebels. If a Cargo Truck is being pursued, slip into one of their bases for protection until the threat is eliminated.

⊕ Citizens can be used to repair the research center if it comes under attack. This can buy some time until the enemy forces are taken out. If the research center is destroyed, you fail the mission!

⊕ If you run too low on stone, you're given a message. By demolishing any of the ancient temples, you can generate stone piles.

The Province has endured some stormy times. But economic equilibrium is returning to the region. Public opinion has been placated for the most part, so the threat of overthrow is comfortably remote. Having achieved Faster-Than-Light travel, UFAR is nearly ready to embark on its expansion into space. The march of progress continues to meet resistance, however, and UFAR must be diligent in protecting its interests. The days ahead could be glorious...or prove disastrous.

LOOK TO THE STARS

Having secured financial and economic stability on the UFAR mainland, the Kwan Do dynasty now turns its attention to the newly revived Space Race, and makes a bid to be the first nation in history to establish a colony on another world. It will not be easy however, as pockets of rebel and fanatical troops have destroyed the two UFAR space centers that had been conducting research and development on the UFAR Space Program.

Turning to its neighbor, Japan, for help, the UFAR government has agreed to help with that countries own Space Exploration program in a joint effort to reach Mars before the Western nations can. Unfortunately, the radical groups that are opposed to the Kwan Do dynasty have now turned against the Japanese and are attacking them as well, straining the relationship between these two powerhouse nations of the East.

If the situation cannot be corrected soon, then the UFAR government could find itself involved in a war on three fronts and the hope of establishing a Martian colony will be nothing more than a dream.

Legend

Ⓝ Naval Yard
Ⓕ Forage
Ⓢ Stone
Ⓓ Dock
Ⓘ Iron
Ⓖ Gold
— Wall

EMPIRE EARTH
THE ART OF CONQUEST

PRIMA'S OFFICIAL STRATEGY GUIDE

Players

U.F.A.R. (you; green; Digital Age)

The Eye of God (enemy; blue; Digital Age to Nano Age)

Rebel Forces (enemy; black; Digital Age)

Novaya Russia (enemy; maroon; Atomic Modern to Digital Age)

Rebel Forces (enemy; orange; Digital Age)

Japan 21st Century (ally; light blue; Digital Age)

Initial Resources

500 Food	500 Wood	500 Stone
500 Gold	500 Iron	

Required Objectives

Establish a military outpost and defend it against terrorist attacks.

Aid the Japanese by rebuilding the Tangeshima Space Complex (missile base and temple).

Launch a manned Colony Ship (FTL nearly complete).

Civ Point/Resource Opportunities

None

Tech Opportunities

New Cyber Unit: Khara Bator.

You Lose If

Hu Kwan Do dies.

Scenario-Specific Stats

Miyazaki (Capitol)

Kagoshima (Town Center)

Kobayashi (Town Center)

Sata (Town Center)

Dr. Webster

HP	5600
Attack	230 (Ms)
Speed	14
Range	8
Armor	10 (Sh)
Morale	

Asian Campaign / Look to the Stars

General Rykov

HP	3650
Attack	55 (Ms)
Speed	14
Range	8
Armor	10 (Sh), 9 (Pr)

Heal, Battle cry

Khara Bator (Mech)

HP	6000
Attack	200 (Ms)
Speed	12
Range	9
Armor	50 (Ar, Pr, Gn), 75 (Ls)

Y-3X Colony Space Transport

Prime Minister Hikaido

HP	5235
Attack	160 (Ms)
Speed	14
Range	8
Armor	10 (Sh), 9 (Pr)

EoG Juggernaut Fleet (Frigate—Juggernauts)

Japanese Tower (Laser)

U-K Machine Gun

HP	400
Attack	16 (Gn)
Speed	12
Range	6
Armor	8 (Gn)

U-K Transport (Atomic)

Walkthrough

Twenty years have passed since the nation of UFAR first rose to power. The Kwan Do family dynasty is now in the hands of the son of the original leader. He's trying to lead his nation into an era of scientific and technological supremacy, and the UFAR's ultimate goal is to be the first nation to establish a colony on Mars.

Their own facilities destroyed by rebel attacks, the UFAR nation is now forced into helping a neighboring country rebuild its Space Center, which was also destroyed in a brutal and violent rebel attack.

When the mission starts, you're granted a parcel of land with which to build a base. You must quickly establish your presence, fend off attacks, and develop a robust economy.

Once you're firmly rooted, you must help rescue a city that has been taken over by rebel factions. You must also clear off the island where the old Space Center used to be housed. Once these two goals have been accomplished, you can finally reconstruct the Space Center. Once it's up and operating, the Colony Ship launches on an inward journey toward Mars.

And with a magnificent roar of fuel and flame, the Huge Colony Ship lifts off from the newly constructed Space Port — and streaks through the atmosphere on its way to Mars.

What destiny awaits the new colonists and what challenges will they face … ?

Only time will tell ….

EMPIRE EARTH
THE ART OF CONQUEST

PRIMA'S OFFICIAL STRATEGY GUIDE

EYE OF GOD

Time is critical. Our colonists on Mars need supplies. Without resources they cannot build the colony, without resources they will not survive. A colony has to be established before competing nations claim all the mineral-rich territories, leaving UFAR an impoverished state. They key to success is the Space Dock. It is the colonists' lifeline. The remote Mongolian Steppes are not monitored by spy satellites, and should help keep the facility a secret. But we must be ever vigilant. If our adversaries - like the Western European Alliance - learn of the facility, they will most certainly attempt to stop us.

Then there's the Eye of God. Their fanaticism endures numerous attempts to thwart them. They cannot see that space is our salvation, not our damnation. Even now they lurk in the desert, waiting for an opportunity to strike at the heart of the Space Program. If the Space Dock is destroyed, the colonists won't last long on their own. It must be protected at all costs.

Legend

- **F** Forage
- **S** Stone
- **D** Dock
- **I** Iron
- **G** Gold
- **—** Wall

Players

UFAR (you; green; Nano Age)

Japan (ally; orange; Nano Age)

Mars Colony (ally; light green; Space Age)

Eye of God (enemy; light blue; Atomic Modern to Nano Age)

European Alliance (enemy; blue; Space Age)

Initial Resources

2000 Food   1000 Wood   500 Stone

1000 Gold   1000 Iron

Required Objectives

Send 20,000 Resources (any type) to the Mars Colony.

Optional Objectives

Destroy Rebel forces.

Civ Point/Resource/Tech Opportunities

None

You Lose If

Space Dock is destroyed.

Scenario-Specific Stats

Ally Transport (Pegasus)

Defense Tank (Centurion)

Enemy Gunships (Spectre AT Helicopters)

Rebel Tank (Gladiator)

Rebel Gunship (Reaper)

Walkthrough

This is a timed mission, so you need to act quickly and decisively. Resources abound in this terrain, but the Eye of God quickly takes notice of anyone who's trying to harvest them. So, before you send your citizens scurrying off to gather resources, set up lines of defense to protect them. To the east, there's a forage patch and some herd animals that can be collected without threat. Wood can also be gathered without much harassment.

Asian Campaign / Eye of God

As you approach the requisite 10,000 resource mark, you probably want to gather a sizeable force and eliminate the rebel bases. If you attempt this too early, though, you'll meet stiffer resistance. When a rebel base is destroyed, you recover more resources, putting you that much closer to meeting your goal.

Once enough resources are gathered, rebuild the Space Dock. Then, dispatch the resources using the Alliances & Tributes screen. Once they're delivered, you must send a second installment of 10,000 resources. You have considerably less time to do so the second time around, but this shouldn't be too difficult, especially if the rebel forces have been eliminated.

Try to respond to request for troops and resources in a timely manner; otherwise enemy forces will arrive. You may also want to invest in building Anti-aircraft units to protect the Space Dock from fighters descending from space.

Other hints:

Build his settlements right next to the resource piles and populate settlements whenever possible. This will generate noticeable gathering bonuses to speed you to victory.

Rebel bases will crumble if the buildings inside are destroyed. Artillery units are ideal for this. Or, they can be reserved for taking down the walls, allowing other units to rush in and destroy the buildings.

UFAR has gained a foothold on the Planet Mars. Our colonists are to be commended for their tireless efforts and continuing bravery in the new frontier. Soon mighty factories will rise above the red landscape, generating plentiful resources for our nation and our people.

The Federation has weathered some truly turbulent events. But now that we have established ourselves as an international - indeed, an interplanetary power, we can look forward to prosperous times and opportunities as limitless as space itself.

PRIMA'S OFFICIAL STRATEGY GUIDE

GHOST SHIP INSURRECTION

"It has been nearly 250 years since the first Mars colonies were founded, and these brave pioneers and workers have made much progress in making this new world their home. The most habitable territories on the Martian surface, those near the Polar Caps, have been well established and are now fully functional towns and cities, each with a stable economy and administrative body backed by differing political Earth-based government. These colonies:

Xin Tong King — * established by the Republic of Japan

Huo Xing Cheng — * established by the UFAR government

Baker's Ridge — * established by the United States/Canadian Conglomerate

Port Chernobyl— * established by the European Union of Nations

... along with five smaller mining communities, have caused quite a few headaches for their earth-based governing bodies, as the distance between Earth and Mars hampers decisive action in settling territorial disputes. Government appointed officials are too easily bribed and cajoled by the mining corporations and financial interests that have holdings on Mars.

However, the first rumblings of civil discontent have been heard in reaction to several new policies and injunctions that have recently been imposed by the Earth governors. Among these is the planned 'Howard Johnson Reclamation Project *' (which basically would force the Martian miners and workers out of there present housing neighborhoods and replace them with resort communities for the rich and famous) and the 'UFAR Contracts and Holdings Act*' (which has resulted in less governmental control of the mining corporations and has lowered wages and benefits packages and increased work loads and costs of goods). These outrageous measures combined with the fact that no 'Martian' has served or been elected to a government position, has led to meetings and marches protesting unfair treatment.

As you may well remember, this month marks the ten-year anniversary of the Baker's Ridge Protest Rally, which ended in violence when the government sent in police and military to break up the protesters and force the workers back to their jobs. Several hundred 'Martians' were either wounded or killed and the populations of the colony cities since that time have been dwindling as disgruntled workers have stolen or appropriated equipment and materials to start shanty communities on the fringes of the terra-formed areas of the established territories. These pockets of discontent have grown quite large over the last two decades throughout the nine established territories and protesting has turned to attacks and well coordinated paramilitary actions against this unfair treatment by the earth-based ruling body.

At the forefront of this rebellion a leader has risen: Khan Sun Do, a descendant of the great hero Hu Kwan Do, who has begun to give the workers not only a sense of solidarity but of nationality as well. The workers are no longer transplanted earthlings, but people born and bred on Martian soil. This has become the driving force in what the workers now see as a war of independence.

Can we here on Earth really afford to ignore the events happening so far away? How long before this war for independence becomes a battle for survival? If these discontents do win out against the colonial governments, how long will it be before they strike out against the originators of their oppression? How long before Earth will be invaded by the Martians?"

Legend

F Forage

S Stone

D Dock

I Iron

G Gold

— Wall

Asian Campaign / Ghost Ship Insurrection

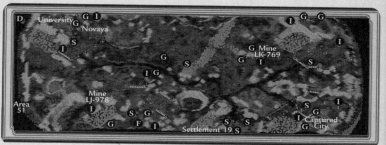

Players

Martian Rebel Alliance (you; green; Nano Age to Space Age)

U.S.C.N. (enemy; yellow; Digital Age to Space Age)

Japan 23rd Century (enemy; light blue; Digital Age to Space Age)

Novaya Russia (enemy; maroon; Space Age)

U.F.A.R. (ally; blue; Nano Age to Space Age)

Initial Resources

None

Required Objectives

Capture Ghost Ship.

Civ Point Opportunities

None

Resource Opportunities

None

Tech Opportunities

Collect 4500 Gold to fund Xinhua's Cyber Ninja research project.

Get the stolen Corporate Mining Unit to your Capitol and it will be added to your build queue.

You Lose If

Khan Sun Do or Xinhua die.

Novaya University is destroyed.

Scenario-Specific Stats

Yamato Ghost Ship
(Yamato Capital Ship)

Kyshu Po (Cyber)

HP	1700
Speed	16
Range	8
Armor	50 (Ar, Pr), 20 (Gn, Ls)

Teleport; Time Warp; Nano Virus

Protocol Unit #579 (Cyber)

HP	3000
Speed	14
Range	8
Armor	50 (Ar, Pr), 20 (Gn, Ls)

Walk underwater; Refractive Cloak; Assimilate other Cybers

Rebel Zeus (Zeus II)
Russian Trooper (Shock Trooper)
Satellite (Spy Satellite)
Settlement 19 Drone

HP	375
Attack	5 (Ms)
Speed	10
Range	2

EMPIRE EARTH
THE ART OF CONQUEST

PRIMA'S OFFICIAL STRATEGY GUIDE

Xinhua (Sergei Molotov)

HP	5600
Attack	230 (Ms)
Speed	14
Range	8
Armor	10 (Sh)
Morale	

Walkthrough

Another 200 years have passed, and the Martian Colonies are well established and thriving. However, the diplomatic relations between the various colonies has been strained to the breaking point. Each colony, sponsored by a different Earth nation, is squabbling over the mineral rights and deposits scattered across the face of the red planet.

The heir to the Kwan Do dynasty has been ousted from his seat of power and now wanders the desolate Martian landscape with a handful of loyal warriors.

Having been granted the opportunity to take over one of the colonies, you must secure the city and defend it from outside attacks.

You're in luck ... a loyal spy has devised a new training technique that can train an evolved unit, the Cyber Ninja. With it, you can subvert other colonies and steal technology.

All of the colonies share one commonality — they all fear the new ship created by the Earth Forces, a Giant Capitol Ship capable of tremendous firepower. You must task your Cyber Ninjas with stealing plans and charts in order to find where this ship is hiding. Only then can you attempt to steal this powerful weapon. Once the Giant Ship is located, you've won the mission.

Congratulations! We have captured the Yamato Capitol Ship!

THINGS TO COME

Ominous rumblings from the USCN Government continue today as President Allison Hardcastle makes it clear that the Earth will not recognize the newly organized Martian Alliance. Khan Sun Do, interim prime minister for the Alliance, worried that the Earth did not take the Alliance seriously, saying that "a military solution to the problem would cost both sides dearly."

When asked if he would consider military action against UCSN holdings on the Moon the Prime Minister would not comment.

Sun Do also spoke about the building unity amongst the members of the Martian Alliance. But private observers have noted that spokespersons for both Baker's Ridge, the North American settlement, and Port Chernobyl, the Russian group, have remained publicly subdued about the prospects of a Pan-Martian alliance, and privately have voiced concerns regarding military "maneuvers" near their bases. Scattered reports of military engagements to the South and West of UFAR base have been reported, but remain unverified at this time.

Legend

F	Forage
S	Stone
D	Dock
I	Iron
G	Gold
—	Wall

Asian Campaign / Things to Come

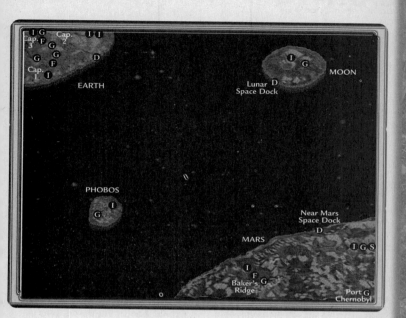

Players

Mars Alliance (you; green; Space Age)

Moon (enemy; maroon; Space Age)

Earth (enemy; maroon; Space Age)

Phobos (enemy; maroon; Space Age)

Baker's Ridge (enemy; red; Nano Age to Space Age)

Port Chernobyl (enemy; blue; Nano Age to Space Age)

Yamato Group (ally; green; Space Age)

Wormholes (ally; black; Space Age)

Initial Resources

1000 Food   1000 Wood   1000 Stone
1000 Gold   1000 Iron

Required Objectives

Coerce or subdue Baker's Ridge and Port Chernobyl on Mars.

Capture Phobos.

Capture the Moon. Capture three Earth capitals to cause Earth to sue for peace.

Civ Point/Resource/Tech Opportunities

None

COPPER AGE		DARK AGE		RENAISSANCE		INDUSTRIAL AGE	
BC	5000 BC	2000 BC	500 BC	0 AD	900 AD	1800 AD	1500 AD	1700 AD	1900 AD
STONE AGE		BRONZE AGE		MIDDLE AGES		IMPERIAL AGE	ATOMIC AG

EMPIRE EARTH
THE ART OF CONQUEST

PRIMA'S OFFICIAL STRATEGY GUIDE

Wonder

Orbital Space Station

You Lose If

Khan Sun Do or General Bhuta die.

Scenario-Specific Stats

Wormhole (Space Fighter)

HP	1400
Attack	175 (Gn)
Speed	24
Range (AE)	5 (0.3)
Armor	10 (Gn, Ls)
W Reinf—Artillery (Colossus Artillery)	
Earth Tank Zone 3 (Gladiator Tank)	

Walkthrough

This is an FSGSB — a Fairly Straightforward Giant Space Battle. The key here is to coerce the other settlements on Mars into harmony, or at least tentative cooperation. Your resource supply is very limited, and if you try to destroy the other settlements, you'll quickly find that it isn't cost-effective.

Persuading the other settlements takes only a Cyber Ninja and a few ground troops. As a result of your efforts, you receive an unending stream of foot soldiers to help you out during the rest of the campaign (okay, the rest of this mission).

With good manpower established, you can attack the western capital by skirting around the edge of the planet and

approaching it from the west. Stand on top of the crater and fire the Logic Bomb, but don't enter the crater by the towers.

Once you get into space you have to capture Phobos. Space fighters work well for taking out the multiple turrets, especially when you follow up with a landing force on Phobos. Watch out for the counterattack, though!

You can stop the harassing attacks by the Earth forces quite easily by positioning some Capital ships by each of the three wormholes. There, your ships can intercept the Earth Forces Transports as they emerge. This is much easier once the Yamato appears — it's very powerful compared to the other Capital ships.

Once you have captured Phobos, you'll have enough resources to build the Orbital Wonder. It's the only way to increase the morale of your spaceships, which is another huge advantage in space battles.

After Phobos is conquered, this scenario is a fairly straightforward "build up and attack" mission. You'll know when you've won; there are no mysteries awaiting here.

———— ✦ ————

By divine right we have triumphed. And we shall generously accede the lands we have taken...in exchange for our own land, our own destiny, our own planet. A dynasty for the future, and the stars.

∽∼∾ Multiplayer ∽∼∾

Empire Earth is essentially two complete games: Multiplayer and Campaign. In general, the two types appeal to two different types of people. A devoted Multiplayer combatant may play the same game for years, and never touch the first Campaign Scenario. It's that different.

Campaign victories are more easily explained than Multiplayer wins. The situations never change. The goals never alter; the enemies are always found in the same place. It's all figuring out what always works and what never does.

Multiplayer isn't like that. You may find a system that works for you, and then your opponents figure out your system and adapt to overcome it. Or you come up against an opponent who uses units in ways you hadn't considered ... or who can focus better on the game than you can ... or who has the uncanny ability to always epoch up a minute before you do.

The best thing you can do is practice. The second best thing to do is to interview experts and learn what they do. That's what this section is all about.

THE EXPERTS

It's generally safe to say that the people who playtest the game know the game better than anyone else ever could. That's because they play anywhere from 8 to 18 hours a day (sometimes even more!) for weeks or months at a time. The testers at Stainless Steel Studios are even better than that. These guys — Ryan "AgeOfEgos" Geiler, Damon "Stratus" Gauthier, Sunny "Crexis" Sihota, Nate "REDLINE" Jacques (pronounced "Jakes") and Mike "YoungGunZ" Echino — are hardcore (sometimes award-winning) RTS tournament players with years of victories behind them.

Asked what they thought the most important elements of the game were, they had essentially the same opinions on nearly everything.

Tournament vs. Regular

Keep in mind that the testers gave advice on what they know best, and by-and-large that means Tournament Multiplayer *Empire Earth*. There's more than one difference between tournament and regular, and you should adjust what you read for that fact.

Tournament is much faster and more intense. On average it takes only half an hour to complete four epochs in Tournament, where it might take an hour or more in a regular game.

Resources are less limited in Tournament play. It costs less to epoch up when you're in Tournament, which makes sense considering the restricted resources.

The variables are also a bit different in Tournament:

| COPPER AGE | DARK AGE | RENAISSANCE | INDUSTRIAL AGE |
| STONE AGE | BRONZE AGE | MIDDLE AGES | IMPERIAL AGE | ATOMIC A |

EMPIRE EARTH
THE ART OF CONQUEST

PRIMA'S OFFICIAL STRATEGY GUIDE

Towers have 50% the HP.

Walls have 70% the HP.

Buildings have 40% the HP.

Resource gathering goes 66% faster.

Epochs cost 50% less.

Maximum morale for a town center or capitol is -2.

Where in standard play, the price of your first "epoch up" is 50% normal, in tournament it's 20% normal. Likewise the second epoch costs 50% normal, compared to the standard 80%.

Towers cost 20% more.

Wonders cost 50% less.

Houses give 1pt morale, and 2 houses give max morale.

It takes 4 citizens populating a settlement to make a town center; 6 in a town center to make a capitol.

For being near a town center/capitol, towers get a morale bonus that reduces damage by 50%.

In a Nutshell

Spend your resources as soon as you get them. Don't hold on to them "just in case." You won't need the resources later any where near as often as you'll need the building, units, or whatever it is that the resources could have bought.

Attack early, attack often, attack with the unit appropriate to the target.

Practice. A lot.

Do Your Homework

Learn the Unit Relationships! Three-quarters of the strategy in *Empire Earth* is to attack units with the best counter-units.

Once you know what the Unit Relationships are, get the feel for fighting with them. Then choose the civilization you're going to play based on your understanding of the units and your skill and experience fighting with them.

Make a list of what works against what. If your three Austrian spearmen make mincemeat out of three macemen, jot that down. You're going to want to remember that later on.

First to Fight

Your goal is to attack first and attack fast. Don't be afraid to be aggressive. Most people are hesitant about attacking, but they shouldn't be. Attacking does a world of good. Early attacks cripple enemy economies before they get established. A mass attack launched as soon as you have a decent number of units can surprise the enemy before he has a chance to get organized. And if you can epoch up before the others and get the newest most powerful unit out, there's everything to gain by using that technology before everyone else has it.

If you haven't attacked your neighbor in the first 20 minutes, you're too slow. If your goal is to build an army and attack, you should be ready to go by then. If that's not working, take a look at your techniques and figure out what's slowing you down. Are insufficient resources keeping you back? Is slow population building your problem? Is it something that can be addressed in future games with the judicious application of Civ Points? If you're consistently slow, you need to figure out why and address the issue.

OPPER AGE   DARK AGE   RENAISSANCE   INDUSTRIAL AGE   INFORMATION
BC   2000 BC   500 BC   0AD   900 AD   1300 AD   1500 AD   1750 AD   1900 AD   2000 AD
BRONZE AGE   MIDDLE AGES   IMPERIAL AGE   ATOMIC AGE

Multiplayer

Send in the Dogs

It's easy to get caught up in the process of building your economy and forget to keep an eye on the other guy. Don't forget to send a dog over to find the enemy. See if you can determine what sort of attack your opponent is most likely to launch, and adjust your economy for an appropriate counter-attack. Does he have an economy that's doing better than yours? Figure out if you can kill some of his workers or take one of his mines. Is he rolling out tanks? Now you know to concentrate primarily on anti-tank units.

> ## ☙ TIP
>
> In games where Wonder victories are not allowed, the tactical advantage of a Wonder is only worth it for long games. In a short game — less than 45 minutes — a Wonder costs too many resources and takes too long to build.
>
> — YoungGunZ

Battles

Right before you go into a battle, check out the home situation. Are all your citizens working? Do you have some more military units queued up? You might be at your Pop Cap, but it's best to have new military being made the moment the enemy starts killing the ones you're sending into battle.

Arrange some of your military to be off to one side during the major battle. It's good to have someone in reserve if things get tough. Having a small group of units off to the side makes it easier

to quickly maneuver them to the place you need them to be.

If you are going to use siege weapons, make sure they have at least a few of their own guards. Siege weapons cost too much, and are too vulnerable, to send off unescorted.

Priests & Prophets

It's never too late to add priests into the mix! The player who associates prophets with the early epochs has no concept of the sheer economic destruction of luring your opponents' people into your camp.

The Power of the People

Make citizens constantly. Your goal is to keep your population at its capacity. They are the key to building a strong economy, and a strong economy is the key to a strong military. If you get distracted and forget, you don't know how much time will go by with your population at a standstill.

The maximum number of people you can put on a patch or a mine is six. Your goal is to have six people on every resource available to you. If you don't have enough population, move them around so that your next construction goal has about the same number of people as your older resources. In other words, say you have a surplus of wood because you have 6 people on trees and only 4 people on gold. If you decide that you want to start building a Hercules AT gun, don't just keep going the way you are and figure you'll find something else to do with the extra wood. Throw two of your tree-workers onto the gold, because you need more gold to make the AT gun.

| COPPER AGE | DARK AGE | RENAISSANCE | INDUSTRIAL AGE |
| STONE AGE | BRONZE AGE | MIDDLE AGES | IMPERIAL AGE | ATOMIC A |

PRIMA'S OFFICIAL STRATEGY GUIDE

EMPIRE EARTH
THE ART OF CONQUEST

Send your very first military unit to the enemy camp as soon as possible and kill as many of his citizens as possible. Making your opponent just a little slower than you are gives you a significant advantage — suddenly he can't build quite as fast, make as much food or crank out as many units as you can.

The hot keys for making citizens are H and then C. Hit H, C, H, C frequently enough that you keep about five citizens in the queue.

Don't, however, queue up a million villagers for future creation. You don't want to have to stop and de-queue villagers if you decide to spend the food on something else.

Go ahead and populate some villagers in the settlements early on. Sacrifice five of your early citizens, pretty much as soon as populating becomes possible.

Keep the Income Outgoing

Spend your resources. Hoarding for hoarding's sake is probably the number one mistake people can make. Unless you're saving for something specific, don't hold on to your resources. Spend them as soon as you have them. Build buildings, make units, get heroes — whatever you need at the moment, that's what you should be spending it on.

That's not to say that you can't save up the resources to get something extraordinary. Of course you can. It just means that when you have a saving goal, that's what you're saving toward. If suddenly you need a lot of iron, get as many guys as you can mining the iron. If you have a lot of wood, make something that requires wood. When in doubt, make farms.

Think of it this way. If you and your opponent have had the same amount of time to harvest wood, and you have 700 wood stored up and he's made farms with his extra wood, he's pulling ahead. The whole trick is to stay ahead of your opponent.

Use your Civ Points on bonuses as soon as you get them.

> ●► TIP
>
> Wonders are good for team games, but not one-on-one or two-on-two. They take too long to build and cost too much. All that time and effort could be going into attacking the enemy.
>
> — REDLINE

Speed is of the Essence

It takes practice, but your goal is to have no "down time" — no periods where you're looking around, wondering what to do. If you can, you want every second to contain some sort of career-advancing command.

Similarly, you want to become an expert at the hotkeys. Taking your eyes (and cursor) off the map to find the correct button to push is a waste of crucial time.

Part of the learning process is to take the time to learn and use the hotkeys until they are second nature. If you keep using the button commands, you'll never get it memorized. If you need a hotkey, look it up, write it down and put it somewhere you can see it easily. Put notes all the way around the monitor until you know them by heart, then take those notes down and put new ones up in their place.

Multiplayer

Stay Smart

Don't forget the mini-map. That's one of the most valuable tools in the game. You should have an eye checking that map every few seconds. It tells you what's going on around your people, and gets you there the fastest.

Become super-sensitive about the enemy colors showing up on the map at all — be practically allergic to having enemy colors near your home base. If you're watching it carefully enough, you always know the direction that the enemy attacked from. That gives you valuable information about unit movement even after the battle is over.

Know the Terrain

Scan the terrain surrounding your home base and decide where the most easily defended places are. Find ground that you can fight from, and defend it well. Build walls, if necessary, to ensure that the enemies come in the way you can best defeat them.

High ground can be valuable ... but sometimes it can be useless. Obviously if you've got the high ground in a place where no one is interested in being, it's not doing you any good. Don't defend somewhere that no one is going to go,

just because it's on your list to "take and defend the high ground."

Where's the gold/iron/stone? Always be aware of the mine locations.

Research the most defensible routes to your enemy's gold, iron and stone mines. Start expanding in that direction.

Man the Mines

Locate the mines (gold, stone and iron) in the vicinity. While you obviously want to have control of the mines nearest your home base, you're equally interested — no, you're more interested — in taking any mines that you can get near your enemy's territory. Throw up a settlement and a tower and, as soon as you can, send some units over as well. Make the settlement a town center as soon as possible, also. That makes the nearby buildings a little harder to destroy. If you have control of all of your local mines and one of the mines nearest your opponent, you're crippling his economy. That's bad for him and really, really good for you. That does mean committing to the defense of the mine, but there's a much better chance you can do that once you have the extra resources at your disposal.

Similarly, if there is a mine that you can grab away from an enemy and keep for yourself, it's worth the battle. You can use priests to convert the guys working at the mines. This obviously works best if your opponent is looking elsewhere at the time. It won't hurt to provide a side battle as a distraction, and meanwhile sneak a priest with some military back-up over to the mine.

➡ TIP

Always move with Attack Move. That's [Control] + 🖱. That way if you meet an enemy, you attack first. If you move without Attack Move, any unexpected encounter with the enemy will have the enemy attacking first.

— Stratus

EMPIRE EARTH
THE ART OF CONQUEST

Don't Waste Your Units

With a few exceptions (canine scouts, for instance), you don't want to send your units off to certain death. It's not good strategy, good tactics or good leadership. At the very least, it's a waste of resources. Don't run your infantry into artillery ... you should know that's a bad combination. Just don't do it.

If you see a well-defended area, don't hesitate to retreat. Use your units against what they'll do best against.

Retreat is also an option for your citizens if your home base is under attack. Scatter them all over the countryside. It can't hurt, it takes the enemy longer to hunt them down and kill everyone, and if you manage to get your military back in time to repel the invaders, you have that many more people to start rebuilding.

Build hospitals so your units last longer.

> ➡ **TIP**
>
> Never "just lose." Figure out why you lost, every time. Learn from every mistake you make. Experiment and see if you can keep that from happening again.
>
> — Crexis

Variety is the Spice of Life

Don't just make one "category" of military units! It doesn't matter how many different kinds of infantry you have, for instance — you need to have something else. You can have musketeers, halberdiers, sharpshooters and hand cannoneers, and all you have is infantry that can be wiped out with a few well-

managed tanks. If you love infantry, you need to add in something to protect them. (In this case it could be either tanks or anti-tanks.)

An example of building a military with variety:

- ⊕ If you only have three units, have two be your main unit "category" and the other be one to defend them.

- ⊕ If you have four units, have them be two in the main category, two in the defense.

- ⊕ If you have five units, have two in the main category, two in the defense, and one in another category.

- ⊕ After five, for every two you add to your main category, add one to each of the other categories.

In fact, you really need to have all your bases covered, just to make sure you're covered from all angles. Build a mix of units with the intention of having a response to any possible attack.

> ➡ **TIP**
>
> A lot of people stick around to watch individual units die. It's a natural thing to do, to stick with a battle to the end. But if you can't save the units — retreat them to somewhere safe — then it's a waste of time. If there isn't anything that you can be doing there, you'd better start doing something else.
>
> — Stratus

Multiplayer

Upgrade ASAP

Upgrades are made to be used. They are an important ingredient to a successful game.

If the battle involves your units fighting the kinds of units that they were intended to fight — planes against citizens, for instance — upgrading may let you take them out with one shot. That's the kind of advantage you want.

If it looks like the game is coming down to your units fighting their "nemesis" units — like your arquebuses being attacked by cuirassiers — an appropriate upgrade is the only thing that can save your skin.

If you're in a naval battle, upgrade Attack and HP.

If you've got tanks against doughboys and machine gunners, upgrade Attack. If your tanks are against Anti-Tank units, you need Gun Armor.

There are all sorts of upgrades available — all the way through the epochs — including Prophet Range and Speed, upgrading Walls and Towers, stone or iron gathering, and Citizen HP and Attack.

Good early upgrades:
Farming = Cheaper citizens
Gathering = Faster buildings and units
Farming + Gathering = Faster town centers

TIP

The reason Crexis is so good is that he never loses focus. Other people tend to get tired or distracted 45 minutes to an hour into the game. He gets off a good early rush, and doesn't ever let up.

— REDLINE

Epochs to Aim For

Most games don't go past 3 or 4 epochs. Plan according to the epochs you'll be in ... the most important epoch is always the next one.

The numbers to remember are 3, 7, 10, 13.

Epoch 3: Copper is good to achieve first. Farming makes a big difference in your economy. Getting farming first gives you a lead on the others.

Epoch 7: Gunpowder becomes available, and the world changes dramatically.

Epoch 10: Atomic is great because your land abilities really begin to shift and become more powerful. Airplanes become the military units to beware. Tanks also become integral to a good military — build them, build them first and fastest, use them as soon as you can.

Epoch 13: Introduction of mech military. It's a big economic shift.

Epoch & Civs

Epochs 1-2. For the first two epochs, Austria is a good civ to choose. The first and second epochs are weak and lame because there's no farming. The Austrians tend to reach epoch 3 first, and they remain effective afterwards.

Epochs 2-9. Franks are good for the earlier epochs. They have good cavalry bonuses, so they make excellent raiders. They also have wood bonuses, so they can make more farms and buildings.

Epoch 7. Spain is a good choice for the seventh epoch because they have infantry bonuses, which carry over to the arquebus. Italy has bonuses on its population, making the citizens unusually cheap. Ottoman can also be fun due to its strong economy and powerful military.

EMPIRE EARTH
THE ART OF CONQUEST

Epochs 8-9. In these epochs you should go ahead and plan for the World War epochs. Russia has bonuses that give it a tank advantage, and that's good. France, however, has wood advantages. Wood is the only limited resource in the game, so the faster it comes, the better.

Epoch 10-12. If you want air superiority, choose the United States. However, it's risky to start off with the intention of being an air power. It takes a lot of resources — a lot! If you won't be able to command that much gold and iron, go for barracks and infantry ... partisans, doughboys and bazookas can hold their own against tanks.

Epoch 12. If you're starting in Epoch 12, choose your civilization based on its mech-friendly bonuses, since the Digital age is only one epoch away.

Epoch 13-14. If you want to go all-cyber, you want Novaya Russia. It also has good range infantry and bombers. If you aren't so interested in the cyber aspect, but like "spell casting" more, you'll probably like China's forces better. Rebels are best for conventional ranged infantry and bombers.

◆◆ TIP

In one-on-one, if I have to sacrifice my lead time to get my military out as early as possible, I will.

— REDLINE

Equal Battle Situation

If you find that you've chosen the same civ as your opponent, you know it's going to be an all-out race. If you can take out even one or two of his early-stage citizens, you're doing well. Send your first military units to attack his resources. Whoever gets the first military advance will probably win.

Know the Pattern

There are three stages to a multiplayer game: early, mid and late.

The early stage is where you want to set up strong and fast. Throw citizens on the local mines. Garrison five citizens as soon as you can. Set up barracks, stables, etc. close to the enemy. Build a wall. Pump up your citizen population. Make an initial, small rush at the enemy encampment. Epoch up as fast as you can.

Mid stage is where you really hammer on building your economy and trying to cripple everyone else's. Epoch up again if at all possible. Prepare for out-and-out war.

Late game strategy revolves around getting your end units. Start any sieges; do as much quick damage as you can while you're building; bring in the final troops.

One vs. Two

One-on-One is usually the preferred method of play for several reasons. With Two-on-Two, if your ally is defeated, there's not much you can do. You'll almost always fall when they double up on you. With Two-on-Two, the good news is that someone can carry you for a while. Still, it always ends up with someone on the losing end with two opponents pounding on him.

Multiplayer

The best way to avoid losing with Two-on-Two is for one player to "slingshot" his partner ahead. One guy won't do much more than build some defenses and then tribute most of his resources to his partner. That allows the other one to afford enough military early on that he can sweep out and knock down one of the enemy, and then concentrate on the last guy.

> ## ⚬ TIP
>
> If you harass their economy, you win. I send over a dog to keep an eye on the enemy, put up towers for an early rush, and do whatever it takes to keep them from building a strong economy.
>
> — YoungGunZ

> ## ⚬ TIP
>
> If it's a Highlands map, I'll definitely build walls. It's worth it to get them where I want them. If it's a Plains or Continental map, I don't bother. Instead, I'll just put down more towers.
>
> — YoungGunZ

> ## ⚬ TIP
>
> Building multiple town centers is a necessity. For 45 minutes of game play, I have 7, maybe 10, TCs.
>
> — YoungGunZ

Playing Defensively

A great offensive strategist wins against an equally great defensive strategist every time. However, a good defensive player has a very good chance against a "regular" opponent. Many people find that they are naturally inclined to take the time to shore up their home base. That strategy can work ... but it's not the best way to win a tournament.

First, make it a priority to put houses around your town center (TC) or capitol. For each house around a TC, the nearby units get a morale boost. That gives them about 10% more HP. Four houses (the max) give the local units 40% more HP and that buys you a little more time.

Place your houses so that they act like walls, protecting your town center from any marauders. You may only get a morale boost for the first four houses around a town center, but the other houses buy you time if the enemy ever gets close enough to attack your home base.

Never leave your home base completely undefended by military. It doesn't matter how many walls you have, or how far away the enemy is. If it doesn't have military support, it's a target.

Good Combos

Experiment to find combinations that work well for mutual backup.

War elephant + elephant archer can't be stopped, but it's expensive in food.

Chariot archer + bronze cavalry is awesome, but costs a lot of gold.

Mounted sword+ arquebus can beat anything. It's easy to think mounted gun and infantry is the way to go, but mounted shock and infantry actually works a little better.

After the Renaissance, add cannon!

| COPPER AGE | | DARK AGE | | RENAISSANCE | | INDUSTRIAL AGE |
| STONE AGE | | BRONZE AGE | | MIDDLE AGES | | IMPERIAL AGE | ATOMIC A |

0 BC 5000 BC 2000 BC 500 BC 0 AD 900 AD 1300 AD 1500 AD 1700 AD 1900 AD

EMPIRE EARTH
THE ART OF CONQUEST

∼∞∼ Civilizations ∼∞∼

Obviously when you're playing Campaign Scenarios, your civilization is automatically assigned to you. Multiplayer, however, allows you to do one of two things — play a civilization that you custom-design, or play one that was created by the game designers. There are 23 in-game civilizations.

They are arranged in general categories of epochs. This is not because you can only play civilizations in their appropriate epochs — you can play any civ in any epoch — but because civilizations do better in their "base" epochs. The civilizations' bonuses are geared toward succeeding in their own times. You can play the United States against the ancient Greeks in the Copper Epoch, but most of the U.S. bonuses are geared toward high-tech military units such as aircraft, tanks and Ships, which aren't available till much later. The Greeks, with their advantages in cavalry and infantry, would mop the map with the Americans in the pre-industrial epochs.

There is no answer to "what is the best civilization to play?" The designers and testers put a great deal of effort into balancing the civilizations against each other. Some bonuses, of course, are more valuable than others, but the sum total of each civilization's power will always give it the ability to stand against the others. Only trial and error and personal preference will establish which civilizations work best for you.

However, in the following pages are some ideas to get you thinking along the right lines.

∼∞∼ Prehistoric to Dark Age ∼∞∼ (I – VI)

Ancient Greece

Greeks are an excellent choice when you are starting a game with the first epoch. Their Hunting and Foraging bonus means you can quickly get out of the first two epochs — and that's the big goal in Epochs I and II. There isn't much to be done in the original two epochs. You can't farm, you can't build up a really powerful army, you can't do much at all beyond throw rocks and eat berries. So do what you do best and forage, forage, forage. Make citizens, cut trees and epoch up as soon as possible. Getting to

Epoch III first will give you a huge advantage over the other civilizations.

Since the Greeks' best form of military units is spear-based, their nemesis would be archers. That means if there are any Babylonians or Assyrians on the map, you can expect real trouble. The first back-up units you'd need to prepare would be macemen, or possibly short sword if you have enough of a head start.

With the fourth epoch, suddenly you have another real advantage: siege weapons. No one else can make or use them as fast as the Greeks.

Civilizations — Greece, Assyria

Civ Power: Flaming Arrows
(III to VII) (15 pts.)

Simple, Composite, and Long bowmen can attack wooden buildings with flaming arrows. Each arrow has a chance of setting the building on fire. Once burning, the building will continue to take damage until the fire goes out. In addition, there is a chance that the fire will spread to adjacent buildings.

- This is one of the most powerful offensive powers in the game, given its limited epochs. Archers would normally be very effective against troops, but few people ever keep troops standing still during battle! Flaming Arrows has given the Archer class another shot at respect, since they now can lay waste to an entire city if managed properly.

- If you can protect your archers, you can wreak havoc.

- When attacking with many Flaming Arrow archers, it's good to divide your flaming arrows to set many buildings on fire, rather than just one or two.

Cavalry — Spear (Melee)

25% Attack
30% Build Time Decrease
20% Hit Points

Citizens & Fishing Boats

20% Speed

Civ — Economy

15% Gold Mining
20% Hunting and Foraging

Civ — General

50% Conversion Resistance

Infantry — Spear (Melee)

25% Attack
20% Hit Points
20% Speed

Ships — Frigates & Cruisers

20% Attack
20% Range

Siege Weapons & Mobile AA

25% Attack
20% Cost Reduction
25% Rate of Fire

Assyrian Empire

The word for Assyrians is fast. First of all, as with the Greeks, they have a Hunting and Foraging bonus, so they can get out of Epochs I and II quickly. They have both ranged and sword cavalry, plus their Foot Archers can fire off more arrows than anyone else. That translates to raiding parties. Get in, do some damage, get out. Heal up and do it again. Harassing other civilizations as they are trying to build their economies is a good thing; every little bit counts. Another thing about raiding parties is that you can be effective with smaller groups of them ... you don't have to wait so long to amass a large group, because you're not actually trying to engage the enemy.

On small maps the hit-and-run method works better than on large maps, simply because there are fewer places for the enemy to hide while building up.

The Assyrians have another serious advantage over many other civs because along with their Hunting and Foraging bonus, they have a higher Pop Cap. That means more people, faster. That, combined with a speedy construction of stronger buildings, walls and towers gives you a home base that can serve you well into the future.

EMPIRE EARTH
THE ART OF CONQUEST

Civ Power: Slavery (All) (20 pts.)

When enemy citizens die, a citizen is created at your capitol, provided you're still under the population cap. As the game progresses, the number of citizens that need to be killed to produce a new citizen increases.

⊕ This is based on global enemy citizen casualties, so it works best in a game with lots of enemies.

⊕ The number one offensive power for the rush-minded player. Not only are you slaughtering your enemy's citizens and economy; you're also creating free citizens for yourself and booming your economy. Take advantage of this early — citizens are crucial units in the first 20 minutes.

Archers — Foot

20% Attack	
20% Speed	

Cavalry — Ranged

25% Hit Points	
20% Range	
20% Speed	

Cavalry — Sword

25% Attack	
20% Hit Points	

Citizens & Fishing Boats

35% Range	

Civ — Bldgs, Walls & Towers

30% Build Time Decrease	
50% Hit Points	

Civ — Economy

20% Farming	
20% Hunting and Foraging	

Civ — General

15% Pop Cap	

Babylon

Babylon has a slower start than the civilizations that have the Hunting and Foraging bonus, but they have their own advantages. The first big advantage is their Wood Cutting bonus. That may not sound like a big deal, but remember that wood is the one finite resource on the map. Gold goes on until the end of time, but when a tree falls, it's not coming back. They also have a stone bonus that makes it easier to get a temple up sooner ... and that leads to the second big advantage: prophets.

Babylonians have an earlier ability to lay down godly smack on their opponents, and that's exactly what they need to do. One good volcano can dramatically retard a growing economy. Early prophets will have to rely on legging it back to safety for survival, but after a while the Babylonian archers or spearmen can ride escort.

Their third big advantage comes in Epoch III when people start wanting to use horses. The Babylonian cavalry is fast and tough. They make excellent raiding parties, especially on small maps where it doesn't take much to get to enemy territory ... or to retreat back to your own home and hospital.

Civ Power: Priest Tower (All) (15 pts.)

Selecting this power lets you build a tower that converts enemy units within its range. The Priest Tower's Hit Points and Range are upgraded when Wall/Tower upgrades are researched. The tower will automatically convert one unit at a time within its range, or you can select the tower and specify certain targets. The University will prevent conversion from Priest Towers.

Civilizations — Babylon, Byzantine Rome

- Great defense for the early rush, but also useful in the later game in greater numbers.

- This power is deliciously powerful in the early epochs, but remains effective deep into the middle epochs, because it upgrades along with your regular towers. Against the AI, this power is just ruthless, but against human opponents, remember to micromanage which units your towers convert, since capturing those rams or elephants first is crucial if your army is too small to help much.

- Priest Towers are better than regular towers against many siege weapons, because siege weapons (such as Howitzers) take very little damage from towers. Priest Towers can just convert these troublesome units.

Archers — Foot

25% Hit Points
20% Range
20% Speed

Cavalry — Spear (Melee)

20% Armor
20% Hit Points
20% Speed

Citizens & Fishing Boats

30% Hit Points

Civ — Bldgs, Walls & Towers

20% Range

Civ — Economy

20% Stone Mining
15% Wood Cutting

Infantry — Spear (Melee)

30% Build Time Decrease
20% Hit Points
20% Speed

Religion — Prophets

20% Range
20% Speed

Byzantine Rome

Here's the trick with Byzantine Rome ... most games tend to be three or four epochs long — about 30 to 40 minutes in a Tournament game, or two hours in a Standard game. The Byz. Romans don't *really* shine until longer game.s Their two important bonuses are their higher Pop Cap and farming. Both come in handy in Epoch III and beyond. But really, they aren't fast enough building up their economy in the critical first days of the game. For longer games, they do well. Farming is the gift that keeps on giving ... if you can get those farms churning out food for your infantry, you can make an impressively large army. Their bonuses cover both ranged and sword, which gives them two legs of the Shock/Arrow/Spear relationship. A large army is a successful army — overwhelming numbers usually win the day.

Moreover, they have good ship bonuses to add to the mix if they survive long enough to get there. You may ask: would the Byz. Romans be a good choice for a later epoch, then? Not as much as you'd think. First of all, they have *good* ship bonuses, not *great* ship bonuses. Secondly, they need at least an epoch's worth of time to get the resources to build the ships. If they start a race against another civilization from scratch, the other civ will probably have some sort of mining bonus to let them pull ahead. So the gist is: Byzantine for the ages, not for the short haul.

EMPIRE EARTH
THE ART OF CONQUEST

Civ Power: Insurance (All) (20 pts.)

When any unit is killed or building is destroyed, this power returns to you a percentage of the resources used in its construction.

- This is a good power both for cautious players and those who rapidly expend resources attacking. Its passive nature makes it very easy to use.

- A solid all-purpose power, Insurance gains in value the longer a game lasts (not through bonuses, just by the fact that you keep getting money back while others just keep losing it), so seriously consider this one for any multi-epoch standard game.

Citizens & Fishing Boats

10% Build Time Decrease

Civ — Bldgs, Walls & Towers

15% Cost Reduction
50% Hit Points

Civ — Economy

20% Farming

Civ — General

15% Pop Cap

Infantry — Ranged

20% Range
20% Speed

Infantry — Sword

25% Attack
20% Hit Points
20% Speed

Ships — Battleships & Carriers

20% Attack
30% Build Time Decrease

Carthage

This is a good, all-around civilization to play. If you've got mountains, you're set. If you've got water, you can make a go of an early epoch. If you've got mountains *and* water, you're ready for anything. They don't have a Hunting and Foraging bonus, but they make up for it with inexpensive Citizens and a solid Fishing bonus. If you're on a water map, that can make a big difference from Epoch II on. Really, they have excellent potential for a strong economy. They also have a nice Stone Mining bonus, which (especially when combined with cost-reduced citizens) gives them an advantage in building walls.

Walls work really well in mountainous regions, and — imagine that — the Carthaginians have a Mountain Combat bonus. That's actually a fairly rare bonus, and can have a big effect on the right map. The Sword/Spear combination gives them two legs of the Shock/Arrow/Spear triangle, so if you keep these units near each other, they're very difficult to stop.

Continuing on the theme of "Water is Good For Carthage," they have a hefty advantage when the Age of Ships comes along. The earliest ships you can make cost less and can usually stay outside the range of the enemy ships. Obviously, Carthage is not so good for the later epochs, but for early epochs, they're solid.

Civ Power: Pathfinding (All) (10 pts.)

Pathfinding allows all citizens and all units produced at barracks and archery ranges (except chariot archer, elephant archer, and cavalry archer) to walk over cliffs and through trees.

Civilizations — Carthage, Israel

- Particularly good on a highlands map, or with ranged units versus non-ranged units.

- Best on non-planets maps, this offensive power has untold advantages. One such advantage is being able to organize early raids on another player from their own forests — very frustrating for the enemy!

Cavalry — Spear (Melee)

25% Attack
30% Build Time Decrease
20% Speed

Cavalry — Sword

20% Armor
20% Hit Points

Citizens & Fishing Boats

20% Cost Reduction

Civ — Economy

20% Fishing
20% Stone Mining

Civ — General

20% Mountain Combat Bonus

Infantry — Ranged

20% Armor
20% Cost Reduction

Ships — Galleys, Transports & Subs

20% Cost Reduction
20% Range

Kingdom of Israel

They're good if you like firepower — literally — but only play the Kingdom of Israel if you've got a buddy willing to back you up economically. These guys are not big into production, they're big into prophets.

In other words, the main strength of the Kingdom of Israel is in its religious capabilities. They can crank out cheap priests in rapid succession and send them out in droves. They can make prophets that can stand outside the range of other prophets and rain down catastrophes behind enemy lines.

This is not to say they're a doomed civilization if they're on their own. They have enough to survive on, and in the hands of a top-notch commander can come out all right. They have Archer and infantry bonuses, can make citizens in a shorter amount of time, and have some good ship bonuses for later epochs — so they have enough to be able to hold their own — but they really don't excel in establishing a flourishing economy, and that can haunt them over time.

They do best as a self-sufficient civilization who can do strategic strikes and provide support for a more military ally.

If you do decide to go it alone, concentrate on attacking early, attacking often and pounding them as rapidly as possible with priests and prophets.

Civ Power: Emissaries (All) (20 pts.)

All this civilization's priests are cloaked.

- Protects your otherwise vulnerable priests, and can have great annoyance value.

- A dominant force in the early epoch games, this offensive power is most potent with Pathfinding, since it will allow you to easily find areas not covered by a university and also to perform some nasty convert-and-run raids. Very hard to defend against, but also very hard to micromanage and build a base simultaneously.

THE ART OF CONQUEST

Archers — Foot

20% Armor

25% Hit Points

20% Range

Citizens & Fishing Boats

10% Build Time Decrease

Civ — Economy

20% Fishing

15% Iron Mining

Infantry — Sword

20% Hit Points

20% Speed

Religion — Priests

30% Build Time Decrease

20% Cost Reduction

20% Hit Points

Religion — Prophets

20% Hit Points

25% Range

Ships — Battleships & Carriers

20% Attack

Ships — Frigates & Cruisers

20% Attack

Ships — Galleys, Transports & Subs

20% Attack

∼∼ Middle Age to Industrial ∼∼ (VII – IX)

Austria

Austria is perhaps the most popular civilization to play. For most pre-WWI epochs, they have ready access to whatever they need. Austria is unusual in that it's a "defensive" (boomer/defender) economy. It has cheaper citizens and faster Hunting and Foraging. On top of that the villagers have a fast enough attack so they can hold their own. The trick is to use the faster Hunting and Gathering to help you get your second town center up quickly. Start your economy by only putting three citizens on gathering food. That will give you about the same food income as anyone else would get with six people. Put your next three people on wood production, and then build settlements and military buildings. Don't forget to garrison people in the town centers to improve your mine income.

Austria has a rich economy during any epoch, but its military bonuses are only particularly useful during epochs VII – IX. With their field cannon and AT guns for long-distance attacks, plus their melee infantry for up-close work, they do pretty well against most comers. Their main military bonuses are focused on sword cavalry and spear infantry. This allows for a good offensive later in the game with your sword cavalry, as well as a good defensive measure early with your Spear infantry. This rounds out Austria well, and certainly ranks it among the top civilizations in its time period.

Civ Power: Adaptation (III to XV) (10 pts.)

Austria can steal advances from other civilizations. When an enemy settlement or town center is converted by Austrian priests, the civilization gets one of the

Civilizations — Austria, England

opponent's advances at random. Unique powers will be chosen first, and advances that the Austrians don't have will be chosen second. If a town center is converted it will change ownership but revert to a settlement. Adaptation priests can convert town centers and settlements beginning in Epoch 3.

- ⊕ Easy to use against the rapidly expanding computer.

- ⊕ More potential bonuses in games with many enemies.

- ⊕ Use several priests and send along a few troops to protect them or to destroy a nearby university. If there's no university, use them for security, because it takes a while to convert a TC, but it's well worth it.

- ⊕ Never loses its potency against the AI, and is very effective against human players well into the middle game.

Cavalry — Sword

| 20% Armor |
| 25% Attack |
| 20% Speed |

Citizens & Fishing Boats

| 30% Attack |
| 20% Cost Reduction |

Civ — Economy

| 20% Hunting and Foraging |

Civ — General

| 50% Conversion Resistance |

Field Cannon & Anti-Tank Guns

| 20% Armor |
| 30% Build Time Decrease |
| 25% Hit Points |

Infantry — Spear (Melee)

| 25% Attack |
| 20% Hit Points |
| 20% Speed |

England

England is the U.S.A. of their time period — meaning that they have a flourishing economy that lends itself to a strong military. Of course, where America rules the skies, England rules the seas. That's what it's all about: naval superiority. If you find yourself on an island map, England is the civilization to choose.

There is one thing tricky about England: it changes its civilization around the time of World War I, when battleships and carriers take more of a dominant role. Up until then it is mostly strong economy and land units. After WWI comes around, it's best to concentrate on ships. If that's when you *start* the game, it's easy to pull ahead of the other civs ... buildings and navy are cheap, and you can get on the water early and hold it.

Don't be afraid of making multiple docks, or any other military buildings. If your strength is in your ships, you're going to need a way of getting more out quickly if you find yourself in a tough battle. Since England's economy is so robust, it's actually possible for you to build more than one ship at a time if you have multiple docks.

Civ Power: Exploration (VI to X) (5 pts.)

With Exploration, each Capital or Town Center constructed reveals a large area of the map around it.

- ⊕ Most useful on smaller maps.

- ⊕ Good defensive power for the price. Choosing this power will allow you to decide where your walls (crucial in standard games) will be placed from the beginning.

EMPIRE EARTH
THE ART OF CONQUEST

Archers — Foot

20% Range
20% Cost Reduction
30% Build Time Decrease

Cavalry — Ranged

20% Cost Reduction

Cavalry — Spear

-20% Armor

Citizens & Fishing Boats

10% Build Time Decrease

Civ — Bldgs, Walls & Towers

15% Cost Reduction
20% Range

Civ — Economy

20% Fishing
15% Gold Mining

Infantry — Ranged

25% Hit Points
20% Range

Ships — Battleships & Carriers

20% Attack
30% Build Time Decrease

Siege Weapons & Mobile AA

30% Hit Points
25% Rate of Fire

Franks

The good thing about Franks is their cavalry ... and that's the bad thing, too. Cavalry is swift and deadly. It is the ultimate raiding unit until tanks appear. You can use it early, it's relatively inexpensive and if you have more than one type (which the Franks do), you have a real advantage.

The bad news is that if you choose the Franks, everyone will know you have a strong cavalry and will begin to plan accordingly.

That makes it even more important to give time and money to your other strengths, as well. Use your priests and prophets. Keep your resources coming in and spend them just as quickly. Build your siege weapons, and use your cavalry to keep them protected. Build your town early on, with a hospital, and keep your cavalry coming back to be healed.

Meanwhile, the goal is to use your horsemen to harass the neighbors from as early on as possible. You can send in cavalry to trim the opponents' citizens and infantry even after artillery is invented and in place ... especially around the mines and town center. Use your spear cav to protect your sword cav, and let the swordsmen do what they do best.

Civ Power: Crusaders (IV to VII) (15 pts.)

This power enables you to train Short Swordsmen, Long Swordsmen, Bronze Cavalry, and Knights that have the ability, like priests, to convert units.

- Convert the units you are most vulnerable to first.

- Like Flaming Arrows, this is pound-for-pound one of the best powers in the game, given that it only exists for a few epochs. The ability to convert your nemesis unit and kill everyone else is almost too good to pass up. The catch? It requires a lot of battlefield micromanagement to fully realize its potential.

- Crusaders can convert their counterunits, making them effective against all enemies.

COPPER AGE	DARK AGE	RENAISSANCE	INDUSTRIAL AGE	INFORMATION
BC	2000 BC	500 BC	0 AD	500 AD	1000 AD	1500 AD	1700 AD	1900 AD	2000 AD
	BRONZE AGE		MIDDLE AGES		IMPERIAL AGE		ATOMIC AGE	

Civilizations — Franks, Italy

Cavalry — Spear (Melee)

> 20% Hit Points

Cavalry — Sword

> 20% Armor
> 20% Cost Reduction
> 20% Hit Points
> 20% Speed

Civ — Bldgs, Walls & Towers

> 20% Attack
> 15% Cost Reduction

Civ — Economy

> 15% Gold Mining
> 15% Wood Cutting

Civ — General

> 50% Conversion Resistance

Religion — Prophets

> 20% Cost Reduction
> 20% Range

Siege Weapons & Mobile AA

> 25% Attack
> 30% Hit Points

Kingdom of Italy

Italy is a great all-around civilization. Depending on the individual situation, it can really shine. Its economy is decent, but not outstanding. It has cheaper citizens and a bonus that decreases the time it takes to build. Use that to its best advantage. Garrison a few of your citizens right off the bat — you can make extra without much of a strain, and the extra workers lost will be made up in the fast building time.

What the Kingdom of Italy (remember the "Kingdom of" bit to keep from being confused with the later Italy) lacks in resource bonuses it makes up for in military. Immediately get the citizens working on wood and throw together a stable right off the bat.

Create sword and ranged cavalry (30% quicker) as soon as possible and send them over to harass the economy of your neighbor. Start cranking out infantry — they do well, being 20% cheaper with 25% more hit points. This helps in both aspects of the rock/paper/scissors triangle, and makes Italy a true military machine.

For the defense-minded player, the combination of their cheap citizens, stone and building bonuses make them great at getting all the basic materials of a solidly defended home base. Don't forget to put houses around the town center for added morale bonus. And if you're working in mountainous territory, that's a plus, too.

Civ Power: Metallurgy (All) (15 pts.)

Metallurgy allows you with this power to pay all costs with gold or iron interchangeably. If the proper resource is exhausted, the alternate will be used until it is also exhausted.

- Great for flexibility, and in particular allows for rapid responses to changes in the RPS.

- This one is practically a must for Deathmatch, but it is equally powerful for all game types, since this great resource power allows the player to change his force composition with regards to RPS far more easily than players without it.

Cavalry — Ranged

> 20% Attack
> 30% Build Time Decrease

Cavalry — Sword

> 30% Build Time Decrease

Citizens & Fishing Boats

> 20% Cost Reduction

EMPIRE EARTH
THE ART OF CONQUEST

PRIMA'S OFFICIAL STRATEGY GUIDE

Civ — Bldgs, Walls & Towers

> 30% Build Time Decrease
> 50% Hit Points

Civ — Economy

> 20% Stone Mining

Civ — General

> 20% Mountain Combat Bonus

Infantry — Ranged

> 20% Cost Reduction
> 25% Hit Points

Religion — Priests

> 20% Hit Points
> 20% Range
> 20% Speed

Ships — Frigates & Cruisers

> 20% Attack

Ottoman Empire

The Ottoman Empire may suffer from poor marketing. While Austria is a popular favorite, and England, Spain and France are familiar territory, the Ottoman Empire suffers from being ... well, gone. But really, in *Empire Earth* it doesn't have to settle for past tense. It has some great economy bonuses that complement each other well.

The Ottoman Empire enjoys quickly made and fast-moving citizens, and on top of that they get a +15% Pop Cap. This immediately spells "economic boom." Add onto this successful start their Farming bonus and you've got a culture that can really start churning out whatever they want. Definitely take advantage of their speedy build time by throwing up some houses near the town center.

The Ottomans have another advantage: their main military bonuses promote ranged cavalry and field cannon, which makes for a truly effective combination!

Priests are a kind of mixed blessing for the Ottomans. While they do have priest bonuses — which are better than nothing — they aren't as good as the bonuses of other priest-friendly civs. Plus, of course, just one university renders priests ineffective as an attacking unit. However, they are excellent as defense. Keeping a handful on duty near the town center never hurts.

Civ Power: Expansionism (All) (20 pts.)

This lets your citizens build Town Centers instead of Settlements right from the start.

- Good not only for speeding up economy but also for survival — one citizen can rebuild a whole civilization!

- This is a great all-around resource bonus power. Boomers and rushers alike will find it hard to resist. The only downside is its vulnerability to Adaptation, since players with Expansionism will often put off garrisoning them up to capitols for longer than they should.

Cavalry — Ranged

> 20% Attack
> 25% Hit Points
> 20% Range

Citizens & Fishing Boats

> 10% Build Time Decrease
> 20% Speed

Civilizations — Ottoman, Spain

Civ — Economy

> 20% Farming
> 20% Stone Mining

Civ — General

> 15% Pop Cap

Field Cannon & Anti-Tank Guns

> 30% Build Time Decrease
> 20% Cost Reduction

Religion — Priests

> 20% Cost Reduction
> 20% Hit Points

Spain

Spain, the birthplace of historic Conquistadors, has a sound economy. It's not magnificent, but it serves to keep their military afloat. Their citizens are fast, their farming is productive and they enjoy a nice little gold boost. Spain has a nice, quick ramp-up time in which to harvest wood, gold and food to give their military a little jump start.

Frankly, Spain has some of the greatest military bonuses in the game. Their main military strength lies in their infantry, both ranged and spear. Infantry is what your start off with, and what will remain the backbone of your military might. They have numerous infantry bonuses, so a smart Spain player will capitalize on these bonuses by building a barracks first. Start rolling those guys out — both types as much as possible. While they're in production, see if you can't scout the enemy camp and see if your infantry will be enough to counter your opponent's forces. Infantry is vital to any good military, but try to send them off with the appropriate backup.

Spain has some decent naval and mountain bonuses to round out their advantages. Mountains are where they really shine, however. Once they have the high ground, these guys are nearly unstoppable.

Civ Power: Conquistadors (VII to IX) (15 pts.)

Cuirassier, Imperial Cuirassier, Carabineer and Dragoon have greatly increased line of sight, and a special power that allows them to temporarily increase it even further.

- Best for early exploration on large maps.
- For the price, this power can be a very nice addition to a strong Cavalry-based custom civ. If you're in a large-to-gigantic game in the middle epochs, there's almost no reason to NOT have this power.
- When Conquistadors have full mana, they can activate their "Reveal" power twice. This gives them an amazing line of sight of twenty tiles!

Cavalry — Ranged

> 20% Speed
> 20% Range

Citizens & Fishing Boats

> 20% Speed

Civ — Buildings, Walls, Towers

> 20% Range

Civ — Economy

> 20% Farming
> 15% Iron Mining

Civ — General

> 20% Mountain Combat Bonus

Infantry — Ranged

> 20% Attack
> 30% Build Time Decrease
> 25% Hit Points

EMPIRE EARTH
THE ART OF CONQUEST

Infantry — Spear (Melee)

> 20% Armor
> 25% Attack
> 20% Hit Points

Religion — Priests

> 20% Hit points
> 20% Range

Ships — Galleys, Transports & Subs

> 20% Attack
> 20% Cost Reduction
> 25% Hit Points

∞∞ Atomic to Nano ∞∞
(X – XIV)

France

France hits the WWI-and-beyond world up to date and ready to rock. France is the anti-tank players dream — if you prefer commanding infantry to tanks, but would rather not get smashed like a pancake, take a look at France's unique advantages. In the first place, their 15% Wood Bonus, 15% Gold Bonus, and 30% Build Time Decrease, along with 20% range on their AT guns all come together in perfect anti-tank harmony. Furthermore, if you're a fan of machine guns and AT guns, this is the civilization for you. And why not? You've got most situations covered: machine guns take care of the army, AT guns take care of approaching tanks.

Their economy is slightly weak, with no other bonuses other then the ones listed, but they more then make up for it with their military later on. Not only do they receive that nasty AT bonus combo, but they also receive 20% attack and 20% range on their machine gun units, making their machine gun/AT combo one of the best pair-

ings in the game. Don't forget to put your anti-tank units toward the back of your regular units, maximizing the function of each one.

Civ Power: Camouflage (All) (15 pts.)

Archers, Ranged Infantry, Tanks, Field Cannons, and Siege weapons can cloak once they have been idle for 10 seconds. If they resume movement or attack, they become visible after a brief time.

- Remember to put your units on flee behavior if you want them to remain invisible without attacking.

- It's really amazing just how effective this offensive power is, since to you it will be almost completely unnoticeable! Not only can you spy on enemy bases by keeping your camouflaged troops on scout behavior, but if you attack with a sizable force, the defending player can't get a good gauge on how many troops you're attacking or prioritize targets.

Citizens & Fishing Boats

> 30% Hit Points
> 35% Range

Civilizations — France, Germany

Civ — Bldgs, Walls & Towers

> 20% Attack
> 50% Hit Points
> 20% Range

Civ — Economy

> 15% Gold Mining
> 15% Wood Cutting

Field Cannon & Anti-Tank Guns

> 30% Build Time Decrease
> 20% Range

Infantry — Ranged

> 20% Attack
> 20% Range

Germany

Germany is a popular civ because it's one of the strongest air militaries in the game. Its bombers cost less and fly farther than normal — and everybody knows if you want something done right, send in the bombers. It is unfortunately weak in the area of infantry, but makes up for that with the ability to send in tanks instead. If you want something done right, send in the bombers ... but never send in planes without first clearing out the anti-aircraft emplacements.

If it has a major drawback, it's that Germany isn't a good rushing military at the outset. Call them a "late game" civilization if you like: Germany takes a little while to get its military really thriving. The good news is that their economy has some bonuses that make it easier to build up some defenses. Their citizens are 20% cheaper, and have 30% more hit points.

It's especially important to remember to build in multiples with Germany. Don't build one tank factory when you can build four. The same rule applies for airports, town centers and whatever else is being built. What you want to avoid is being crippled in one big battle without the capability to recover in a short time. If you can roll out four planes at once when you need to, you have a much better chance of staying in the game. It takes a while to get there, but that's what resources are for, building military factories.

Civ Power: Bundeswehr (IX to XII) (15 pts.)

With Bundeswehr, Citizens can instantly be converted to Partisans at a cost.

- ⊕ A great defensive power for the price, this ability allows you to not only effectively nullify someone's early rush attempt, but also to have limited defense against pathfinding raiders and anti-air in your base.

- ⊕ Good for scouting and instant air defense, especially against balloons.

- ⊕ Allows you to breathe easy in the early game if you gather iron and produce numerous citizens, safe in the knowledge that your defense is ready, even against airplanes.

Aircraft — Bombers

> 20% Cost Reduction
> 20% Flight Time

Aircraft — Fighters

> 20% Attack
> 30% Build Time Decrease
> 25% Hit Points

Citizens & Fishing Boats

> 20% Cost Reduction
> 30% Hit Points

Civ — Economy

> 20% Stone Mining

Ships — Galleys, Transports & Subs

> 20% Attack
> 25% Hit Points
> 20% Range

EMPIRE EARTH
THE ART OF CONQUEST

Tanks

10% Armor
20% Attack
25% Hit Points

Great Britain

Great Britain, like its earlier counterpart England, is simply one of the best water civilizations in the game. If you see a water map, this is the civ to choose. It's that easy, and everyone else will be doing it too, so there's a really good chance it will turn into a race.

And you'll have to hustle. Things happen fast with this civ. Its economy offers a 15% bonus on gold mining, and that combined with its quick building of military buildings (30%) and its strong hunting/foraging, you have a civilization that ramps up with frightening speed. What to do? Two things have priority. The first one is to shore up your homeland defenses. Never have a settlement when you can arrange to have a town centers, and surround each TC with a few — four if you can swing it — houses for the morale boost. The second priority is to try to sucker-punch your opponents. That's tough unless you build a barracks early on ... and that's not what you want to be doing. The method is up to your own style and preference, but in a race, the one who trips first comes in last. Send in a fighter or battleship if you can swing it.

Civ Power: SAS Commando
(X to XV) (15 pts.)

Great Britain's barracks can construct this special military unit. The SAS Commando can attack like a normal Marine, but can also swim through water and plant explosive charges on a building, which then automatically detonate and do significant damage.

- Has both explosives and swimming abilities, so is most useful on water maps.

- This offensive power is like having Cyber Ninjas starting in WWI, but even better because these guys swim! The coolness factor alone should sell you, but in addition to their snazzy goggles, they bring along some bombs that pack a pretty decent punch (with some area effect damage), and they have their own machine gun ranged attack, so they're not completely helpless if intercepted.

Aircraft — Fighters

30% Build Time Decrease
20% Cost Reduction
20% Range

Citizens & Fishing Boats

20% Speed

Civ — Bldgs, Walls & Towers

20% Attack
30% Build Time Decrease
20% Range

Civ — Economy

15% Gold Mining
20% Hunting and Foraging

Field Cannon & Anti-Tank Guns

20% Attack
25% Hit Points
20% Speed

Ships — Frigates & Cruisers

30% Build Time Decrease
25% Hit Points
20% Speed

Italy

Italy is strong right off the bat. It has two major advantages. For one thing, it has excellent farming ... something that gets lost in all the high technology of later epochs. More food means more people in less time, which is the single best ingredient for a thriving, early economy. Make the most of a good thing and garrison some citizens in the town center ... you can afford it more than many civs, and it gives a nice gold advantage.

Nearly as important as its food production is its infantry production. Italy can create cheap and inexpensive ranged infantry practically from the start. That's good because it means Italy has the ability to send early raids to the enemy encampments.

Not much later in the game comes the next big bonus: helicopters. Like infantry, the helicopter is another unit that is handy for early raiding. Even better, combining infantry and helicopters can be devastating. Once the first helicopter is created, use the early infantry to create a distraction. The opponent will almost always concentrate on the battle. Meanwhile, the helicopters can sneak around and wreak utter devastation on the fledgling economy. Target mining citizens and factories whenever possible.

Civ Power: Paratroopers
(XII to 15) (15 pts.)

Italy's airports can build the Paratrooper Transport plane. Once the plane is built, and the Paratrooper Rally location is specified, the plane takes off and drops off 8 ranged infantry at the rally flag. If the plane is destroyed, so are the paratroopers. If the plane runs out if fuel, it drops the troopers immediately.

- Transport planes must be wary of AA, but eight units suddenly or in an unexpected location can be crucial.

- This offensive power is great for grabbing neutral ground/islands before anyone else, but also for quickly reinforcing an attacking force that is starting to lose momentum.

Aircraft — Helicopters

| 30% Build Time Decrease |
| 20% Range |
| 20% Speed |

Civ — Bldgs, Walls & Towers

| 20% Attack |
| 30% Build Time Decrease |
| 20% Range |

Civ — Economy

| 20% Farming |
| 20% Stone Mining |

Civ — General

| 50% Conversion Resistance |

Field Cannon & Anti-Tank Guns

| 20% Range |

Infantry — Ranged

| 30% Build Time Decrease |
| 20% Cost Reduction |

Siege Weapons & Mobile AA

| 25% Attack |
| 30% Hit Points |
| 25% Rate of Fire |

EMPIRE EARTH
THE ART OF CONQUEST

Russia

There's not much to say about Russia — it's very straightforward. You've got your tanks. You've got your doughboys. Tanks and doughboys, doughboys and tanks. They're your lifeblood, and the only chance you have. If you try anything else, you're doomed.

You've also got the ability to make citizens faster, and a higher than normal Pop Cap. Russians tend to solve their problems the old fashioned way — throwing enough people at any given problem until it is overcome. That should be your mantra, too. Use this citizen surplus to garrison extra people and get a head start on other civs.

Your first doughboy or two should be sent to kill your opponent's miners. Even one or two can make a difference in the early stages. Since you can probably make more people before they can, the loss in resources is well spent. It's an investment on the future, you might say.

Remember that other players will know that your goal is to crank out tanks. Take all necessary precautions to protect your tank factory — put it near a town center, get some houses up near the TC, and don't neglect your infantry.

Civ Power: Advanced Mining (All) (20 pts.)

Russia can send up to seven citizens to mine stone, gold and iron, and gather from forage patches.

- ⊕ Make use of this power if you have it!

- ⊕ This is a solid resource bonus power, but it is most effective when used with Expansionism in a standard game. It'll almost feel like you're playing tournament rules while everyone else desperately tries to boom sluggish economies.

Citizens & Fishing Boats

> 10% Build Time Decrease

Civ — Bldgs, Walls & Towers

> 20% Attack

Civ — Economy

> 20% Fishing
> 15% Iron Mining

Civ — General

> 15% Pop Cap

Infantry — Ranged

> 30% Build Time Decrease
> 25% Hit Points

Ships — Frigates & Cruisers

> 20% Cost Reduction

Siege Weapons & Mobile AA

> 20% Area Damage
> 20% Range

Tanks

> 20% Armor
> 20% Range

United States

The United States is a very powerful civilization. It has a strong economy and excels at making tanks and aircraft. The associated bonuses — gold and iron — only increase the speed with which it can bring its military up to full strength.

Civilizations — Russia, United States

The United States has a unusually strong capability for self-defense. Its citizens have 30% Attack. With the addition of cheaper houses (15% less), it's difficult to sweep in and destroy the home base while the player is distracted. Of course the player has to manually tell the citizens to attack — otherwise they'll just run away — but only someone who is not paying attention will lose the homestead to a sneak attack.

Another advantage is that the U.S. citizens are 20% faster. That means that it can react more swiftly to upcoming threats. It's a good tactic to scout and see what the other guy's making. If he's making barracks, the U.S. should create a tank factory. If he makes anti-tank units, make doughboys. The economy itself helps out here. Even from a disadvantage, there's nearly always enough time to make the counter to what your opponent is making.

Primarily concentrate on aircraft, and the infrastructure that will allow you to make the skies safe enough to fly.

Civ Power: Market (X to XV) (20 pts.)

The United States can build a Market which allows the player to exchange one resource for another. Four buttons allow you to sell Food, Iron, Stone and Wood. All resources sold are converted to Gold. Four more buttons allow you to buy Food, Iron, Stone and Wood. All resources purchased cost a specific amount of Gold, which is removed from your reserves. Each transaction costs a small amount of extra gold, and as the amount of resource purchased or sold increases, so does the cost.

⊕ This allows great flexibility. It's at its best if you continue to mine all resources, as it keeps the prices down.

⊕ The only thing that keeps this power from being one of the prominent resource powers of the game is its epoch limitation. Beyond that, there's very little reason a player concentrating on booming wouldn't take this power.

Aircraft — Bombers

20% Attack
20% Flight Time
20% Speed

Aircraft — Fighters

20% Flight Time
20% Range

Aircraft — Helicopters

25% Hit Points

Citizens & Fishing Boats

30% Attack
20% Speed

Civ — Bldgs, Walls & Towers

30% Build Time decrease
15% Cost Reduction

Civ — Economy

15% Gold Mining
15% Iron Mining

Civ — General

15% Pop Cap

Ships — Battleships & Carriers

25% Hit Points
20% Range

Tanks

20% Cost Reduction

PRIMA'S OFFICIAL STRATEGY GUIDE

EMPIRE EARTH
THE ART OF CONQUEST

∽∽ Digital to Nano ∽∽ (XIII – XIV)

China

China's got a little bit of everything, and in the case of citizens, a little bit more. First of all, use the higher Pop Cap to get your economy going as quickly as possible. You're going to need it, especially if you decide to go cyber. Be aware that if you're playing against the Rebels, you're going to need every second of economic buildup, since their economy will rocket them ahead, and their weapons are cheaper to produce.

China is the only future civilization that really has a choice of whether to go down the cyber road. You can base this decision either on your own preferences or in opposition to what your neighbors are doing — it's up to you. Just be aware that because China only has ultra cyber bonuses, fighting means advanced-tech "spellcasting." Still, it's nice to be able to counter your opponent ... or in the case of playing against another China, to keep 'em guessing as long as possible.

Despite a booming economy, cybers are expensive to make, and are not the answer to all ills. They're expensive, and losing even one can hurt. The good news is that AT guns work on both tanks and cybers, so get those guys out and strategically placed.

Civ Power: Just-In-Time Manufacturing (All) (20 pts.)

China can build units instantly for additional cost. Each unit producing building has a toggle button. When JIT is toggled "on," the build queue for that building is cleared, and any units selected are instantly produced at extra cost. If the button is toggled "off" or another building is selected, production resumes as normal. (Clicking on a building that is already selected turns off Just-In-Time for that building).

- Great for long games where your whole army attacks and gets wiped out — you can instantly replace it!

- Surprisingly, this good all-purpose power is not a Deathmatch must, since it is more expensive to produce troops this way in Deathmatch and it has a five-minute activation timer. In other game types, this is a handy power to have, much like Cloaking in its "in-a-pinch" base defense capacity.

- JIT manufacturing provides excellent defense. With only one of each military building, you can instantly produce the right units to smash the incoming attackers.

Aircraft — Fighters

20% Cost Reduction

Aircraft — Helicopters

20% Attack
30% Build Time Decrease
25% Hit Points

Citizens & Fishing Boats

20% Cost Reduction

Civilizations — China, Novaya Russia

Civ — Economy

20% Farming

Civ — General

15% Pop Cap

Cybers — Ultra

20% Armor

30% Build Time Decrease

25% Hit Points

Field Cannon & Anti-Tank Guns

20% Armor

20% Cost Reduction

25% Hit Points

Ships — Galleys, Transports & Subs

20% Attack

Tanks

20% Attack

Novaya Russia

Novaya Russia — not to be confused with the earlier Russia! — is cyber, cyber, cyber. Mega-carnage and destruction is the way they play the game. You've got ranged and up-close-and-personal attacks. Conventional and "spellcasting" ultras are an amazing force to be unleashed on the unwary ... which is of course where you encounter your first problem. It's not secret what you're going to be swinging when you come out of the gate, and everyone else will have had plenty of time to prepare for your debut.

The good news is that you have a wood bonus. That may not sound like much when it takes food and iron and gold to make a cyber, but it only takes wood to make a factory. What you want is a surplus of factories, enough that you can crank out as many cybers as you want, when you need them.

Of course, Novaya Russia has such a powerful inertia once it gets started that it will be your opponent's goal to keep you from getting started. You can safely assume you're going to be rushed at the earliest opportunity. There are two things you can do. First is to boost the morale in your town by putting houses near your town centers. You've got lots of wood; you can do it fairly quickly. Your second factory should be AA. You don't need a lot once you get really rolling, but you need them fast.

Civ Power: Missile Base
(XIII to XV) (15 pts.)

Novaya Russia's Citizens can construct missile bases. These bases can construct Nuclear Missiles, which can travel across land, sea and space to attack a target. Anti Missile Batteries are the only units that can destroy a Nuclear Missile.

- This power is at its best in a longer game, when plentiful resources make missiles affordable.

- This offensive power is too expensive and too easily countered to be readily chosen for any and all late epoch games, but it never loses the threat of being devastating. Choose this power on large, small, or satellite planets and conduct quick teleporter or transport raids on enemy planets to hunt down and destroy their anti-missile batteries. While your troops are destroying them, fire off as many missiles as you can. Most of the time, the defending player has no way to re-establish his ballistic missile defenses in time. You'll lose your raiders, but the defender will lose a whole lot more.

COPPER AGE   DARK AGE   RENAISSANCE   INDUSTRIAL AGE
0 BC   5000 BC   2000 BC   500 BC   0 AD   900 AD   1000 AD   1500 AD   1700 AD   1900 AD
STONE AGE   BRONZE AGE   MIDDLE AGES   IMPERIAL AGE   ATOMIC A

EMPIRE EARTH
THE ART OF CONQUEST

Citizens & Fishing Boats

| 20% Cost Reduction |
| 30% Hit Points |

Civ — Bldgs, Walls & Towers

| 50% Hit Points |
| 20% Range |

Civ — Economy

| 15% Wood Cutting |

Cybers — Combat

| 20% Attack |
| 25\0% Range |
| 20% Speed |

Cybers — Ultra

| 20% Cost Reduction |
| 25% Hit Points |
| 20% Speed |

Siege Weapons & Mobile AA

| 30% Hit Points |
| 20% Range |
| 25% Rate of Fire |

Rebel Forces

The Rebel Forces are the courageous underdogs of the Future epochs. Their strengths are in the more old-fashioned ways of combat, and that sets them apart from the other world powers. What they do well is infantry and tanks, and they do that very well. That may seem a little primitive and unfair, but remember that there have been advances in the air and tank arenas as well. These guys can hold their own in the field. Now that's not saying they *can't* use cybers. They can, and even have some good cyber combat bonuses. It's just that they aren't designed to specialize in that area. Note that combat cybers take gold to create, and the

Rebels only have an iron bonus. With the Rebels, cybers are the backup, not the backbone of the military.

Of course, their main advantage is that they can get some decent stuff up quickly, and potentially cripple their opponents before they have time to get their economy rolling. They excel at ground attacks. Figure on infantry to take out the AA, tanks for all-purpose destruction, including the Zeus and Pandora lines of combat cybers, and maybe a few bombers to destroy the factories if you can get them up in time.

Civ Power: Cloaking (All) (15 pts.)

Rebel Forces' Capitols have the special ability to totally cloak areas of the town. They have a mana-based ability that cloaks all units within an area of effect. If a group of Capitols share an area of effect and one of them cloaks, any Capitols in that group that have enough power will also cloak.

⊕   Good combined with static defense (AA guns, towers, etc.)

⊕   Take this power and never worry about being caught off-guard in your base. Using this effective defensive power can buy your troops in the field precious seconds to hurry back for base defense. It also cloaks your own troops in your base, so they can keep defending and not take any damage for the duration of the cloak.

⊕   If you have Cloaking in a team game, be sure to build capitols in your ally's bases so that they can benefit too!

Civilizations — Rebel Forces, Japan

Aircraft — Bombers

> 25% Hit Points

> 20% Speed

Citizens & Fishing Boats

> 10% Build Time Decrease

> 35% Range

Civ — Bldgs, Walls & Towers

> 50% Hit Points

Civ — Economy

> 15% Iron Mining

Civ — General

> 20% Mountain Combat Bonus

Cybers — Combat

> 25% Hit Points

> 20% Range

Infantry — Ranged

> 20% Attack

> 20% Range

Tanks

> 20% Attack

> 20% Range

∞∞ Nano to Space ∞∞ (XIV – XV)

Japan

An empire founded by mythological "Divine Warriors" about 660 B.C., Japan enjoyed a long prehistoric period of tribal rule. Around 300 B.C., the Yamato clan emerged and established close ties with other Asian mainland countries. Under the next millennium of Yamato rule, Buddhism and kana emerged. The Yamato dynasty slowly splintered, and many years of war followed. Finally, in the 16th century, the regions were once again unified. Japan enjoyed an isolationist stance until the late 1860s, developing a rigid social structure and feudal system. The first country to make lasting contact this new Japan was the United States. The doors once again open, Japan spent the next few decades establishing itself as a superpower. However, this rising empire suffered a stinging blow during World War II, and in the aftermath turned into a parliamentary nation. Today, Japan is a major economic and global force.

Like Korea, Japan is capable of fighting Space-epoch battles. Its bonuses in this regard differ from those of Korea, and

Japan also receives a cost bonus that makes it cheaper for them to fight galactic battles. Cyber production plays an important role for Japan; this civilization receives cost breaks on Combat and Ultra Cybers, and can build Combat Cybers more quickly than other civilizations.

Civ Power: Cyber Ninja (XV) (15 pts.)

Japan's Barracks can produce the Cyber Ninja, a cloaking unit that employs the "Logic Bomb" spell. A building attacked with a Logic Bomb will be disabled for a short amount of time. The Cyber Ninja also has an up-close sword attack.

- ⊕ Great against towers and cloaking capitols.

- ⊕ A good offensive power, these women can ruin the best laid defenses of L33ts and n00bs alike. Put four to six of them on a hotkey when you launch an attack and cripple a swath of towers/AA guns with Logic Bombs. There's no defense against it, but the effect has a duration that is strangely too short for the attacker and all too long for the defender.

| STONE AGE | COPPER AGE | BRONZE AGE | DARK AGE | MIDDLE AGES | RENAISSANCE | IMPERIAL AGE | INDUSTRIAL AGE | ATOMIC A |

EMPIRE EARTH
THE ART OF CONQUEST

Civ — Economy

> 15% Iron Mining

Citizens & Fishing Boats

> 20% Speed

Civ — General

> 15% Pop Cap

Infantry — Ranged

> 20% Armor
> 20% Speed

Tanks

> 30% Build Time Decrease
> 20% Speed

Cybers — Combat

> 30% Build Time Decrease
> 20% Cost Reduction

Cybers — Ultra

> 20% Cost Reduction

Spacecraft — Space Fighters

> 25% Hit Points

Spacecraft — Spaceships

> 30% Build Time Decrease
> 20% Cost Reduction
> 20% Speed

Korea

A fractured nation to this day, Korea has a long history of clan-based rulers. The rich, historical story of this nation's government began with Tan'gun, who by legend established the Joseon Kingdom in 2333 B.C. — which was also known as the Land of the Morning Calm. Many dynasties passed, from Koryo to the Choson, and in the early 1900s Korea fell under Japanese control. The end of World War II granted freedom to this nation, which was again tested during the Korean War. Even today, peace and harmony are elusive.

The Korean civilization in the game has the ability to engage in Space epoch battles and boasts several bonuses in that area. Not surprisingly, Korea also gets a Mountain Combat bonus — good for those high-altitude games! The Pop Cap increase doesn't hurt either, especially since you can use all of those extra citizens to take advantage of your Gold Mining bonus. Your military abilities are also boosted due to your Build Time Decrease — you can churn out several different military units in about two-thirds of the time it takes other civs.

Civ Power: Fanaticism (All) (15 pts.)

All foot soldiers of Korea have the ability to become "fanatic." When this ability is used the units take some damage, but then gain the ability to do extra damage for a short time.

- ⊕ If possible, use with medics or near a hospital.

- ⊕ Depending on the epoch, this offensive power becomes weaker or stronger, but when used as described above, it will never disappoint.

Civ — Economy

> 15% Gold Mining
> 20% Mountain Combat

Infantry — Ranged

> 20% Armor
> 25% Hit Points

Field Cannon & Anti-Tank Guns

> 30% Build Time Decrease

Siege Weapons & Mobile AA

> 20% Range
> 25% Rate of Fire

Civilizations — Korea, Custom-Made Civilizations

Tanks

> 20% Attack

Cybers — Combat

> 20% Attack

Aircraft — Fighters

> 20% Attack
> 25% Hit Points

Spacecraft — Space Fighters

> 20% Attack
> 30% Build Time Decrease
> 20% Speed

Spacecraft — Spaceships

> 20% Attack

∽ Custom-Made ∽ Civilizations

You start off with 100 points to be allotted during the creation of your custom-made civ. The cost is noted to the right of each bonus.

It's important to be aware that for any bonus you take from a category, the rest of the bonuses in that category increase in cost by a certain amount. The amount varies according to the category — this amount is part of each category description on the following pages. Increasing subsequent costs within a category is intended to act as a balancing tool: you can have a large number of different kinds of bonuses, but once you start amassing a lot of capability in one category, you have to give up bonuses in other areas.

Example:
The Aircraft — Bombers category.

Bonus	Original Cost
20% Area Damage	5
20% Attack	2
30% Build Time Decrease	1
20% Cost Reduction	6
20% Flight Time	3
25% Hit Points	2
20% Speed	2

If you took 20% Speed for 2 points, all the remaining bonuses in the bombers category would increase by 2.

Bonus	Original Cost
20% Area Damage	7
20% Attack	4
30% Build Time Decrease	3
20% Cost Reduction	8
20% Flight Time	5
25% Hit Points	4

If you then took 25% Hit Points for 4 points, all the remaining bonuses in the bombers category would again increase by 2.

Bonus	Original Cost
20% Area Damage	9
20% Attack	6
30% Build Time Decrease	5
20% Cost Reduction	10
20% Flight Time	7

Again, taking bonuses in one category has no effect on bonus costs for other categories. Aircraft — Fighters bonuses, for instance, would remain unchanged.

EMPIRE EARTH
THE ART OF CONQUEST

PRIMA'S OFFICIAL STRATEGY GUIDE

Aircraft — Bombers

Bomber. The bomber's job is to kill buildings and military units. It's important to remember that they do best in packs — don't try to launch one at a time. Hold back until you have four bombers and then send them out as a force. Obviously, you don't want to fly them out over AA positions, although if you can find a path with only one AA, you'll be okay. Be sure you don't wait so long between your infantry attack and your bombing run that your opponent can put up new AA. Don't forget that you can use air as a defensive support. If you start to lose a battle and decide to retreat, you can send bombers out to support retreating troops.

Atomic Bomber. Unlike other bombers, the atomic version is *very* expensive and *very* fragile — it can go down with one AA. When you're sending this one in, you have to make absolutely sure that there is no AA. First send tanks, then send infantry, *then* send in a B-29. It's definitely worth the hassle to upgrade Fuel Gauge so they can fly longer. They don't last long in the air, so they're not good for buzzing around until you need them. Instead, keep them at the base and use the [Shift][A] command to summon them when you need them.

Cost increase: +2
Epoch X: WWI — End

Bonus	Original Cost
20% Area Damage	5
20% Attack	2
30% Build Time Decrease	1
20% Cost Reduction	6
20% Flight Time	3
25% Hit Points	2
20% Speed	2

Aircraft — Fighters

There are three different kinds of fighters. It's important to grab the right one in an emergency.

Regular. Run-of-the-mill fighters cannot shoot land targets; they only kill other planes. These are great for clearing the skies of bombers.

Strafe Fighter. A strafer can shoot land targets or air targets, but they aren't really great at either. Strafe fighters are used more often to attack infantry, because the infantry can't shoot back. Still, it's not an extremely popular unit.

AT Fighter. On the other hand, anti-tank fighters are extremely useful. If you have a civilization that's going to be devoted to aircraft, and you're up against a tank-based civ, the Typhoon (and its upgrade the A-10) is definitely a handy plane to crank out.

Cost increase: +2
Epoch X: WWI — End

Bonus	Original Cost
20% Attack	2
30% Build Time Decrease	1
20% Cost Reduction	6
20% Flight Time	3
25% Hit Points	2
20% Range	3
20% Speed	2

Aircraft — Helicopters/Balloons

Balloons. As they were in pre-WWI days, balloons are extremely useful for reconnaissance. There are some artillery that do well firing over walls, but only if you have Line-of-Sight. In other words,

Custom Civilizations — Aircraft - Cavalry

if you want to shoot at something, you have to be able to see it. It doesn't have to be LOS for the attacking unit, it just can't be affected by the Fog of War. That's where balloons come in handy. They're a bit harder to kill than a regular scout, and can lift the Fog of War for long distances. They are excellent for revealing snipers. Of course they can be killed by AA, but usually not before your units have gotten their target.

Helicopters. First of all, helicopters are great raiders. They don't require fueling at the home base, so you can hide them in corners and bring them in when the enemy is distracted for surprise attacks. Of course they die to AA fire, so you'll need to keep those in mind, but you won't ever have to take the shortest route (i.e., the route with the most AA) to get to the enemy. Used in a double-attack with infantry, helicopters can deal a crippling blow to the enemy's economy.

Anti-Sub. With the helicopters you get the Sea King, the killer of subs. If you're enemy has the battleship-submarine combo, you can use the Sea King to make a quick dash in to take out the sub, leaving the battleship much more vulnerable.

Cost increase: +2

Epoch XII: Modern Age — End

Bonus	Original Cost
20% Attack	2
30% Build Time Decrease	1
20% Cost Reduction	6
25% Hit Points	2
20% Range	3
20% Speed	2

Archers — Foot

Archers are truly excellent for ranged combat up through Epoch VI. They are a valuable and necessary leg of the Rocks/Paper/Scissors triangle, used as the counter for spearmen. However, after the invention of guns, the archer is suddenly not so useful anymore. That's not an issue unless you're building a military in Epoch VI ... at which point you might want to reconsider building your archery forces up very high. Remember, they will not upgrade ... suddenly the only thing they'll be good for is target practice for your opponent.

Cost increase: +4

Epoch II: Stone — VI: Middle Ages

Bonus	Original Cost
20% Armor	2
20% Attack	4
30% Build Time Decrease	3
20% Cost Reduction	8
25% Hit Points	4
20% Range	5
20% Speed	4

Cavalry — Ranged

Mounted archers/gun cavalry make up the world's first truly outstanding raiding unit. They can get in, kill enemy citizens like wolves among sheep, and then ride right back out before they get hammered. Take them in groups ... for instance, have eight cuirassiers make a mounted raid on an enemy mine. Remember that they have a ranged attack, so keep them behind your infantry in battle. Even better is using them as a flanking unit, sending them around to attack from the side when your infantry is engaged. An excellent combination is gun cavalry and musketeers; you're prepared for pretty much anything.

EMPIRE EARTH
THE ART OF CONQUEST

PRIMA'S OFFICIAL STRATEGY GUIDE

Cost increase: +4

Epoch IV: Bronze — Epoch IX: Industrial

Bonus	Original Cost
20% Armor	2
20% Attack	4
30% Build Time Decrease	3
20% Cost Reduction	8
25% Hit Points	4
20% Range	5
20% Speed	4

Cavalry — Spear (Melee)

Bronze spear, and their later counterpart, the knights, are astonishingly ferocious. It is a common tactic for nations with cheap building bonuses and quickly raised cavalry to send the citizens out foraging and gold mining, put up a few quick stables and mount a raid on nearby towns within a few minutes of the start of the game. It's an effective way of slowing down the other's economy, and you usually have the element of surprise on your side. However, there is a counter to that practice that the raiding cavalry should be aware of. The attacked player will send most of his people scattering over the countryside. A few citizens put down two houses near the town center while the raiders are chasing the running villagers. With two houses up, the citizens have the hit points to hold their own and can repulse the raiders.

Cost increase: +3

Epoch IV: Bronze — Epoch IX: Industrial

Bonus	Original Cost
20% Armor	2
25% Attack	3
30% Build Time Decrease	2
20% Cost Reduction	7
20% Hit Points	3
20% Speed	3

Cavalry — Sword

Sword cavalry is an important military unit to control. They are useful against any infantry; you've got to have them to take out siege weapons and ranged infantry. Just as important, they are a raiding force that really shows results.

Be certain to use Attack Move to move them from one place to another, so that if they come across opposition they'll fight rather than to continue trying to travel while they're being injured. Also, you want them to wade into the infantry and attack whomever they come across, not have them run over, kill a single targeted enemy and then start to mill around.

Cost increase: +3

Epoch III: Copper — Epoch IX: Industrial

Bonus	Original Cost
20% Armor	2
25% Attack	3
30% Build Time Decrease	2
20% Cost Reduction	7
20% Hit Points	3
20% Speed	3

Custom Civilizations — Cavalry/Spear - Civ/Economy

Citizens & Fishing Boats

Notice that the costs of the Build Time Decrease and Cost Reduction bonuses are much more expensive than any other bonus offered. That's because they're *that much more* valuable than any other bonus. Citizen bonuses translate immediately into economic well-being, and that's what builds up a good military.

Cost increase: +2
All Epochs

Bonus	Original Cost
30% Attack	1
10% Build Time Decrease	20
20% Cost Reduction	25
30% Hit Points	3
35% Range	2
20% Speed	4

Civ — Bldgs, Walls & Towers

Walls. First of all, walling off your home base is usually a waste of resources. If you don't have a big enough military to defend your own territory, you're already in a world of hurt. Mining enough stone to build walls around a place is usually a waste of precious time. Those same workers harvesting wood would have built enough military buildings to protect the town just as well. However, walls are great when they funnel your enemy up a hill, where your people can have the tactical advantage of the higher ground.

Buildings. Don't hesitate to spend resources on buildings. Your goal is to be able to instantly replace your lost citizens and military units as quickly as possible. Also, town centers and houses are a formidable form of home defense

when they raise the nearby morale. It's nice to have a safe place to go home and recuperate after a hard day of conquest.

Towers. Consider towers to be the fire alarm of your civilization. Put them up, make sure they're in the right place, pay attention to them when they go off.

Cost increase: +3
All Epochs

Bonus	Original Cost
20% Attack	3
30% Build Time Decrease	4
15% Cost Reduction	11
50% Hit Points	11
20% Range	4

Civ — Economy

Obviously, economy is important. You should always have at least one of these bonuses to your civ, always enabling you to go forward to your ultimate military setup. Notice that bonus prices increase by 6 for every bonus chosen, so you can't have very many ... but you should have one or two. Foraging, Farming and Fishing affect how quickly you can command your full Pop Caps. Mining (primarily) affects how quickly you can establish your military.

Cost increase: +6
All Epochs

Bonus	Original Cost
20% Farming	9
20% Fishing	9
15% Gold Mining	11
20% Hunting and Foraging	11
15% Iron Mining	11
20% Stone Mining	9
15% Wood Cutting	13

EMPIRE EARTH
THE ART OF CONQUEST

Civ — General

Conversion Resistance. This is extremely valuable, but only in very specific circumstances. Since you can keep people from converting your own populace by installing a university, conversion resistance is primarily useful for keeping priests from converting your outlying areas (usually mines) ... and for keeping the priests from converting your attacking forces. Remember, every unit lost is a bite out of your economic forward momentum.

Mountain Combat Bonus. Obviously this is an enormous help on a mountainous map, not much help elsewhere.

Pop Cap. This is an enormous shot in the arm, because you can use the extra people to either speed up production of multiple buildings or — even better — use them to garrison town centers to increase your production.

Cost increase: +0

All Epochs

Bonus	Original Cost
50% Conversion Resistance	10
20% Mountain Combat Bonus	4
15% Pop Cap	9

Cybers — Combat

There are two problems with choosing cyber bonuses, and one very large plus. The plus is that you get the world's ultimate fighting machine. It can kick your opponents across the map if they don't come up with a counter quickly enough.

The problems are timing and timing. In the first place, you cannot upgrade to get a cyber unit. If you're playing a game that starts off before cybers are available, you'll need to build them from scratch. That wouldn't normally be a problem because you could be building up your resources in preparation for slamming down a cyber factory/laboratory ... the problem is, if you have given yourself some decent cyber bonuses, then you are missing other bonuses that might help you get to the Nano Age on time. It hurts to be late to the next epoch! Keep this inequity in mind when you're building your civ. (Of course, if you're starting off in the Nano Age, this is a non-issue.)

The second timing problem is that cybers take longer than "normal" units to create. If you emphasize your cyber industry too much, you'll be unable to defend them from raiding parties, etc.

Cost increase: +4
Epoch XIII: Digital — End

Bonus	Original Cost
20% Armor	2
20% Attack	4
30% Build Time Decrease	3
20% Cost Reduction	9
25% Hit Points	4
20% Range	4
20% Speed	4

Cybers — Ultra

The ultra cybers are the spellcasters of the game. If you mourned the passing of the prophets earlier on, you'll have a good time with these bad boys. They suffer from some of the same shortcomings as the conventional cybers — they're slow and expensive to mass-produce.

Custom Civilizations — Civ/General - Infantry/Ranged

The Anti-Matter Storm is excellent in removing aircraft, and makes the Tempest a popular model vs. non-cyber civs. The Hades' Nano Virus and the Poseidon's Assimilate power make them particularly useful against other cyber civs. The Apollo is a good, multi-use fighter.

Cost increase: +2

Epoch XIV: Nano — End

Bonus	Original Cost
20% Armor	1
30% Build Time Decrease	2
20% Cost Reduction	5
25% Hit Points	2
20% Speed	2

Field Cannon & Anti-Tank Guns

There are a variety of field cannon, changing in purpose only a little as the epochs roll by. Siege weapons can kill infantry, but it's almost not worth the reload time vs. amount of damage. They were designed for destroying buildings, and that's what they do best. The culverin is an excellent anti-infantry weapon, and upgrades to the even more destructive bronze cannon. They do splash damage on the units surrounding your target, so try to use them when the target has allies clustered nearby.

Most cannon can fire over walls, but you must be able to see the target. If you have line of sight (usually via balloon or a spotter unit), you can do considerable damage to the buildings inside a fortified area.

Anti-tank guns are absolutely vital. Tanks are the killing machine of the modern age, and anyone who can't hold them back is going to be cut to shreds.

Cost increase: +4

Epoch VII: Renaissance — End

Bonus	Original Cost
20% Armor	2
20% Attack	4
30% Build Time Decrease	3
20% Cost Reduction	8
25% Hit Points	4
20% Range	5
20% Speed	4

Infantry — Ranged

Historically, ranged infantry has been the majority of the army. In *Empire Earth* it's still definitely the backbone. Ranged infantry is what you should build first, and usually build biggest.

Arquebus/Grenadier. Slam a barracks down and get some of these guys out, then churn out some of whatever else you need to counter what your opponent is building. (Always, always check to see what your opponent is doing!) Whatever it is, though, ranged infantry should be one of the legs of your Rock/Paper/Scissors triangle.

Cannoneer. This is the guy who runs up and shoots over walls. He's essentially a siege unit. Have a spotter on a hill somewhere so you can see targets (or a sniper or a balloon), and let the cannoneer do his thing. Cannoneers en masse can take out siege units such as the serpentine if you use a spotter unit so the cannoneers can make use of their long range without getting fired on.

Sharpshooter/Sniper. Sharpshooter is invisible from a distance, and one-shot/one-kill on infantry. He's particularly useful in the atomic ages. This guy is really good at stopping rushes. If you're in the situation where you are going to need more time to get your

EMPIRE EARTH
THE ART OF CONQUEST

PRIMA'S OFFICIAL STRATEGY GUIDE

army up and out than your opponent needs, place a sharpshooter near the place where your opponent will take his troops to attack you. If you use a sharpshooter and a balloon, you'll benefit from an amazing Line of Sight. Three or four are a great complement to your army in battle. If, however, they use a balloon, they'll be able to see him. If you think you're being hit by a sharpshooter, look for the puff of smoke his gun makes and send cavalry (or something fast) over to find and kill him.

Musketeer. This is the unit for knocking out gun cavalry, but they're also great for whittling down enemy citizens. They kill everything but cannon (including bombards) and sword cavalry. Musketeers are an absolute mainstay for their epochs.

Elite Guard. These act like an advanced musketeer with better gun armor, only a little more vulnerable to more types of attack. Still, they're high-risk, high-reward. They work well against infantry (especially musketeers), so if you're playing someone (such as Italy) who is flooding the world with musketeers, respond by making elite guards.

Partisan. If you're up against aircraft, one of your best defenses is a lot of partisans. They work especially well in Epoch X, when your opponent suddenly gets access to planes and starts building an air army. Use them as mobile anti-aircraft and place them in strategic positions. Be careful about fighting bombers ... they'll drop their loads on your partisans in a heartbeat. Keep your guys spread out, and don't hesitate to scatter and run away when necessary.

One of the truly great things about partisans is that they can walk through woods ... which means they can walk right up to many enemy camps, kill citizens left and right and walk back through the woods — and the enemy can't follow them. That's the kind of raiding that keeps people from sleeping at night.

Grenade Launcher. These are one of the safest bets for a defensive player. If you've got gold coming in, and these guys coming out of the barracks, you've got a pretty good start. For instance, grouped together, they're good against tanks — you'll still want anti-tank units, but these guys can hold down the fort long enough for you to get together whatever will counter the enemy. They can't stand one-on-one with much, but three-on-one is a good ratio for them.

Machine Gun. The anti-infantry infantry unit is the machine gunner. It can take on anything that comes out of a barracks. If you're fighting a ton of doughboys, make a bunch of machine gunners. They are a good combo with AT units. They are also good as a stand-in for a sniper if you are better at mining gold.

Doughboy. Upgrade from a grenadier. These units kill anything from a siege factory, although they aren't good with artillery. Enough of them will even kill tanks. One of the important things about a doughboy is that at the beginning of Epoch X, the machine gun becomes available. However, anyone making machine guns will have to start from scratch, while grenadiers can upgrade and outnumber them instantly.

Custom Civilizations — Infantry/Ranged - Religion/Priests

Cost increase: +5   All
Epochs

Bonus	Original Cost
20% Armor	3
20% Attack	5
30% Build Time Decrease	4
20% Cost Reduction	9
25% Hit Points	5
20% Range	6
20% Speed	5

Infantry — Spear (Melee)

There's only one thing that you do with a spearman, and that's fight cavalry. Unlike infantry or cavalry, it's not intended to be the main branch of your military, but if you're facing down the horses, you'd better have a good number of pikes to slow them down.

It's up to you to know when to make spear infantry. When you scout the enemy camp and see stables, it's time. When you bring up the diplomat screen and you're fighting Prussia, it's time. When a horde of angry horses sweep into your town and kill all your citizens, it's too late.

Cost increase: +3

Epoch II: Stone — Epoch IX: Industrial

Bonus	Original Cost
20% Armor	2
25% Attack	3
30% Build Time Decrease	2
20% Cost Reduction	7
20% Hit Points	3
20% Speed	3

Infantry — Sword

Swordsmen aren't as widely used as you might thing. History trains us to think of battles as being fought by two screaming hordes of men, rushing into each other's ranks like two waves meeting and annihilating each other. Maybe that's the way it was, maybe it wasn't. In *Empire Earth*, swordsmen exist to fight pikemen. Since pikemen are (usually) only around to fight cavalry, the only time you'll see a swordsman is as an escort unit for mounted units. If you have cavalry, you need swordsmen to counter any pikemen you encounter.

After Epoch VI, swordsmen need to be retired and replaced with arquebus gun infantry. Don't even try to use them in Epoch VII. War doesn't have to be that ugly.

Cost increase: +3

Epoch I: Prehistoric — Epoch VI: Middle Ages

Bonus	Original Cost
20% Armor	2
25% Attack	3
30% Build Time Decrease	2
20% Cost Reduction	7
20% Hit Points	3
20% Speed	3

Religion — Priests

Priests add an element of fun to the game, but they're not really much used by the serious players. They do a good early-game rush to the unexpected, but they are fairly easy to counter. Placing a university in your town usually pulls the teeth out of their bite, and of course they don't stand much of a chance against any sort of ranged attack. They're more of a help in a defensive game, keeping the home safe from invaders, but frankly there's usually better things you could do with your resources than build up an army of priests.

EMPIRE EARTH
THE ART OF CONQUEST

Cost increase: +2   All
Epochs

Bonus	Original Cost
30% Build Time Decrease	2
20% Cost Reduction	4
20% Hit Points	2
20% Range	4
20% Speed	2

Religion — Prophets

Like priests, prophets are good for the home defense. Unlike priests, prophets are great for going on the offensive. For one thing, their spells have a lasting effect. Bring one along on a raiding party and let him cast volcano near the gold mine. Even after you've been and gone, the volcano is still there for a while, disrupting the normal flow of gold. Plague is excellent for "softening up" the opponent before a battle. There's nothing simpler than fighting people who are weak and getting weaker before you even strike the first blow. A prophet is a little used, but quite efficient siege weapon. If you're on a water map, try the Hurricane.

Like other long-range attacks, prophets really benefit from some sort of spotter to lift the fog of war from the battlefield. A sniper or a balloon will do the trick. The biggest drawback to a prophet is that it takes a long time for him to build up enough mana to cast his spell. If you think you're going to use one, make him as soon as possible and hide him somewhere safe while he builds up enough power.

Cost increase: +2

Epoch I: Prehistoric — Epoch VI: Imperial

Bonus	Original Cost
30% Build Time Decrease	1
20% Cost Reduction	3
20% Hit Points	2
20% Range	4
20% Speed	2

Ships — Battleships & Carriers

Battleships. This is *the* main ship. It kills frigates and cruisers, and it's good at bombing land targets in support of your regular troops. Always put your battleships in the rear of any collection of ships that you have out. Battleships are far too expensive to risk getting fired upon when they could easily stay out of enemy range and still be effective.

The downside to battleships is that they are easy prey to submarines and are very expensive. Pairing a battleship with a submarine makes for a good combo.

Carriers. Carriers, and the planes they carry, do very well against naval units in general, plus their planes can go ashore and provide strafing support for ground troops. It's a great way to surprise the enemy in the middle of a land-based sting. Like the battleship, the carrier can be destroyed by a submarine. A frigate or submarine escort will usually take care of that problem.

Cost increase: +3

Battleships = Epoch III: Copper — Epoch XIII: Digital

Carriers = Epoch XI: WWII — Epoch XIII: Digital

Custom Civilizations — Religion/Prophets - Ships/Galleys…

Bonus	Original Cost
20% Attack	3
30% Build Time Decrease	2
20% Cost Reduction	7
25% Hit Points	3
20% Range	4
20% Speed	3

Ships — Frigates & Cruisers

Frigates. Frigates are primarily used as backup ships to protect another ship from submarines. In the earlier epochs they kill galleys/galleons, again making the seas safe for battleships. Of course, an enemy battleship can make short work of a frigate no matter what epoch it's sailing in. Frigates and submarines make a nice combination, but they both share the same resource: iron. If you don't have a flood of iron coming in, frigate/submarine combos can be slow to build.

Cruisers. When the skies above the water are filled with planes, the cruiser is your buddy. Shooting down aircraft is the only thing it does, so you don't want to make many unless you're sure you've got airpower headed your way. However, if the skies are a threat, you better have a few of these along to protect your battleships.

Cost increase: +3

Frigate = Epoch II: Stone — Epoch XIII: Digital

Cruiser = Epoch VIII: Imperial — Epoch XIII: Digital

Bonus	Original Cost
20% Attack	3
30% Build Time Decrease	2
20% Cost Reduction	7
25% Hit Points	3
20% Range	4
20% Speed	3

Ships — Galleys, Transports, Subs

Galleys. They kill battleships. Frigates kill them, and they aren't particularly good at taking out land targets, but galleys eat battleships for breakfast.

Transports. Take your land troops from one shore to the next, by loading them on a Transport. It's strongly recommended that you only use transports in pairs: one with citizens, one with military. When you're in enemy territory, far from home and no quick way to get back, you need citizens to establish the basics like a town center, hospital, etc.

Submarines. These are your second most important ship, once available. Subs kill battleships and carriers, but are destroyed by frigates. The battleship/submarine combo is a tough one to beat — especially because you can "stack" the submarine directly below the battleship and have your fire concentrated. Even better, submarines and battleships do not share resources. One's iron, the other's gold.

Cost increase: +3

Galley = Epoch III: Copper — Epoch IX: Industrial

Transport = Epoch II: Stone — Epoch XIII: Digital

Subs = Epoch X: WWI — End

Bonus	Original Cost
20% Attack	3
30% Build Time Decrease	2
20% Cost Reduction	7
25% Hit Points	3
20% Range	4
20% Speed	3

EMPIRE EARTH
THE ART OF CONQUEST

Siege Weapons & Mobile AA

Siege. Siege weapons are for killing buildings, a pastime that's very important for the up-and-coming conqueror. There are two different kinds: melee (like the ram) and range (like the trebuchet). You should always have some siege weapons on hand for destroying the economy of whatever civ you're attacking. If you're both injured the same amount, and you can rebuild your forces quickly while your enemy can't ... then you've all but won.

Mobile Anti-Aircraft. You pay a price for having the convenience of mobility. Mobile AA is not as effective as a traditional AA gun. You use them to protect your troops when they're on the move — especially against the devastating nuclear bomber. Mass them in groups of five and take them with you as you travel.

Cost increase: +2

Siege Weapons = Epoch IV: Bronze — End

Mobile AA = Epoch X: WWI — Epoch XIII: Digital

Bonus	Original Cost
20% Area Damage	5
20% Armor	1
25% Attack	2
30% Build Time Decrease	1
20% Cost Reduction	3
30% Hit Points	2
20% Range	2
25% Rate of Fire	2
25% Speed	2

Spacecraft

Space Carrier Fighters. The Space Carrier Fighters are lethal space superiority units. With their long range and great speed, they can hit an enemy fleet from seemingly out of nowhere. They must be launched in force, however, because they don't last very long in any confrontation, but in numbers they can deliver a good amount of damage and occupy enemy capitol ships' guns as your own big ships move in for the kill. Be sure to keep the carrier fighters from straying too close to a fortified enemy planet, however, as Space Turrets and Missile Towers will wipe out a large number of them without even breaking a sweat.

Planetary Fighters. The great thing about Planetary Fighters is their ability to launch from an airport and attack space units or even enemy planets. This makes them unique, but they are relatively weak otherwise. Although they can do more damage than the Space Fighters, they are slower, more vulnerable and have a much shorter range. Their best used in reserve for when an enemy tries to muscle past your turrets to land an invasion force. A good-sized group of these fighters could easily dismantle a space transport and harass the enemy fleet until you can bring your own ships into the engagement.

Cost Increase: +4

Epoch XV

Bonus	Original Cost
20% Attack	4
30% Build Time Decrease	3
20% Cost Reduction	8
25% Hit Points	4
20% Range	5
20% Speed	4

Custom Civilizations — Siege Weapons - Tanks

Spaceships

Capital Ship. The dreadnought of the galaxy is an impressive military machine. Not only can it withstand a huge amount of punishment, but it can dish it out like no other – except the ICBM, of course. The Capitol ship comes equipped with the appropriately named Devastating Beam of Death (DBOD), which can be used against other ships and planetary structures with equal effect. Although they are hugely expensive, they are not hard to keep alive, thus the initial investment could easily be recouped for the attentive player.

Space Carrier. If the Capitol ship is the king of the stars, then the carrier is the queen. The carrier's capacity of fifteen space fighters makes having just one in service a great tactical weapon. With two fully loaded carriers, there are few military objectives that are beyond your reach. The Carrier has no weaponry, however, but can take more than a few hits before being destroyed. Nonetheless, Carriers should never leave your home planet without at least a couple of screening Corvettes.

Corvette. The unfortunate crew of any Corvette have little to look forward to as they embark on any given mission. Fast and cheap, they are best used as scouts in the early game, but, sadly, as cannon fodder in the late game. Although they do decent damage to Space/Planetary fighters, they can be easily overwhelmed and won't last much longer than a blink of the eye in front of a Capitol ship's guns. They can, however, screen your carriers and, if

deployed in force, distract Space Turrets just long enough to land ground forces on an enemy planet.

Space Transport. The impressive capacity of the space transport is not to be underrated. With just two of these mammoth ships, a player can unload no less than sixty units onto an unfortunate enemy! The trick, of course, is getting there. Although, with a speed and HP upgrade, they can probably muscle past one or two space turrets to unload a force, they won't be coming back - and once the turrets get the range upgrade, they won't make it at all.

Cost Increase: +4

Epoch XV

Bonus	Original Cost
25% Attack	4
30% Build Time Decrease	2
30% Cost Reduction	8
25% Hit Points	4
20% Range	5
25% Speed	4

Tanks

Anti-Aircraft Tanks. Skywatcher tanks have the specialized duty of patrolling for aircraft. Keep them to the rear of your army, and move them in groups of four. Four should be able to take out 2-3 bombers, which is an excellent day's work on top of costing the enemy a lot of time and resources. Because speed is of the essence, assign the AA tanks to a control key, so you can grab and move them at a moment's notice to where the enemy bombers are going, without having to find them, select them, group them and send them out.

EMPIRE EARTH
THE ART OF CONQUEST

German Tanks. Tanks like the A7V are the master unit of the modern war. They are expensive, and worth it. If you've got them and the other side doesn't, you're doing great. If the other side has German tanks and you're still sending out the regular MkV-level tanks, you can expect to get pounded.

Regular Tanks. If you can't make the German tank, use the weaker tank and some anti-tank infantry in tandem. That's a combo almost as formidable— if not more so — than the German tank when facing other regular tanks and infantry. However, if the enemy is producing German tanks and anti-tank infantry on its own, it's really best to meet them with German tanks. Tanks are not the kind of units that do well with subtle tactics ... it's more a "smash 'em, smash 'em hard" kind of thing.

Cost increase: +4

Epoch X: WWI — End

Bonus	Original Cost
10% Armor	3
20% Attack	4
30% Build Time Decrease	3
20% Cost Reduction	8
25% Hit Points	4
20% Range	5
20% Speed	4

∽∽∽ World Statistics ∽∽∽

Knowledge is power. If you're serious about playing Empire Earth *the way it should be played — wielded like a studded mace to crush your enemies and conquer the map — it really helps if you know the mechanics of the game.*

In this chapter are the cold hard facts about what does what, from which unit works best against a trebuchet to how great Alexander is, really.

All listed stats are for scenario play. Only units marked with an "*" are available in Skirmish play.

Source. Where it comes from when it's created (Pop Count if applicable and not 1).

Build. How long it takes to build it / the resources necessary to finish the build. F = Food, G = Gold, I = Iron, S = Stone, W = Wood.

Hit Points. The amount of damage it can take before it's destroyed.

Speed. Its relative velocity (Air and Sea: also lists maximum number of units it can transport).

Line of Sight. How far it can see, in tiles. Tiles are a standard unit of measurement in the game. A house is one tile square, while a settlement is two tiles by two tiles. LOS can be boosted by tech.

A/D. Attack class / Defense class. If these are the same, they're only listed once. For Heroes, Strategist = Restores health to troops, Battle Cry demoralizes enemies; Warrior = Strong fighter, provides morale to troops.

Attack. How much damage it does (what type of damage it does) / how many seconds before it can attack again. Ar = Arrow, Gn = Gun, Ls = Laser, Ms = Missile, Pr = Pierce, Sh = Shock.

Range (AE). The range of its attack (and the radius of the area effect, if any), in tiles.

AA = Anti-Aircraft, AC = Aircraft, AS = Anti-Sub-marine, AT = Anti-Tank, BM = Ballistic Missile.

Heroes

* All heroes that can be "built" by a player are created at a Town Center (or Capitol).

ACHILLES (IV)

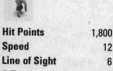

Hit Points	1,800
Speed	12
Line of Sight	6
A/D	Warrior Hero
Attack	52 (Ms) / 2
Range (AE)	0.5
Armor	3 (Sh, Pr)

ALEXANDER THE GREAT (IV) *

Build	160 s. / 430 F, 360 G
Hit Points	1,235
Speed	16
Line of Sight	6
A/D	Strategist Hero
Attack	14 (Ms) / 2
Range (AE)	0.6
Armor	3 (Sh, Pr)

OTTO VON BISMARCK (IX) *

Build	160 s. / 430 F, 360 G
Hit Points	3,000
Speed	16
Line of Sight	9
A/D	Strategist Hero
Attack	33 (Ms) / 2
Range (AE)	8
Armor	10 (Sh), 8 (Pr)

EMPIRE EARTH
THE ART OF CONQUEST

PRIMA'S OFFICIAL STRATEGY GUIDE

BLACK PRINCE (VI)

Hit Points	1,950
Speed	16
Line of Sight	6
A/D	Strategist Hero
Attack	19 (Ms) / 2
Range (AE)	0.6
Armor	5 (Sh, Pr)

BLACK ROBE OFFICER (XIII)

Hit Points	3,600
Speed	14
Line of Sight	9
A/D	Strategist Hero
Attack	90 (Ms) / 2
Range (AE)	8
Armor	10 (Sh)

RW BRESDEN (XII) *

Build	180 s. / 600 F, 500 I
Hit Points	4,000
Speed	14
Line of Sight	9
A/D	Strategist Hero
Attack	60 (Ms) / 2
Range (AE)	8
Armor	10 (Sh), 9 (Pr)

CHARLEMAGNE (V) *

Build	160 s. / 430 F, 360 G
Hit Points	1,575
Speed	16
Line of Sight	6
A/D	Strategist Hero
Attack	16 (Ms) / 2
Range (AE)	0.6
Armor	4 (Sh, Pr)

OLIVER CROMWELL (VIII) *

Build	160 s. / 530 F, 450 I
Hit Points	3,750
Speed	16
Line of Sight	6
A/D	Warrior Hero
Attack	110 (Ms) / 2
Range (AE)	0.6
Armor	8 (Sh), 7 (Pr)

DEVERRAN (X) *

Build	180 s. / 480 F, 400 G
Hit Points	3,330
Speed	14
Line of Sight	9
A/D	Strategist Hero
Attack	43 (Ms) / 2
Range (AE)	8
Armor	10 (Sh), 9 (Pr)

HAUPTMANN DURER (XI)

Hit Points	5,235
Speed	14
Line of Sight	9
A/D	Warrior Hero
Attack	160 (Ms) / 2
Range (AE)	0.5
Armor	10 (Sh), 9 (Pr)

PROPHET DURER (XI)

Hit Points	2,500
Speed	14
Line of Sight	7
A/D	Strategist Hero
Attack	10 (Ms) / 180
Range (AE)	6
Armor	10 (Sh), 9 (Pr)

EL CID (VI)

Hit Points	2,775
Speed	16
Line of Sight	6
A/D	Strategist Hero
Attack	75 (Ms) / 2
Range (AE)	0.6
Armor	5 (Sh, Pr)

Hero Stats

ELIZABETH I (VIII) *

Build	160 s. / 430 F, 360 G
Hit Points	2,610
Speed	16
Line of Sight	7
A/D	Strategist Hero
Attack	25 (Ms) / 2
Range (AE)	0.6
Armor	8 (Sh), 7 (Pr)

GAIUS MARIUS (IV)

Hit Points	1,235
Speed	16
Line of Sight	6
A/D	Strategist Hero (Conscript)
Attack	14 (Ms) / 2
Range (AE)	0.6
Armor	3 (Sh, Pr)

GERMAN OFFICER (XI)

Build	180 s. / 480 F, 400 G
Hit Points	2,430
Speed	14
Line of Sight	9
A/D	Strategist Hero
Attack	55 (Ms) / 2
Range (AE)	8
Armor	10 (Sh), 9 (Pr)

GILGAMESH (III) *

Build	160 s. / 530 F, 450 I
Hit Points	1,275
Speed	16
Line of Sight	6
A/D	Warrior Hero
Attack	41 (Ms) / 2
Range (AE)	0.6
Armor	2 (Sh, Pr)

HANNIBAL (IV) *

Build	160 s. / 530 F, 450 I
Hit Points	1,800
Speed	16
Line of Sight	6
A/D	Warrior Hero
Attack	46 (Ms) / 2
Range (AE)	0.6
Armor	3 (Sh, Pr)

HENRY V (VII) *

Build	160 s. / 530 F, 450 I
Hit Points	3,270
Speed	16
Line of Sight	6
A/D	Warrior Hero
Attack	90 (Ms) / 2
Range (AE)	0.6
Armor	6 (Sh, Pr)

HIERAKLES (IV)

Hit Points	825
Speed	12
Line of Sight	6
A/D	Strategist Hero
Attack	14 (Ms) / 2
Range (AE)	0.6
Armor	3 (Sh, Pr)

HU KWAN DO (XIV) *

Build	185 s. / 750 F, 600 G
Hit Points	8,100
Speed	16
Line of Sight	9
A/D	Warrior Hero
Attack	360 (Ms) / 2
Range (AE)	8
Armor	10 (Sh)

ISABELLA OF CASTILE (VII) *

Build	160 s. / 430 F, 360 G
Hit Points	2,300
Speed	16
Line of Sight	6
A/D	Strategist Hero
Attack	22 (Ms) / 2
Range (AE)	0.6
Armor	6 (Sh, Pr)

EMPIRE EARTH
THE ART OF CONQUEST

JULIUS CAESAR (V) *

Build	160 s. / 530 F, 450 I
Hit Points	2,250
Speed	16
Line of Sight	6
A/D	Warrior Hero
Attack	52 (Ms) / 2
Range (AE)	0.6
Armor	4 (Sh, Pr)

KHAN SUN DO (XIV) *

Build	180 s. / 600 F, 500 G
Hit Points	6,000
Speed	14
Line of Sight	9
A/D	Strategist Hero
Attack	85 (Ms) / 2
Range (AE)	8
Armor	10 (Sh)

SERGEI MOLOTOV (XIII) *

Build	180 s. / 675 F, 560 I
Hit Points	5,600
Speed	14
Line of Sight	9
A/D	Warrior Hero
Attack	230 (Ms) / 2
Range (AE)	8
Armor	10 (Sh)

CYBORG MOLOTOV (XIV) *

Build	180 s. / 675 F, 560 I
Hit Points	6,075
Speed	16
Line of Sight	9
A/D	Warrior Hero
Attack	360 (Ms) / 2
Range (AE)	8
Armor	10 (Sh)

NAPOLEON (IX) *

Build	160 s. / 530 F, 450 I
Hit Points	4,245
Speed	16
Line of Sight	9
A/D	Warrior Hero
Attack	140 (Ms) / 2
Range (AE)	8
Armor	10 (Sh), 8 (Pr)

PERICLES (IV)

Hit Points	1,235
Speed	16
Line of Sight	6
A/D	Strategist Hero
Attack	14 (Ms) / 2
Range (AE)	0.6
Armor	3 (Sh, Pr)

THE POPE (V)

Hit Points	2,800
Speed	12
Line of Sight	6
A/D	Strategist Hero
Attack	(Ms) / 180
Range (AE)	6
Armor	4 (Sh, Pr)

BULLDOG RAMSEY (XI)

Hit Points	5,500
Speed	14
Line of Sight	9
A/D	Warrior Hero
Attack	160 (Ms) / 2
Range (AE)	8
Armor	10 (Sh), 9 (Pr)

RICHARD LIONHEART (VI) *

Build	160 s. / 530 F, 450 I
Hit Points	2,775
Speed	16
Line of Sight	6
A/D	Warrior Hero
Attack	60 (Ms) / 2
Range (AE)	0.6
Armor	5 (Sh, Pr)

Hero Stats

MANFRED V. RICHTOFEN (X) *

Build	180 s. / 600 F, 500 I
Hit Points	4,740
Speed	14
Line of Sight	9
A/D	Warrior Hero
Attack	150 (Ms) / 2
Range (AE)	8
Armor	10 (Sh), 9 (Pr)

ERWIN ROMMEL (XI) *

Build	180 s. / 480 F, 400 G
Hit Points	3,650
Speed	14
Line of Sight	9
A/D	Strategist Hero
Attack	55 (Ms) / 2
Range (AE)	8
Armor	10 (Sh), 9 (Pr)

MOLLY RYAN (XIV) *

Build	180 s. / 540 F, 450 G
Hit Points	5,000
Speed	14
Line of Sight	9
A/D	Strategist Hero
Attack	85 (Ms) / 2
Range (AE)	8
Armor	10 (Sh)

DENNIS ST. ALBANS (XII) *

Source	Town Center
Build	180 s. / 480 F, 400 G
Hit Points	5,730
Speed	14
Line of Sight	8
A/D	Warrior Hero
Attack	180 (Ms) / 2
Range (AE)	7
Armor	10 (Sh), 9 (Pr)

SARGON OF AKKAD (III) *

Build	160 s. / 430 F, 360 G
Hit Points	900
Speed	16
Line of Sight	6
A/D	Strategist Hero
Attack	12 (Ms) / 2
Range (AE)	0.6
Armor	2 (Sh, Pr)

ALEXI SEPTIMUS (XIII) *

Build	180 s. / 540 F, 450 G
Hit Points	4,725
Speed	16
Line of Sight	9
A/D	Strategist Hero
Attack	70 (Ms) / 2
Range (AE)	8
Armor	10 (Sh)

TRAVIS SHACKELFORD (XI) *

Build	180 s. / 600 F, 500 I
Hit Points	5,235
Speed	14
Line of Sight	9
A/D	Warrior Hero
Attack	160 (Ms) / 2
Range (AE)	8
Armor	10 (Sh), 9 (Pr)

LT. STOCK (XI)

Hit Points	5,235
Speed	14
Line of Sight	9
A/D	Warrior Hero
Attack	160 (Ms) / 2
Range (AE)	8
Armor	10 (Sh), 9 (Pr)

GRIGOR STOYANOVICH (XIII)

Hit Points	6,500
Speed	14
Line of Sight	9
A/D	Warrior Hero
Attack	95 (Ms) / 2
Range (AE)	8
Armor	10 (Sh)

EMPIRE EARTH
THE ART OF CONQUEST

PRIMA'S OFFICIAL STRATEGY GUIDE

TARIQ (VI)

Hit Points	2,775
Speed	12
Line of Sight	6
A/D	Warrior Hero
Attack	75 (Ms) / 2
Range (AE)	0.6
Armor	5 (Sh, Pr)

TITUS LABENIUS (III)

Hit Points	2,250
Speed	16
Line of Sight	6
A/D	Warrior Hero
Attack	52 (Ms) / 2
Range (AE)	0.6
Armor	4 (Sh, Pr)

DUKE OF WELLINGTON (IX)

Hit Points	4,245
Speed	16
Line of Sight	9
A/D	Warrior Hero
Attack	145 (Ms) / 2
Range (AE)	8
Armor	10 (Sh), 8 (Pr)

WILLIAM CONQUEROR (VI) *

Build	160 s. / 430 F, 360 G
Hit Points	1,950
Speed	16
Line of Sight	6
A/D	Strategist Hero
Attack	19 (Ms) / 2
Range (AE)	0.6
Armor	5 (Sh, Pr)

WILLIAM ON FOOT (VI)

Hit Points	1,300
Speed	12
Line of Sight	6
A/D	Strategist Hero
Attack	19 (Sh) / 2
Range (AE)	0.5
Armor	5 (Sh, Pr)

Personnel

ARQUEBUS (VII) *

Source	Barracks
Build	40 s. / 40 F, 40 I
Hit Points	270
Speed	12
Line of Sight	6
A/D	Primitive Gun / Musket
Attack	44 (Gn) / 5
Range (AE)	5
Armor	10 (Pr)

ASHIKAGU ARQUEBUS (VI)

Source	Barracks
Build	40 s. / 40 F, 40 I
Hit Points	270
Speed	12
Line of Sight	6
A/D	Primitive Gun / Musket
Attack	44 (Gn) / 5
Range (AE)	5
Armor	10 (Pr)

BARBARIAN (V) *

Source	Barracks
Build	40 s. / 35 F, 35 I
Hit Points	325
Speed	14
Line of Sight	6
A/D	Barbarian / Foot Shock
Attack	16 (Sh) / 2
Range (AE)	0.5
Armor	2 (Sh, Pr), 4 (Ar)

Walks through forests

Personnel Stats

BAZOOKA (XI) *

Source	Barracks
Build	25 s. / 55 F, 40 G
Hit Points	625
Speed	12
Line of Sight	8
A/D	Bazooka / Human
Attack	20 (Ms) / 4
Range (AE)	7

BLACK ROBE (XIII)

Source	Barracks
Build	40 s. / 40 F, 40 I
Hit Points	800
Speed	12
Line of Sight	7
A/D	Rifle
Attack	74 (Ls) / 2
Range (AE)	6
Armor	15 (Ms)

BRITISH INFANTRY (IX)

Source	Barracks
Build	40 s. / 40 F, 40 I
Hit Points	390
Speed	12
Line of Sight	7
A/D	Primitive Gun / Human
Attack	44 (Gn) / 3
Range (AE)	6
Armor	10 (Pr)

BRONZE CAVALRY (IV) *

Source	Stable (PC 2)
Build	43 s. / 60 F, 60 G
Hit Points	290
Speed	16
Line of Sight	4
A/D	Mounted Spear
Attack	23 (Pr) / 2
Range (AE)	0.6
Armor	5 (Sh), 2 (Pr)

CANINE SCOUT (ALL) *

Source	Town Center
Build	28 s. / 50 F
Hit Points	60 (I), 102 (IV), 144 (VI), 186 (VIII), 228 (X), 305 (XII), 365 (XIV)
Speed	16
Line of Sight	4
A/D	Animals / Human
Attack	(Ms) / 2
Range (AE)	0.5

CARABINEER (VII) *

Source	Stable (PC 2)
Build	43 s. / 70 F, 65 G
Hit Points	425
Speed	16
Line of Sight	5
A/D	Mounted Gun
Attack	55 (Gn) / 5
Range (AE)	4
Armor	20 (Sh)

CATAPHRACT (V) *

Source	Stable (PC 2)
Build	43 s. / 60 F, 60 G
Hit Points	440
Speed	16
Line of Sight	4
A/D	Mounted Shock
Attack	24 (Sh) / 2
Range (AE)	0.6
Armor	2(Sh), 6(Ar), 20(Gn)

CAVALRY ARCHER (VI) *

Source	Archery Range (PC 2)
Build	38 s. / 45 G, 60 W
Hit Points	275
Speed	16
Line of Sight	6
A/D	Ranged Cav
Attack	23 (Ar) / 2
Range (AE)	5
Armor	6 (Sh), 4 (Pr)

CELTIC WARRIOR (V)

Source	Barracks
Build	40 s. / 35 F, 35 I
Hit Points	350
Speed	14
Line of Sight	6
A/D	Barbarian
Attack	18 (Sh) / 2
Range (AE)	0.5
Armor	2 (Ar, Pr)

EMPIRE EARTH
THE ART OF CONQUEST

PRIMA'S OFFICIAL STRATEGY GUIDE

CHARIOT ARCHER (IV) *

Source	Archery Range (PC 2)
Build	38 s. / 45 G, 60 W
Hit Points	180
Speed	16
Line of Sight	5
A/D	Ranged Cav
Attack	17 (Ar) / 2
Range (AE)	4
Armor	1 (Ar), 4 (Pr)

CHILD (ALL)

Hit Points	20 (I), 34 (IV), 48 (VI), 62 (VIII), 76 (X), 96 (XII), 116 (XIV)
Speed	8
Line of Sight	2
A/D	NA / Citizen
Range (AE)	0.5

CHINESE INFANTRY (IV)

Source	Barracks
Build	32 s. / 30 F, 30 I
Hit Points	155
Speed	12
Line of Sight	4
A/D	Foot Spear / Human
Attack	24 (Pr) / 2
Range (AE)	0.5
Armor	3 (Sh)

CITIZEN (M OR F) (ALL) *

Source	Town Center
Build	28 s. / 50 F
Hit Points	65 (I), 110 (IV), 155 (VI), 200 (VIII), 245 (X), 310 (XII), 375 (XIV)
Speed	10
Line of Sight	3
A/D	Citizen
Attack	5 (Ms) / 2
Range (AE)	2

CLUBMAN (I) *

Source	Barracks
Build	32 s. / 30 F, 30 I
Hit Points	135
Speed	12
Line of Sight	4
A/D	Foot Shock
Attack	8 (Sh) / 2
Range (AE)	0.5
Armor	1 (Ar)

COMPANION CAVALRY (IV)

Source	Stable (PC 2)
Build	43 s. / 60 F, 60 G
Hit Points	290
Speed	16
Line of Sight	4
A/D	Mounted Spear
Attack	23 (Pr) / 2
Range (AE)	0.6
Armor	5 (Sh), 2 (Pr)

COMPOSITE BOW (V) *

Source	Archery Range
Build	38 s. / 30 G, 40 W
Hit Points	145
Speed	11
Line of Sight	6
A/D	Primitive Ranged / Archer
Attack	13 (Ar) / 2
Range (AE)	5
Armor	2 (Ar), 7 (Pr)

COURT JESTER (VI)

Hit Points	215
Speed	12
Line of Sight	4
A/D	Foot Shock
Attack	15 (Sh) / 2
Range (AE)	0.5
Armor	6 (Ar)

CROSSBOW (V) *

Source	Archery Range
Build	100 s. / 100 G, 100 W
Hit Points	125
Speed	10
Line of Sight	8
A/D	Sniper / Archer
Attack	40 (Ar) / 10
Range (AE)	7

1 shot = 1 kill vs. infantry in basic armor

Personnel Stats

CYBER NINJA (XV) * (JAPAN)

Source	Barracks
Build	30 s./50 F,100 G,100 I
Hit Points	1800
Speed	12
Line of Sight	11
A/D	Foot Shock / Human
Attack	120 (Sh) / 2.4
Range (AE)	0.5 (0.1)

DIPLOMAT (ALL)

Source	Settlement
Build	25 s. / 250 F, 100 G
Hit Points	40 (I), 68 (IV), 96 (VI), 124 (VIII), 152 (X), 192 (XII), 232 (XIV)
Speed	12
Line of Sight	3
A/D	Citizen
Attack	3 (Ar) / 2
Range (AE)	2

DOUGHBOY (X) *

Source	Barracks
Build	40 s. / 40 F, 40 I
Hit Points	370
Speed	12
Line of Sight	7
A/D	Rifle
Attack	44 (Gn) / 2
Range (AE)	6

DRAGOON (IX) *

Source	Stable (PC 2)
Build	43 s. / 70 F, 65 G
Hit Points	480
Speed	16
Line of Sight	6
A/D	Mounted Gun
Attack	65 (Gn) / 3
Range (AE)	5
Armor	25 (Sh)

EGYPTIAN WARRIOR (II)

Source	Barracks
Build	32 s. / 35 F, 35 I
Hit Points	125
Speed	12
Line of Sight	4
A/D	Foot Spear / Spear
Attack	16 (Pr) / 2
Range (AE)	0.5
Armor	2 (Sh)

ELEPHANT ARCHER (IV) *

Source	Archery Range (PC 2)
Build	40 s. / 120 F, 80 G
Hit Points	600
Speed	10
Line of Sight	5
A/D	Prim. Ranged / Elephant Archer
Attack	25 (Ar) / 2
Range (AE)	4
Armor	3 (Ar), 5 (Pr)

ELITE GUARD (IX) *

Source	Barracks
Build	55 s. / 85 F, 80 I
Hit Points	350
Speed	12
Line of Sight	6
A/D	Elite Guard
Attack	35 (Gn) / 1.5
Range (AE)	5
Armor	10 (Gn)

EMISSARY (II +) * (ISRAEL)

Source	Temple
Build	45 s. / 50 F, 125 G
Hit Points	100 (II), 200 (III), 300 (VII), 370 (X), 440 (XIII)
Speed	9
Line of Sight	6
A/D	Priest
Attack	Conversion(Sh)/25
Range (AE)	4

ENGINEER (X)

Source	Barracks
Build	40 s. / 40 F, 40 I
Hit Points	470
Speed	12
Line of Sight	7
A/D	NA / Human
Range (AE)	0.5

EMPIRE EARTH
THE ART OF CONQUEST

PRIMA'S OFFICIAL STRATEGY GUIDE

FIELD MEDIC - WWII (XI)

Source	Barracks
Build	30 s. / 75 F, 50 G
Hit Points	600
Speed	12
Line of Sight	3
A/D	NA / Human

FLAME THROWER (XI) *

Source	Barracks
Build	40 s. / 80 F, 65 G
Hit Points	430
Speed	12
Line of Sight	4
A/D	Modern Siege / Human
Attack	25 (Gn) / 2
Range (AE)	3 (0.8)

GALLIC WARRIOR (V)

Source	Barracks
Build	32 s. / 35 F, 35 I
Hit Points	300
Speed	12
Line of Sight	6
A/D	Barbarian
Attack	16 (Sh) / 2
Range (AE)	0.5
Armor	3 (Sh), 5 (Ar), 2 (Pr)

GERMAN INFANTRY (X)

Source	Barracks
Build	40 s. / 40 F, 40 I
Hit Points	470
Speed	12
Line of Sight	7
A/D	Rifle
Attack	52 (Gn) / 2
Range (AE)	6

GERMAN MACHINE GUN (X)

Source	Barracks
Build	60 s. / 95 F, 85 G
Hit Points	400
Speed	12
Line of Sight	7
A/D	Machine Gun
Attack	16 (Gn) / 1
Range (AE)	6
Armor	8 (Gn)

GRENADE LAUNCHER (X) *

Source	Barracks
Build	25 s. / 55 F, 40 G
Hit Points	525
Speed	12
Line of Sight	7
A/D	Bazooka / Human
Attack	16 (Ms) / 4
Range (AE)	6

GRENADIER (IX) *

Source	Barracks
Build	40 s. / 40 F, 40 I
Hit Points	390
Speed	12
Line of Sight	7
A/D	Primitive Gun / Musket
Attack	44 (Gn) / 3
Range (AE)	6
Armor	10 (Pr)

GUARDIAN (XIV) *

Source	Barracks
Build	40 s. / 40 F, 40 I
Hit Points	800
Speed	12
Line of Sight	7
A/D	Rifle
Attack	74 (Ls) / 2
Range (AE)	6

HALBERDIER (VIII) *

Source	Barracks
Build	25 s. / 30 F, 30 I
Hit Points	350
Speed	12
Line of Sight	4
A/D	Halberdier / Spear
Attack	40 (Pr) / 2
Range (AE)	0.5
Armor	4 (Sh)

Personnel Stats

HAND CANNONEER (VIII) *

Source	Barracks
Build	40 s. / 50 F, 40 G
Hit Points	350
Speed	12
Line of Sight	8
A/D	Hand Cannon/Human
Attack	65 (Gn) / 8
Range (AE)	8 (0.5)

Fires over walls

HEAVY MORTAR (XII) *

Source	Barracks
Build	40 s. / 45 F, 35 G
Hit Points	425
Speed	12
Line of Sight	8
A/D	Mortar / Human
Attack	120 (Gn) / 8
Range (AE)	11 (0.5)

HORSEMAN (III) *

Source	Stable (PC 2)
Build	43 s. / 60 F, 60 G
Hit Points	240
Speed	16
Line of Sight	4
A/D	Mounted Shock
Attack	17 (Sh) / 2
Range (AE)	0.6
Armor	6 (Ar)

HUSKARL (VI)

Source	Barracks
Build	32 s. / 30 F, 30 I
Hit Points	400
Speed	12
Line of Sight	4
A/D	Foot Shock
Attack	29 (Sh) / 2
Range (AE)	0.5
Armor	6 (Ar)

IMPERIAL CUIRASSIER (IX)*

Source	Stable (PC 2)
Build	43 s. / 60 F, 60 G
Hit Points	655
Speed	16
Line of Sight	5
A/D	Mounted Shock
Attack	60 (Sh) / 2
Range (AE)	0.6
Armor	9 (Ar), 31 (Gn)

INCAN WARRIOR (III)

Source	Archery Range
Build	38 s. / 30 G, 30 W
Hit Points	70
Speed	11
Line of Sight	4
A/D	Primitive Ranged / Human
Attack	9 (Ar) / 2
Range (AE)	3
Armor	2 (Pr)

JAVELIN (IV) *

Source	Archery Range
Build	38 s. / 30 G, 40 W
Hit Points	130
Speed	11
Line of Sight	4
A/D	Prim. Ranged / Spear Thrower
Attack	11 (Pr) / 2
Range (AE)	3
Armor	4 (Sh)

KNIGHT (VI) *

Source	Stable (PC 2)
Build	43 s. / 60 F, 60 G
Hit Points	400
Speed	16
Line of Sight	4
A/D	Mounted Spear
Attack	38 (Pr) / 2
Range (AE)	0.8
Armor	10 (Sh), 8 (Pr)

LONG BOW (VI) *

Source	Archery Range
Build	38 s. / 30 G, 40 W
Hit Points	190
Speed	11
Line of Sight	7
A/D	Ranged / Archer
Attack	17 (Ar) / 2
Range (AE)	6
Armor	3 (Ar), 7 (Pr)

LONG SWORD (VI) *

Source	Barracks
Build	32 s. / 30 F, 30 I
Hit Points	400
Speed	12
Line of Sight	4
A/D	Foot Shock
Attack	29 (Sh) / 2
Range (AE)	0.5
Armor	6 (Ar)

MACEMAN (III) *

Source	Barracks
Build	32 s. / 30 F, 30 I
Hit Points	150
Speed	12
Line of Sight	4
A/D	Foot Shock
Attack	13 (Sh) / 2
Range (AE)	0.5
Armor	4 (Ar)

MACHINE GUN (X) *

Source	Barracks
Build	58 s. / 95 F, 85 G
Hit Points	400
Speed	12
Line of Sight	7
A/D	Machine Gun
Attack	16 (Gn) / 1
Range (AE)	6
Armor	9 (Gn)

MARINE (XI) *

Source	Barracks
Build	40 s. / 40 F, 40 I
Hit Points	470
Speed	12
Line of Sight	7
A/D	Rifle
Attack	52 (Gn) / 2
Range (AE)	6

MEDIC - ATOMIC (XI) *

Source	Barracks
Build	30 s. / 75 F, 50 G
Hit Points	425
Speed	12
Line of Sight	3
A/D	NA / Human

MEDIC - DIGITAL (XIII) *

Source	Barracks
Build	30 s. / 75 F, 50 G
Hit Points	500
Speed	12
Line of Sight	3
A/D	NA / Human

MEDIC - IMPERIAL (IX) *

Source	Barracks
Build	30 s. / 75 F, 50 G
Hit Points	360
Speed	12
Line of Sight	3
A/D	NA / Human

MISSILE TROOPER (XIII)

Source	Barracks
Build	32 s. / 60 F, 50 G
Hit Points	265
Speed	12
Line of Sight	7
A/D	AA / Land AA
Attack	55 (Ms) / 4
Range (AE)	6
Armor	8 (Gn)

MOORISH CAVALRY (V)

Source	Stable (PC 2)
Build	43 s. / 60 F, 60 G
Hit Points	440
Speed	16
Line of Sight	4
A/D	Mounted Shock
Attack	24 (Sh) / 2
Range (AE)	0.6
Armor	2(Sh),6(Ar),20(Gn)

Personnel Stats

MOORISH INFANTRY (V)

Source	Barracks
Build	32 s. / 30 F, 30 I
Hit Points	400
Speed	12
Line of Sight	4
A/D	Foot Shock
Attack	29 (Sh) / 2
Range (AE)	0.5
Armor	6 (Ar)

MUSKETEER (VIII) *

Source	Barracks
Build	40 s. / 40 F, 40 I
Hit Points	325
Speed	12
Line of Sight	6
A/D	Primitive Gun / Musket
Attack	44 (Gn) / 4
Range (AE)	5
Armor	10 (Pr)

PARTISAN (IX) *

Source	Barracks
Build	40 s. / 40 F, 40 I
Hit Points	325
Speed	12
Line of Sight	7
A/D	Partisan / Human
Attack	20 (Gn) / 3
Range (AE)	6
Armor	10 (Pr)
Walks through forests	

PERSIAN CAVALRY (V) *

Source	Stable (PC 2)
Build	40 s. / 55 F, 55 G
Hit Points	225
Speed	16
Line of Sight	6
A/D	Persian Cav
Attack	18 (Pr) / 2
Range (AE)	5
Armor	7 (Sh)

PERSIAN IMMORTAL (IV)

Source	Barracks
Build	32 s. / 30 F, 30 I
Hit Points	155
Speed	12
Line of Sight	4
A/D	Foot Spear / Human
Attack	24 (Pr) / 2
Range (AE)	0.5
Armor	3 (Sh)

PHALANX (IV) *

Source	Barracks
Build	32 s. / 30 F, 30 I
Hit Points	155
Speed	12
Line of Sight	4
A/D	Foot Spear / Spear
Attack	24 (Pr) / 2
Range (AE)	0.5
Armor	3 (Sh)

PIKEMAN (VI) *

Source	Barracks
Build	32 s. / 30 F, 30 I
Hit Points	240
Speed	12
Line of Sight	4
A/D	Foot Spear / Spear
Attack	40 (Pr) / 2
Range (AE)	0.5
Armor	6 (Sh), 4 (Pr)

PILUM (V) *

Source	Archery Range
Build	38 s. / 30 G, 40 W
Hit Points	155
Speed	11
Line of Sight	5
A/D	Prim. Ranged / Spear Thrower
Attack	13 (Pr) / 2
Range (AE)	4
Armor	5 (Sh)

PRIEST (II +) *

Source	Temple
Build	45 s. / 50 F, 125 G
Hit Points	100 (II), 200 (III), 300 (VII), 370 (X), 440 (XIII)
Speed	9
Line of Sight	6
A/D	Priest
Attack	Conversion (Sh) / 25
Range (AE)	4

| COPPER AGE | | DARK AGE | | RENAISSANCE | | INDUSTRIAL AGE | |
| STONE AGE | BRONZE AGE | | MIDDLE AGES | | IMPERIAL AGE | | ATOMIC AG |

BC 5000 BC 2000 BC 500 BC 0AD 900 AD 1300 AD 1500 AD 1700 AD 1900 AD 2

EMPIRE EARTH
THE ART OF CONQUEST

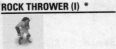

PROPHET (ALL) *

Source	Temple (PC 5)
Build	50 s. / 200 F, 200 G
Hit Points	150 (I), 240 (II), 330 (VI), 420 (IX)
Speed	9
Line of Sight	8
A/D	Other / Human
Attack	Calamity (Sh) / 180
Range (AE)	6
Armor	6 (Ar, Pr), 10 (Gn)

RADIO MAN (X)

Source	Barracks
Build	40 s. / 40 F, 40 G
Hit Points	500
Speed	12
Line of Sight	8
A/D	Rifle/Human
Attack	50 (Gn) / 3
Range (AE)	8

RIOT POLICE (XIII)

Source	Barracks
Build	120 s. / 600 G, 600 I
Hit Points	600
Speed	12
Line of Sight	7
A/D	Rifle
Attack	30 (Ls) / 2.4
Range (AE)	6

ROCK THROWER (I) *

Source	Barracks
Build	38 s. / 30 F, 30 G
Hit Points	75
Speed	11
Line of Sight	3
A/D	Other / Human
Attack	5 (Sh) / 2
Range (AE)	2
Armor	2 (Ar, Pr)

ROMAN CENTURION (VI)

Hit Points	350
Speed	12
Line of Sight	4
A/D	Foot Shock
Attack	30 (Sh) / 2
Range (AE)	0.5
Armor	2 (Sh), 4 (Ar)

ROMAN LEGIONNAIRE (IV)

Source	Barracks
Build	32 s. / 35 F, 35 I
Hit Points	215
Speed	12
Line of Sight	4
A/D	Foot Shock
Attack	20 (Sh) / 2
Range (AE)	0.5
Armor	2 (Sh), 6 (Ar)

ROMAN SENATOR (II)

Hit Points	100
Speed	9
Line of Sight	6
A/D	NA / Citizen

ROYAL CUIRASSIER (VII) *

Source	Stable (PC 2)
Build	43 s. / 60 F, 60 G
Hit Points	605
Speed	16
Line of Sight	4
A/D	Mounted Shock
Attack	40 (Sh) / 2
Range (AE)	0.6
Armor	1 (Sh), 8 (Ar), 20 (Gn)

ROYAL GUARD (IV)

Source	Barracks
Build	32 s. / 30 F, 30 I
Hit Points	215
Speed	12
Line of Sight	4
A/D	Foot Shock
Attack	15 (Sh) / 2
Range (AE)	0.5
Armor	6 (Ar)

Personnel Stats

SAMPSON (II) *

Source	Barracks
Build	40 s. / 65 G, 65 W
Hit Points	105
Speed	10
Line of Sight	4
A/D	Ram / Siege
Attack	60 (Gn) / 4
Range (AE)	1.3

SAMURAI (VI)

Source	Barracks
Build	32 s. / 30 F, 30 I
Hit Points	400
Speed	12
Line of Sight	4
A/D	Foot Shock
Attack	29 (Sh) / 2
Range (AE)	0.5
Armor	6 (Ar)

SAS COMMANDO (XI)* (GB)

Source	Barracks
Build	40 s. / 40 G, 40 I
Hit Points	650
Speed	12
Line of Sight	7
A/D	Rifle
Attack	52 (Gn) / 2
Range (AE)	6
Armor	5 (Gn, Ls, Ms)
Bomb	1500 (Sh)

SENTINEL (XIII) *

Source	Barracks
Build	40 s. / 40 F, 40 I
Hit Points	600
Speed	12
Line of Sight	7
A/D	Rifle
Attack	62 (Ls) / 2
Range (AE)	6

SHARPSHOOTER (VIII) *

Source	Barracks
Build	100 s. / 150 F, 150 G
Hit Points	315
Speed	9
Line of Sight	9
A/D	Sniper / Human
Attack	50 (Gn) / 12
Range (AE)	8

1 shot = 1 kill vs. infantry in basic armor

SHOCK TROOPER (XIII)

Source	Barracks
Build	100 s. / 150 F, 150 G
Hit Points	405
Speed	9
Line of Sight	11
A/D	Sniper / Human
Attack	60 (Gn) / 12
Range (AE)	9

SHORT SWORD (IV) *

Source	Barracks
Build	32 s. / 30 F, 30 I
Hit Points	215
Speed	12
Line of Sight	4
A/D	Foot Shock
Attack	15 (Sh) / 2
Range (AE)	0.5
Armor	6 (Ar)

SIMPLE BOWMAN (III) *

Source	Archery Range
Build	38 s. / 30 G, 40 W
Hit Points	95
Speed	11
Line of Sight	5
A/D	Primitive Ranged / Archer
Attack	9 (Ar) / 2
Range (AE)	4
Armor	1 (Ar), 3 (Pr)

SLINGER (II) *

Source	Archery Range
Build	38 s. / 30 G, 30 W
Hit Points	70
Speed	11
Line of Sight	4
A/D	Primitive Ranged / Archer
Attack	9 (Ar) / 2
Range (AE)	3
Armor	2 (Pr)

EMPIRE EARTH
THE ART OF CONQUEST

PRIMA'S OFFICIAL STRATEGY GUIDE

SNIPER (X) *

Source	Barracks
Build	100 s. / 150 F, 150 G
Hit Points	405
Speed	9
Line of Sight	11
A/D	Sniper / Human
Attack	60 (Gn) / 12
Range (AE)	9

1 shot = 1 kill vs. infantry in basic armor

SPANISH CAVALRY (VII)

Source	Stable (PC 2)
Build	43 s. / 70 F, 65 G
Hit Points	425
Speed	16
Line of Sight	5
A/D	Mounted Gun
Attack	55 (Gn) / 5
Range (AE)	4
Armor	20 (Sh)

SPANISH INFANTRY (VII)

Source	Barracks
Build	25 s. / 30 F, 30 I
Hit Points	350
Speed	12
Line of Sight	4
A/D	Halberdier / Spear
Attack	40 (Pr) / 2
Range (AE)	0.5
Armor	4 (Sh)

SPEARMAN (II) *

Source	Barracks
Build	32 s. / 30 F, 30 I
Hit Points	85
Speed	12
Line of Sight	4
A/D	Foot Spear / Spear
Attack	15 (Pr) / 2
Range (AE)	0.5
Armor	2 (Sh)

SPY (X)

Source	Espionage HQ
Build	25 s. / 250 F, 100 G
Hit Points	1,000
Speed	12
Line of Sight	7
A/D	Other / Human
Attack	50 (Sh) / 2
Range (AE)	0.5

STANDARD BEARER (III)

Source	Barracks
Build	40 s. / 50 F, 50 I
Hit Points	250
Speed	12
Line of Sight	4
A/D	Viking
Attack	2 (Sh, Pr) / 2
Range (AE)	0.5

STINGER SOLDIER (XII) *

Source	Barracks
Build	32 s. / 60 F, 50 G
Hit Points	265
Speed	12
Line of Sight	7
A/D	AA / Land AA
Attack	55 (Ms) / 4
Range (AE)	6
Armor	8 (Gn)

TRENCH MORTAR (X) *

Source	Barracks
Build	40 s. / 45 F, 35 G
Hit Points	375
Speed	12
Line of Sight	8
A/D	Mortar / Human
Attack	90 (Gn) / 8
Range (AE)	10 (0.5)

VIKING (V) *

Source	Barracks
Build	40 s. / 35 F, 35 I
Hit Points	160
Speed	12
Line of Sight	4
A/D	Viking
Attack	10 (Ms) / 2
Range (AE)	0.5

Building Stats

WAR ELEPHANT (IV) *

Source	Stable (PC 2)
Build	48 s. / 120 F, 80 G
Hit Points	600
Speed	10
Line of Sight	4
A/D	Siege / War Elephant
Attack	23 (Ms) / 2
Range (AE)	0.6 (1.1)

WATCHMAN (XV) *

Source	Barracks
Build	40 s. / 50 F, 50 I
Hit Points	1200
Speed	12
Line of Sight	9
A/D	Rifle
Attack	85 (Ls) / 2
Range (AE)	7 (0.1)
Armor	5 (Gn, Ls, Ms)

Buildings

88MM AA GUN (X) *

Source	Citizen
Build	40 s. / 80 G, 80 W
Hit Points	600
Line of Sight	8
A/D	AA / AA Building
Attack	25 (Ms) / 1
Range (AE)	7
Armor	7 (Gn)

AA MISSILE TOWER (XIII +) *

Source	Citizen
Build	40 s. / 80 G, 80 W
Hit Points	900
Line of Sight	8
A/D	AA / AA Building
Attack	100 (Ms) / 3
Range (AE)	7
Armor	7 (Gn)

AIRPORT (X +) *

X

XIII

Source	Citizen
Build	70 s. / 425 W
Hit Points	11,000 (X - XII), 16,500 (XIII)
Line of Sight	3
A/D	NA / Building

ARC LAMP

Hit Points	100
Line of Sight	2
A/D	NA / Building
Range (AE)	0.5

ARCHERY RANGE (II +) *

II, IV

VI

Source	Citizen
Build	45 s. / 225 W
Hit Points	1,250 (II - IV), 1,875 (V - VIII), 2,500 (IX - XII), 3,125 (XIII+)
Line of Sight	3
A/D	NA / Building

BARBED WIRE (X)

Source	Engineer
Build	3 s. / 5 W
Hit Points	500
Line of Sight	1
A/D	NA / Wall

EMPIRE EARTH
THE ART OF CONQUEST

PRIMA'S OFFICIAL STRATEGY GUIDE

BARRACKS (I +) *

I, III

IV, VI

VIII, X

XIII

Source	Citizen
Build	45 s. / 225 W
Hit Points	1,500 (I - IV), 2,250 (V - VIII), 3,000 (IX - XII), 3,750 (XIII+)
Line of Sight	3
A/D	NA / Building

BUCKINGHAM PALACE (IX)

Hit Points	10,000
Line of Sight	3
A/D	NA / Building

CAPITOL (I +) *

I

III, IV

VI, VIII

X

XIII, XV

Source	Citizen
Build	45 s. / 100 W
Hit Points	5,000 (I - IV), 7,500 (V - VIII), 10,000 (IX - XII), 12,500 (XIII+)
Line of Sight	5
A/D	NA / Building
Range (AE)	0.5

CASTLE KEEP (VI)

Hit Points	5,000
Line of Sight	2
A/D	NA / Building

CASTLE TOWER (VI)

Hit Points	2,000
Line of Sight	1
A/D	NA / Wall

CASTLE WALL - LEFT, RT. (VI)

Hit Points	2,000
Line of Sight	1
A/D	NA / Wall

CHURCH

Hit Points	1,000
Line of Sight	3
A/D	NA / Building

COMPUTER PANEL

Hit Points	100
Line of Sight	0

Building Stats

CYBER FACTORY (XIII +) *

Source	Citizen
Build	70 s. / 475 W
Hit Points	6,000
Line of Sight	3
A/D	NA / Building
Armor	50 (Ar, Pr)

CYBER LABORATORY(XIII +)*

Source	Citizen
Build	70 s. / 475 W
Hit Points	6,000
Line of Sight	3
A/D	NA / Building

DOCK (I +) *

I, IV

VI, X

XIII, XV

Source
Citizen
Build 45 s. / 175 W (I - XIV)
50 s. / 500 W (XV)
Hit Points 2,000 (I - IV),
3,000 (V - VIII), 4,000 (IX -
XII), 5,000 (XIII - XIV),
6,000 (XV)
Line of Sight 3
A/D NA / Building

EIFFEL TOWER (IX)

Hit Points	5,000
Line of Sight	3
A/D	NA / Building

FORTRESS (I +) *

I, IV

VI, X

XIII

Source	Citizen
Build	45 s. / 350 W
Hit Points	2,000 (I - IV), 3,000 (V - VIII), 4,000 (IX - XII), 5,000 (XIII+)
Line of Sight	3
A/D	NA / Building
Range (AE)	2

GASLIGHT

Hit Points	100
Line of Sight	2
A/D	NA / Building
Range (AE)	0.5

GRANARY (III +) *

III

IV

VI

X

XIII

XV

Source	Citizen
Build	30 s. / 125 W
Hit Points	2,000 (III - IV), 3,000 (V - VIII), 4,000 (IX - XII), 5,000 (XIII+)
Line of Sight	5
A/D	NA / Building

FARM (III) / ROBOTIC FARM (XV) *

Build	Around Granary (8 tiles) 30 s. / 50 W
Hit Points	100
Line of Sight	2
A/D	NA / Building

EMPIRE EARTH
THE ART OF CONQUEST

GREEK RUINS (IV)

Hit Points	2,000
Line of Sight	0
A/D	NA / Building
Range (AE)	0.5

HOSPITAL (III +) *

III, IV

VI, X

XIII

Source	Citizen
Build	110 s./100 S, 250 W
Hit Points	1,000 (III - IV), 1,500 (V - VIII), 2,000 (IX - XII), 2,500 (XIII+)
Line of Sight	3
A/D	NA / Building

HOUSE (ALL) *

All houses have the following stats; their hit points vary by epoch.

Source	Citizen
Build	35 s. / 40 S, 50 W
Hit Points	Varies
Line of Sight	2
A/D	NA / Building

+1 Morale per House

HOUSE - PREHISTORIC (I) *

Hit Points	500

HOUSE - STONE (II) *

Hit Points	600

HOUSE - COPPER (III) *

Hit Points	700

HOUSE - BRONZE (IV) *

Hit Points	450

HOUSE - DARK (V) *

Hit Points	1,100

HOUSE - ASIAN (VI)

Hit Points	1,300

HOUSE - MIDDLE AGES(VI) *

Hit Points	1,300

HOUSE - RENAISSANCE (VII) *

Hit Points	1,500

HOUSE - IMPERIAL (VIII) *

Hit Points	1,700

HOUSE - INDUSTRIAL (IX) *

Hit Points	1,900

Building Stats

HOUSE - ATOMIC (X) *

Hit Points	500

HOUSE - DIGITAL (XIII) *

Hit Points	2,100
Armor	50 (Ar, Pr)

HOUSE - NANO (XIV) *

Hit Points	2,300

HOUSE - SPACE (XV) *

Hit Points	2,500

LIGHTHOUSE (X)

Source	Citizen
Build	900 s. / 500 I, 500 S, 500 W
Hit Points	3,500
Line of Sight	5
A/D	NA / Building

MARKET (X) *

Source	Citizen
Build	45 s. / 500 W, 250 S
Hit Points	1000
Line of Sight	3
A/D	NA / Wall

MINARET (V)

Hit Points	2,000
Line of Sight	2
A/D	NA / Building

MISSILE BASE (XI +) *

XI, XIV

Source	Citizen
Build	50 s. / 2000 W
Hit Points	6,000 (XI - XII), 9,000 (XIII+)
Line of Sight	2
A/D	Tower
Attack	15,000 (Ms) / 30
Range (AE)	99 (3.5)

MISSILE BASE (NOV. RUSSIA)

Source	Citizen
Build	50 s. / 2000 W
Hit Points	6,000
Line of Sight	3
A/D	ICBM / Building
Attack/Delay	20,000 (Ms) / 30
Range (AE)	99 (3.5)
Capacity	5

MOSQUE (V)

Source	Citizen
Build	100 s. / 50 S, 300 W
Hit Points	1,000
Line of Sight	3
A/D	NA / Building

NAVAL YARD (X +) *

X, XIII

Source	Citizen
Build	45 s. / 225 W
Hit Points	10,000 (X - XII), 15,000 (XIII)
Line of Sight	3
A/D	NA / Building

EMPIRE EARTH
THE ART OF CONQUEST

ORTHODOX CHURCH (VI)

Source Citizen
Build 100 s. / 50 S, 300 W
Hit Points 1,000
Line of Sight 3
A/D NA / Building

PAGODA (VI)

Source Citizen
Build 45 s. / 250 W
Hit Points 1,300
Line of Sight 2
A/D NA / Building

PILLBOX

Source Engineer
Build 12 s. / 150 S
Hit Points 1,500
Line of Sight 9
A/D Machine Gun / Building
Attack 16 (Gn) / 1
Range (AE) 8

PORTABLE COMPUTER

Hit Points 100
Line of Sight 0

RADAR CENTER (XI +)

Hit Points 8,000
Line of Sight 13
A/D NA / Building

SETTLEMENT (I +) *

I, III

IV, V

VIII, X

XIII

Source Citizen
Build 45 s. / 100 W
Hit Points 2,000 (I - IV), 3,000 (V - VIII), 4,000 (IX - XII), 5,000 (XIII+)
Line of Sight 4
A/D NA / Building

SIEGE FACTORY (IV +) *

IV, VI

VII, X

XIII

Source Citizen
Build 55 s. / 275 W
Hit Points 1,250 (IV), 1,875 (V - VIII), 2,500 (IX - XII), 3,125 (XIII+)
Line of Sight 3
A/D NA / Building

STABLE (III +) *

III, IV

VI

Source Citizen
Build 45 s. / 225 W
Hit Points 1,250 (III - IV), 1,875 (V - VIII), 2,500 (IX - XII), 3,125 (XIII+)
Line of Sight 3
A/D NA / Building

Building Stats

STATUE - BUDDHA (VI)

Hit Points	1,300
Line of Sight	2
A/D	NA / Building

STATUE - IWO JIMA

Hit Points	500
Line of Sight	2
A/D	NA / Building

STATUE - MOAI, NIKE, MOUNTED, OLMEC (I)

Hit Points	500
Line of Sight	2
A/D	NA / Building

STREETLAMP

Hit Points	100
Line of Sight	2
A/D	NA / Building

TANK BARRIER (X)

Hit Points	3,500
Line of Sight	1
A/D	AT Gun / Building
Attack	100 (Gn)

TANK FACTORY (X +) *

X, XIII

Source	Citizen
Build	70 s. / 375 W
Hit Points	3,500 (X - XII), 5,250 (XIII)
Line of Sight	3
A/D	NA / Building

TELEPORTER (XV) *

Source	Citizen
Build	55 s. / 1000 W, 500 S, 125 G, 250 I
Hit Points	2,000
Line of Sight	3
A/D	NA / Building
Range (AE)	2
Capacity	15

TEMPLE (I +) *

I, IV

VI, IX

XIII

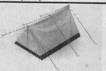

Source	Citizen
Build	100 s. / 50 S, 225 W
Hit Points	1,000 (I - IV), 1,500 (V - VIII), 2,000 (IX - XII), 2,500 (XIII+)
Line of Sight	3
A/D	NA / Building

TENT (III +)

Hit Points	400
Line of Sight	2
A/D	NA / Building

TOWER OF LONDON (VI)

Hit Points	5,000
Line of Sight	3
A/D	NA / Building

| STONE AGE | COPPER AGE | DARK AGE | RENAISSANCE | INDUSTRIAL AGE |
| | BRONZE AGE | MIDDLE AGES | IMPERIAL AGE | ATOMIC AGE |

EMPIRE EARTH
THE ART OF CONQUEST

TOWN CENTER (I +) *

II, III

IV, VI

VIII, X

XIII

Source	Citizen
Build	45 s. / 100 W
Hit Points	4,000 (I - IV), 6,000 (V - VIII), 8,000 (IX - XII), 10,000 (XIII+)
Line of Sight	5
A/D	NA / Building

UNIVERSITY (III +) *

III, IV

VI, VIII

XIII

Source	Citizen
Build	55 s. / 50 S, 175 W
Hit Points	1,000 (III - IV), 1,500 (V - VIII), 2,000 (IX - XII), 2,500 (XIII+)
Line of Sight	3
A/D	NA / Building

Towers, Walls & Gates

TOWER - PRIMITIVE (I) *

Source	Citizen
Build	150 s. / 175 S
Hit Points	1,000
Line of Sight	5
A/D	Tower
Attack	50 (Ms) / 4
Range (AE)	4 (0.3)

TOWER - COPPER (III) *

Source	Citizen
Build	150 s. / 175 S
Hit Points	1,450
Line of Sight	5
A/D	Tower
Attack	68 (Ms) / 4
Range (AE)	4 (0.3)

TOWER - BRONZE (IV) *

Source	Citizen
Build	150 s. / 175 S
Hit Points	1,750
Line of Sight	6
A/D	Tower
Attack	75 (Ms) / 4
Range (AE)	5 (0.3)

Tower, Wall & Gate Stats

TOWER - MEDIEVAL (VI) *

Source	Citizen
Build	150 s. / 175 S
Hit Points	3,125
Line of Sight	6
A/D	Tower
Attack	140 (Ms) / 4
Range (AE)	5 (0.3)

TOWER - PALISADES (VI) *

Source	Citizen
Build	150 s. / 175 W
Hit Points	1,000
Line of Sight	6
A/D	Tower
Attack	40 (Ms) / 4
Range (AE)	5 (0.3)

TOWER - IMPERIAL (VIII) *

Source	Citizen
Build	150 s. / 175 S
Hit Points	4,625
Line of Sight	7
A/D	Tower
Attack	180 (Ms) / 4
Range (AE)	6 (0.3)

TOWER - CONCRETE (X) *

Source	Citizen
Build	150 s. / 175 S
Hit Points	4,875
Line of Sight	8
A/D	Tower
Attack	225 (Ms) / 4
Range (AE)	7 (0.3)

TOWER - LASER (XIII +) *

Source	Citizen
Build	150 s. / 175 S
Hit Points	5,250
Line of Sight	9
A/D	Tower
Attack	350 (Ms) / 4
Range (AE)	8

TOWER - SPACE (XV) *

Source	Citizen
Build	150 s. / 175 S
Hit Points	5,500
Line of Sight	10
A/D	Tower
Attack	350 (Ms) / 4
Range (AE)	9

Common Stats for Walls & Gates

WALL

Source	Citizen
Build	15 s. / 10 S
Line of Sight	1
A/D	NA / Wall

GATE

Source	Wall - of same type
Build	10
Line of Sight	2
A/D	NA / Gate

COPPER (III) *

WALL Hit Points	7,000
GATE Hit Points	14,000

PALISADES (III) *

WALL	
Build	15 s. / 10 W
Hit Points	3,500
GATE	
Hit Points	10,000

BRONZE (IV) *

WALL Hit Points	7,750
GATE Hit Points	16,000

EMPIRE EARTH
THE ART OF CONQUEST

MEDIEVAL (VI) *

WALL Hit Points	10,000
GATE Hit Points	20,000

IMPERIAL (VIII) *

WALL Hit Points	12,000
GATE Hit Points	24,000

CONCRETE (X) *

WALL Hit Points	15,000
GATE Hit Points	30,000

LASER (XIII) *

WALL Hit Points	18,000
GATE Hit Points	36,000

SPACE (XV) *

WALL Hit Points	18,000
GATE Hit Points	36,000

PRIEST TOWER (ALL) *
(BABYLON)

Source	Citizen
Build	50 s. / 60 G, 100 W

Hit Points	950 (I - II), 1140 (III - IV) 1330 (V - VI), 1520 (VII) 1710 (VIII - X), 1900 (XI - XIII), 2090 (XIV - XV)
Line of Sight	5
A/D	Priest / Tower
Attack	Priest / 25
Range (AE)	5

SPACE TURRET (XV) *

Source	Citizen
Build	75 s. / 100 G, 200 I
Hit Points	8,500
Line of Sight	10
A/D	Anti-Space / Tower
Attack	425 (Ls) / 4
Range (AE)	9

Wonders

All costs listed here are for Epoch III Wonders. At each higher epoch, resource costs increase by 50: 550 at Epoch IV, 600 at Epoch V, etc., until 1050 at Epoch XIV.

The Espionage HQ and Time Machine have the same price progression, beginning at Epochs XI and XIV, respectively.

COLISEUM *

Source	Citizen
Build	900 s. / 500 G, 500 S, 500 W
Hit Points	3,500
Line of Sight	5
A/D	NA / Building

ISHTAR GATES *

Source	Citizen
Build	900 s. / 500 I, 500 S, 500 W
Hit Points	3,500
Line of Sight	5
A/D	NA / Building

Wonder Stats

LIBRARY OF ALEXANDRIA *

Source	Citizen
Build	900 s. / 500 G, 500 S, 500 W
Hit Points	3,500
Line of Sight	5
A/D	NA / Building

PHAROS LIGHTHOUSE *

Source	Citizen
Build	900 s. / 500 I, 500 S, 500 W
Hit Points	3,500
Line of Sight	5
A/D	NA / Building

TEMPLE OF ZEUS *

Source	Citizen
Build	900 s. / 500 I, 500 S, 500 W
Hit Points	3,500
Line of Sight	5
A/D	NA / Building

TOWER OF BABYLON *

Source	Citizen
Build	900 s. / 500 G, 500 S, 500 W
Hit Points	3,500
Line of Sight	5
A/D	NA / Building

ESPIONAGE HEADQUARTERS (XI+)

Source	Citizen
Build	480 s. / 500 I, 500 S, 500 W
Hit Points	3,500
Line of Sight	5
A/D	NA / Building

TIME MACHINE (XIV+)

Source	Citizen
Build	900 s. / 2000 I, 1000 S, 2000 W
Hit Points	3,500
Line of Sight	5
A/D	NA / Building

ORBITAL SPACE STATION (XV)

Source	Citizen
Build	900 s. / 2000 G, 1000 I, 2000 W
Hit Points	3,500
Line of Sight	5
A/D	NA / Building

EMPIRE EARTH
THE ART OF CONQUEST

PRIMA'S OFFICIAL STRATEGY GUIDE

Armor

A7V (X) *

Source Tank Factory (PC 2)
Build 50 s. / 130 F, 130 I
Hit Points 405
Speed 12
Line of Sight 7
A/D Tank (German)
Attack 85 (Gn) / 4
Range (AE) 6
Armor 60 (Sh, Pr, Gn), 50 (Ar, Ls)

ANTI-MISSILE BATTERY (XIII) *

Source Tank Factory (PC 2)
Build 40 s. / 100 G, 100 I
Hit Points 200
Speed 12
Line of Sight 8
A/D Attacks ICBMs / Land AA
Attack 100 (Ls) / 3
Range (AE) 7
Armor 30 (Ar, Pr), 10 (Gn, Ls)

CARGO TRUCK (X)

Source Tank Factory
Build 50 s. / 100 F, 100 I
Hit Points 500

Speed 14
Line of Sight 7
A/D NA / Tank
Armor 60 (Sh, Gn, Ls), 10 (Ar, Pr)

CENTURION TANK (XIV) *

Source Tank Factory (PC 2)
Build 50 s. / 100 F, 100 I
Hit Points 750
Speed 16
Line of Sight 7
A/D Tank
Attack 145 (Gn) / 4
Range (AE) 6
Armor 75 (Sh,Gn), 50 (Ar), 60 (Pr), 82 (Ls)

DUNE PATROL (XV)

Source Tank Factory
Build 25 s. / 50 G, 100 I
Hit Points 400
Speed 28
Line of Sight 11
A/D Tank
Attack 35 (Gn) / 1
Range (AE) 9
Armor 25 (Sh, Ls), 20 (Pr, Gn), 15 (Ar)

FLAK HALFTRACK (X) *

Source Tank Factory
Build 45 s. / 100 F, 100 I
Hit Points 450
Speed 12
Line of Sight 8
A/D AA / Land AA
Attack 50 (Ms) / 2
Range (AE) 7
Armor 30 (Ar, Pr), 8 (Gn), 10 (Ls)

GLADIATOR TANK (XIII) *

Source Tank Factory (PC 2)
Build 50 s. / 100 F, 100 I
Hit Points 600
Speed 16
Line of Sight 7
A/D Tank
Attack 110 (Gn) / 4
Range (AE) 6
Armor 75 (Sh), 50 (Ar), 60 (Pr, Gn), 72 (Ls)

Armor Stats

HOVER TANK (XIV)

Source	Tank Factory
Build	50 s. / 100 F, 100 I
Hit Points	750
Speed	16
Line of Sight	7
A/D	Tank
Attack	145 (Gn) / 4
Range (AE)	6
Armor	60 (Sh, Pr), 50 (Ar), 76 (Gn), 82 (Ls)

LEOPARD TANK (AP) (XII) *

Source	Tank Factory (PC 2)
Build	50 s. / 130 F, 130 I
Hit Points	600
Speed	12
Line of Sight	7
A/D	Tank (German)
Attack	110 (Gn) / 4
Range (AE)	6
Armor	75 (Sh), 50 (Ar), 60 (Pr, Gn), 72 (Ls)

M1 TANK (HE) (XII) *

Source	Tank Factory (PC 2)
Build	50 s. / 100 F, 100 I
Hit Points	450
Speed	16
Line of Sight	7
A/D	Tank
Attack	110 (Gn) / 4
Range (AE)	6
Armor	75 (Sh), 50 (Ar), 60 (Pr, Gn), 72 (Ls)

MINING UNIT (XV)

Source	Tank Factory (PC 2)
Build	20 s. / 100 G, 100 I
Hit Points	500
Speed	20
Line of Sight	9
A/D	Tank
Attack	85 (Gn) / 3
Range (AE)	8
Armor	75 (Sh), 60 (Pr), 50 (Ar,Ls), 40 (Gn)

MKV TANK (HE) (X) *

Source	Tank Factory (PC 2)
Build	50 s. / 100 F, 100 I
Hit Points	315
Speed	14
Line of Sight	7
A/D	Tank
Attack	85 (Gn) / 4
Range (AE)	6
Armor	60 (Sh, Pr, Gn), 50 (Ar, Ls)

PANZER TANK (AP) (XI) *

Source	Tank Factory (PC 2)
Build	50 s. / 130 F, 130 I
Hit Points	500
Speed	12
Line of Sight	7
A/D	Tank (German)
Attack	100 (Gn) / 4
Range (AE)	6
Armor	60 (Sh, Pr, Gn), 50 (Ar, Ls)

SHERMAN TANK (HE) & FLAMETHROWER (XI) *

Source	Tank Factory (PC 2)
Build	50 s. / 100 F, 100 I
Hit Points	400
Speed	16
Line of Sight	7
A/D (HE)	Tank
(Flamethrower)	Modern Siege / Tank
Attack	100 (Gn) / 4
Range (AE)	6
Armor	60 (Sh, Pr, Gn), 50 (Ar, Ls)

SKYWATCHER AA (XIII) *

Source	Tank Factory
Build	45 s. / 100 F, 100 I
Hit Points	575
Speed	12
Line of Sight	8
A/D	AA / Land AA
Attack	100 (Ms) / 3
Range (AE)	7
Armor	30 (Ar, Pr), 10 (Gn, Ls)

STAFF CAR (XI)

Hit Points	315
Speed	14
Line of Sight	7
A/D	NA / Car
Armor	60 (Sh, Gn, Ls), 10 (Ar, Pr)

EMPIRE EARTH
THE ART OF CONQUEST

PRIMA'S OFFICIAL STRATEGY GUIDE

Siege & Aritillery

120MM AT GUN (XII) *

Source	Siege Factory
Build	40 s. / 55 G, 70 W
Hit Points	455
Speed	12
Line of Sight	7
A/D	AT Gun
Attack	44 (Gn) / 4
Range (AE)	6
Armor	10 (Gn), 25 (Ls)

57MM AT GUN (X) *

Source	Siege Factory
Build	40 s. / 55 G, 70 W
Hit Points	440
Speed	12
Line of Sight	7
A/D	AT Gun
Attack	35 (Gn) / 4
Range (AE)	6
Armor	8 (Gn)

ARTILLERY (X) *

Source	Siege Factory (PC 2)
Build	60 s. / 200 I, 200 W
Hit Points	225
Speed	10
Line of Sight	5
A/D	Siege / Artillery
Attack	175 (Gn) / 12
Armor	20 (Gn), 8 (Ms)

BALLISTA (VI) *

Source	Siege Factory (PC 2)
Build	50 s. / 160 G, 160 W
Hit Points	200
Speed	8
Line of Sight	7
A/D	Field Piece
Attack	75 (Ms) / 10
Armor	5 (Ar), 4 (Pr), 12 (Gn)

BASILISK (VII) *

Source	Siege Factory (PC 2)
Build	55 s. / 170 I, 170 W
Hit Points	360
Speed	10
Line of Sight	9
A/D	Siege
Attack	145 (Gn) / 8
Armor	13 (Ar, Gn), 10 (Ms)

BOMBARD (VIII) *

Source	Siege Factory (PC 2)
Build	60 s. / 200 I, 200 W
Hit Points	175
Speed	10
Line of Sight	5
A/D	Siege / Artillery
Attack	140 (Gn) / 12
Armor	20 (Gn), 8 (Ms)

BRONZE CANNON (IX) *

Source	Siege Factory (PC 2)
Build	55 s. / 175 I, 200 W
Hit Points	280
Speed	10
Line of Sight	9
A/D	Field Cannon
Attack	90 (Gn) / 10
Armor	10 (Ar), 43 (Gn)

CATAPULT (IV) *

Source	Siege Factory (PC 2)
Build	50 s. / 150 G, 150 W
Hit Points	160
Speed	8

Siege & Artillery Stats

Line of Sight	8
A/D	Siege
Attack	85 (Gn) / 8
Range (AE)	7
Armor	8 (Ar), 6 (Pr), 4 (Ms)

COLOSSUS ARTILLERY (XIII)*

Source	Siege Factory (PC 2)
Build	60 s. / 200 I, 200 W
Hit Points	300
Speed	10
Line of Sight	5
A/D	Siege / Artillery
Attack	200 (Gn) / 12
Armor	20 (Gn), 10 (Ms)

CULVERIN (VII) *

Source	Siege Factory (PC 2)
Build	55 s. / 175 I, 200 W
Hit Points	215
Speed	10
Line of Sight	8
A/D	Field Cannon
Attack	80 (Gn) / 10
Armor	11 (Ar), 43 (Gn)

HEAVY RAM (VI) *

Source	Siege Factory
Build	40 s. / 80 G, 80 W
Hit Points	325

Speed	10
Line of Sight	4
A/D	Ram
Attack	200 (Sh) / 4
Range (AE)	1.1

HEAVY SIEGE TOWER (VI) *

Source	Siege Factory
Build	30 s. / 25 G, 80 W
Hit Points	720
Speed	10
Line of Sight	3
A/D	Siege / Ram
Attack	(Sh) / 2

Transports units over walls

HERCULES AT GUN (XIV) *

Source	Siege Factory
Build	40 s. / 55 G, 70 W
Hit Points	680
Speed	16
Line of Sight	7
A/D	AT Gun
Attack	62 (Gn) / 4
Range (AE)	6
Armor	50 (Ar,Pr), 15 (Gn), 40 (Ls), 5 (Ms)

HOWITZER CANNON (X) *

Source	Siege Factory (PC 2)
Build	55 s. / 170 I, 170 W
Hit Points	500
Speed	10
Line of Sight	10
A/D	Modern Siege / Siege
Attack	250 (Gn) / 8
Armor	13 (Gn), 15 (Ms)

PALADIN CANNON (XIII) *

Source	Siege Factory (PC 2)
Build	55 s. / 170 I, 170 W
Hit Points	800
Speed	10
Line of Sight	11
A/D	Modern Siege / Siege
Attack	425 (Gn) / 8
Armor	50 (Ar, Pr), 18 (Gn), 25 (Ms)

RAM (IV) *

Source	Siege Factory
Build	40 s. / 80 G, 80 W
Hit Points	275
Speed	10
Line of Sight	4
A/D	Ram
Attack	125 (Sh) / 4
Range (AE)	0.7

EMPIRE EARTH
THE ART OF CONQUEST

PRIMA'S OFFICIAL STRATEGY GUIDE

SCORPION (IV)

Source	Siege Factory
Build	20 s. / 150 G, 150 W
Hit Points	180
Speed	8
Line of Sight	6
A/D	Field Piece
Attack	75 (Ms) / 10
Range (AE)	2 - 5 (0.5)
Armor	5 (Ar), 4 (Pr)

SERPENTINE (IX) *

Source	Siege Factory (PC 2)
Build	55 s. / 170 I, 170 W
Hit Points	405
Speed	10
Line of Sight	10
A/D	Siege
Attack	205 (Gn) / 8
Armor	13 (Gn), 10 (Ms)

SIEGE TOWER (IV) *

Source	Siege Factory
Build	30 s. / 25 G, 80 W
Hit Points	675
Speed	8
Line of Sight	3
A/D	Siege / Ram
Attack	(Sh) / 2

Transports units over walls

STONE THROWER (IV) *

Source	Siege Factory
Build	50 s. / 160 G, 160 W
Hit Points	180
Speed	8
Line of Sight	6
A/D	Field Piece
Attack	65 (Ms) / 10
Range (AE)	2 - 5 (1.2)
Armor	5 (Ar), 4 (Pr)

THOR AT GUN (XIII) *

Source	Siege Factory
Build	40 s. / 55 G, 70 W
Hit Points	550
Speed	16
Line of Sight	7
A/D	AT Gun
Attack	52 (Gn) / 4
Range (AE)	6
Armor	12 (Gn), 33 (Ls)

TREBUCHET (VI) *

Source	Siege Factory (PC 2)
Build	55 s. / 150 G, 150 W
Hit Points	215
Speed	10
Line of Sight	10
A/D	Siege
Attack	150 (Gn) / 8
Armor	13 (Ar), 4 (Pr)
	17 (Gn), 4 (Ms)

TROJAN HORSE (IV)

Hit Points	1,500
Speed	8
Line of Sight	3
A/D	Siege / Ram
Attack	(Sh) / 2

UPPER AGE		DARK AGE		RENAISSANCE		INDUSTRIAL AGE		INFORMATION
2000 BC	500 BC	0 AD	900 AD	1000 AD	1500 AD	1700 AD	1900 AD	2000 AD
BRONZE AGE			MIDDLE AGES		IMPERIAL AGE		ATOMIC AGE	

Cyber Stats

Cybers

All Cybers count 2 pop units.

APOLLO (XIII) *

Source	Cyber Lab
Build	50 s. / 180 F, 180 I
Hit Points	2,500
Speed	16
Line of Sight	8
A/D	NA / Apollo
Attack	(Ls) / 2
Range (AE)	7
Armor	50 (Ar, Pr), 20 (Ms)

Flying; Diffraction Shield; Repairs other Cybers; Ion Pulse

ARES (XIII) *

Source	Cyber Factory
Build	60 s. / 200 F, 200 G
Hit Points	1,200
Speed	18
Line of Sight	6
A/D	Ares
Attack	65 (Ls) / 1
Range (AE)	5
Armor	50 (Ar, Pr), 30 (Gn), 20 (Ls), 14 (Ms)

Flying; Self-Repair

ARES II (XIV) *

Source	Cyber Factory
Build	60 s. / 200 F, 200 G
Hit Points	1,500
Speed	18
Line of Sight	7
A/D	Ares
Attack	75 (Ls) / 1
Range (AE)	6
Armor	50(Ar,Pr), 30(Gn), 27(Ls), 14(Ms)

Flying; Self-Repair

COMMAND UNIT (XIII) (GRIGOR II)

Hit Points	6,000
Speed	12
Line of Sight	8
A/D	Hyperion
Attack	200 (Ms) / 2
Range (AE)	9
Armor	50 (Ar, Pr, Gn), 75 (Ls)

FURIES (XIII) *

Source	Cyber Lab
Build	70 s. / 180 F, 180 I
Hit Points	900
Speed	18
Line of Sight	3

A/D	Other / Furies
Attack	150 (Sh) / 2
Range (AE)	0.6
Armor	50 (Ar, Pr)

Self-Destruct

HADES (XIV) *

Source	Cyber Lab
Build	50 s. / 160 F, 160 I
Hit Points	1,700
Speed	16
Line of Sight	9
A/D	Hades
Range (AE)	8
Armor	50 (Ar, Pr), 20 (Gn, Ls)

Teleport; Time Warp; Nano Virus

HYPERION (XIII) *

Source	Cyber Factory
Build	60 s. / 230 F, 230 G
Hit Points	2,200
Speed	16
Line of Sight	7
A/D	Hyperion
Attack	105 (Ls) / 2
Range (AE)	6
Armor	50(Ar,Pr), 35(Gn), 46(Ls), 19(Ms)

Walk underwater and over cliffs

| COPPER AGE | | DARK AGE | | RENAISSANCE | | INDUSTRIAL AGE |
| STONE AGE | BRONZE AGE | MIDDLE AGES | | IMPERIAL AGE | | ATOMIC A |

00 BC 5000 BC 2000 BC 500 BC 0AD 900 AD 1800 AD 1500 AD 1700 AD 1900 AD

EMPIRE EARTH
THE ART OF CONQUEST

HYPERION II (XIV) *

Source	Cyber Factory
Build	60 s. / 230 F, 230 G
Hit Points	2,500
Speed	16
Line of Sight	7
A/D	Hyperion
Attack	130 (Ls) / 2
Range (AE)	6
Armor	50(Ar,Pr), 36(Gn), 59(Ls), 26(Ms)

Walk underwater and over cliffs

MINOTAUR (XIII) *

Source	Cyber Factory
Build	50 s. / 180 F, 180 G
Hit Points	1,500
Speed	16
Line of Sight	8
A/D	Minotaur
Attack	72 (Ms) / 3
Range (AE)	7
Armor	50(Ar,Pr), 30(Gn), 40(Ls), 10(Ms)

MINOTAUR II (XIV) *

Source	Cyber Factory
Build	50 s. / 180 F, 180 G
Hit Points	1,800
Speed	16
Line of Sight	8
A/D	Minotaur
Attack	82 (Ms) / 3
Range (AE)	7
Armor	50(Ar,Pr), 42(Gn), 48(Ls), 1 (Ms)

PANDORA (XIII) *

Source	Cyber Factory
Build	50 s. / 180 F, 180 G
Hit Points	550
Speed	14
Line of Sight	7
A/D	Pandora
Attack	67 (Gn) / 3
Range (AE)	6 (1.5)
Armor	50 (Ar, Pr), 60 (Gn), 66 (Ls), 35 (Ms)

PANDORA II (XIV) *

Source	Cyber Factory
Build	50 s. / 180 F, 180 G
Hit Points	660
Speed	14
Line of Sight	8
A/D	Pandora
Attack	80 (Gn) / 3
Range (AE)	7 (1.5)
Armor	50(Ar,Pr), 65(Gn), 78(Ls), 35(Ms)

POSEIDON (XIV) *

Source	Cyber Lab
Build	50 s. / 240 F, 240 I
Hit Points	3,000
Speed	14
Line of Sight	8
A/D	Poseidon
Range (AE)	8
Armor	50 (Ar, Pr), 20 (Gn, Ls)

Walk underwater; Refractive Cloak; Assimilate other Cybers

TEMPEST (XIII) *

Source	Cyber Lab
Build	50 s. / 200 F, 200 I
Hit Points	800
Speed	19
Line of Sight	8
A/D	Sniper / Tempest
Attack	115 (Ls) / 2
Range (AE)	0.9
Armor	50(Ar,Pr), 30(Gn), 45(Ls), 2(Ms)

Anti-Matter Storm; Resonator

ZEUS (XIV) *

Source	Cyber Factory
Build	70 s. / 280 F, 280 G
Hit Points	2,300
Speed	16
Line of Sight	7
A/D	Zeus
Attack	350 (Ms) / 5
Range (AE)	6
Armor	50(Ar,Pr), 35(Gn), 40(Ls), 1 (Ms)

Sea Stats

Sea

Battleships

BATTLESHIP - COPPER (III)*

Source	Dock
Build	100 s. / 250 G, 250 W
Hit Points	900
Speed	10
Line of Sight	6
A/D	Battleship
Attack	62 (Ms) / 4
Range (AE)	5 (1)
Armor	6 (Ar, Pr)

BATTLESHIP - BRONZE (IV)*

Source	Dock
Build	100 s. / 250 G, 250 W
Hit Points	1,180
Speed	10
Line of Sight	6
A/D	Battleship
Attack	72 (Ms) / 4
Range (AE)	6 (1)
Armor	7 (Ar, Pr)

BATTLESHIP - BYZANT. (V)*

Source	Dock
Build	100 s. / 250 G, 250 W
Hit Points	1,560
Speed	10
Line of Sight	7
A/D	Battleship
Attack	90 (Ms) / 4
Range (AE)	7 (1)
Armor	8 (Ar, Pr)

BATTLESHIP - MID. AGES (VI) *

Source	Dock
Build	100 s. / 250 G, 250 W
Hit Points	2,025
Speed	10
Line of Sight	8
A/D	Battleship
Attack	108 (Ms) / 4
Range (AE)	7 (1)
Armor	10 (Ar, Pr, Gn)

BATTLESHIP - RENAIS. (VII) *

Source	Dock
Build	100 s. / 250 G, 250 W
Hit Points	2,450
Speed	11
Line of Sight	8
A/D	Battleship
Attack	150 (Ms) / 4
Range (AE)	7 (1)
Armor	15 (Ar, Pr), 18 (Gn)

BATTLESHIP - IMPER. (VIII)*

Source	Dock
Build	100 s. / 250 G, 250 W
Hit Points	3,060
Speed	11
Line of Sight	9
A/D	Destroyer / Ship
Attack	175 (Ms) / 4
Range (AE)	8 (1)
Armor	18 (Ar, Pr), 20 (Gn)

BATTLESHIP - AGINCOURT (IX)

Source	Dock
Build	100 s. / 250 G, 250 W
Hit Points	4,525
Speed	11
Line of Sight	9
A/D	Destroyer / Battleship
Attack	200 (Ms) / 4
Range (AE)	8 (1)
Armor	20 (Ar, Pr), 22 (Gn)

BATTLESHIP - ROYAL (IX) *

Source	Dock
Build	100 s. / 250 G, 250 W
Hit Points	4,525
Speed	11
Line of Sight	9
A/D	Battleship
Attack	200 (Ms) / 4
Range (AE)	8 (1)
Armor	20 (Ar, Pr), 22 (Gn)

BATTLESHIP - DREADNOUGHT (X) *

Source	Dock
Build	100 s. / 250 G, 250 W
Hit Points	5,750
Speed	12
Line of Sight	9
A/D	Battleship
Attack	230 (Ms) / 4
Range (AE)	8 (1)
Armor	20 (Ar, Pr), 25 (Gn)

EMPIRE EARTH
THE ART OF CONQUEST

BATTLESHIP - BISMARCK (XI) *

Source	Dock
Build	100 s. / 250 G, 250 W
Hit Points	6,625
Speed	12
Line of Sight	9
A/D	Battleship
Attack	276 (Ms) / 4
Range (AE)	8 (1)
Armor	20(Ar, Pr, Ls),30(Gn)

BATTLESHIP - LEVIATH. (XIII)*

Source	Dock
Build	100 s. / 250 G, 250 W
Hit Points	8,600
Speed	12
Line of Sight	9
A/D	Battleship
Attack	380 (Ms) / 4
Range (AE)	8 (1)
Armor	20(Ar, Pr),30(Gn, Ls)*

Carriers

CARRIER - ENTERPRISE (XI)*

Source	Navy Yard (PC2)
Build	120 s. / 300 G, 300 W
Hit Points	6,000
Speed (Capacity)	10 (15)
Line of Sight	4
A/D	AA / Aircraft Carrier
Armor	20 (Ar, Pr, Gn, Ls)

CARRIER - JAPANESE FLATTOP (XI)

Source	Navy Yard (PC2)
Build	100 s. / 300 G, 300 W
Hit Points	6,000
Speed (Capacity)	10 (15)
Line of Sight	4
A/D	NA / Aircraft Carrier
Armor	20 (Ar, Pr, Gn, Ls)

CARRIER - NEXUS (XIII)

Source	Navy Yard (PC 2)
Build	140 s. / 300 G, 300 W
Hit Points	8,000
Speed	12
Line of Sight	4
A/D	AA / Aircraft Carrier
Armor	50(Ar, Pr),20(Gn, Ls)

CATAPULT SHIP (VI)

Source	Dock
Build	40 s. / 250 G, 250 W
Hit Points	1,460
Speed	10
Line of Sight	9
A/D	Siege / Ship
Attack	150 (Ms) / 10
Range (AE)	8 (1.2)

Cruisers

CRUISER - GUNBOAT (VIII)*

Source	Dock
Build	72 s. / 150 G, 150 W
Hit Points	1,400
Speed	14
Line of Sight	8
A/D	Air Superiority / Ship
Attack	30 (Ms) / 2
Range (AE)	7
Armor	15 (Ar, Pr, Gn)

CRUISER - DARDO (X) *

Source	Dock
Build	72 s. / 150 G, 150 W
Hit Points	2,300
Speed	14
Line of Sight	9
A/D	Air Superiority / Ship
Attack	70 (Ms) / 2
Range (AE)	8
Armor	20 (Ar, Pr), 25 (Gn)

CRUISER - SAGITTAR. (XIII)*

Source	Dock
Build	72 s. / 150 G, 150 W
Hit Points	3,800
Speed	14
Line of Sight	9
A/D	Air Superiority / Ship
Attack	110 (Ms) / 2
Range (AE)	8
Armor	30 (Ar, Pr, Gn, Ls)

Fishing Boats

FISHING RAFT (II) *

Source	Dock
Build	30 s. / 50 W
Hit Points	120
Speed	13
Line of Sight	4
A/D	Fishing Boat / Ship
Attack	1 (Ms)
Range (AE)	0.5

FISHING BOAT - BRONZE (IV)*

Source	Dock
Build	30 s. / 50 W
Hit Points	280
Speed	14
Line of Sight	4
A/D	Fishing Boat / Ship
Attack	1 (Ms)
Range (AE)	0.5

FISHING BOAT - IMPER. (VIII) *

Source	Dock
Build	30 s. / 50 W
Hit Points	420
Speed	15
Line of Sight	4
A/D	Fishing Boat / Ship
Attack	1 (Ms)
Range (AE)	0.5

FISHING BOAT - TRAWL. (XI) *

Source	Dock
Build	30 s. / 50 W
Hit Points	700
Speed	16
Line of Sight	4
A/D	Fishing Boat / Ship
Attack	1 (Ms)
Range (AE)	0.5

FISHING BOAT - DIGIT. (XIII) *

Source	Dock
Build	30 s. / 50 W
Hit Points	900
Speed	16
Line of Sight	3
A/D	Fishing Boat / Ship
Attack	1 (Ms)
Range (AE)	0.5

Frigates

FRIGATE - COPPER (III) *

Source	Dock
Build	72 s. / 125 I, 125 W
Hit Points	240
Speed	15
Line of Sight	8
A/D	Destroyer / Ship
Attack	15 (Ms) / 2
Range (AE)	5
Armor	6 (Ar, Pr)

Sea Stats

FRIGATE - BRONZE (IV) *

Source	Dock
Build	72 s. / 125 I, 125 W
Hit Points	310
Speed	16
Line of Sight	8
A/D	Destroyer / Ship
Attack	18 (Ms) / 2
Range (AE)	5
Armor	7 (Ar, Pr)

FRIGATE - BYZANTINE (V) *

Source	Dock
Build	72 s. / 125 I, 125 W
Hit Points	400
Speed	16
Line of Sight	9
A/D	Destroyer / Ship
Attack	21 (Ms) / 2
Range (AE)	6
Armor	8 (Ar, Pr)

FRIGATE - MIDDLE AGES (VI) *

Source	Dock
Build	72 s. / 125 I, 125 W
Hit Points	540
Speed	16
Line of Sight	10
A/D	Destroyer / Ship
Attack	25 (Ms) / 2
Range (AE)	7
Armor	10 (Ar, Pr, Gn)

EMPIRE EARTH
THE ART OF CONQUEST

PRIMA'S OFFICIAL STRATEGY GUIDE

FRIGATE - RENAISSANCE (VII) *

Source	Dock
Build	72 s. / 125 l, 125 W
Hit Points	625
Speed	17
Line of Sight	9
A/D	Destroyer / Ship
Attack	33 (Ms) / 2
Range (AE)	7
Armor	15 (Ar, Pr), 18 (Gn)

FRIGATE - IMPERIAL (VIII) *

Source	Dock
Build	72 s. / 125 l, 125 W
Hit Points	750
Speed	17
Line of Sight	9
A/D	Destroyer / Ship
Attack	38 (Ms) / 2
Range (AE)	7
Armor	18 (Ar, Pr), 20 (Gn)

FRIGATE - ROYAL (IX) *

Source	Dock
Build	72 s. / 125 l, 125 W
Hit Points	1,060
Speed	17
Line of Sight	10
A/D	Destroyer / Ship
Attack	51 (Ms) / 2
Range (AE)	8
Armor	20 (Ar, Pr), 22 (Gn)

FRIGATE - GOOD HOPE (X)*

Source	Dock
Build	72 s. / 125 l, 125 W
Hit Points	1,350
Speed	17
Line of Sight	11
A/D	Destroyer / Ship
Attack	55 (Ms) / 2
Range (AE)	8
Armor	20 (Ar, Pr), 25 (Gn)

FRIGATE - WARRINGTON (XI) *

Source	Dock
Build	72 s. / 125 l, 125 W
Hit Points	1,600
Speed	17
Line of Sight	10
A/D	Destroyer / Ship
Attack	68 (Ms) / 2
Range (AE)	8
Armor	20(Ar, Pr, Ls),30(Gn)

FRIGATE - JUGGERNAUT (XIII) *

Source	Dock
Build	72 s. / 125 l, 125 W
Hit Points	2,100
Speed	17
Line of Sight	11
A/D	Destroyer / Ship
Attack	100 (Ms) / 2
Range (AE)	8
Armor	20(Ar, Pr),30(Gn, Ls)

Galleys & Galleons

GALLEY - COPPER (III) *

Source	Dock
Build	72 s. / 125 l, 125 W
Hit Points	260
Speed	12
Line of Sight	6
A/D	Galley
Attack	6 (Ms) / 2
Range (AE)	5

GALLEY - BRONZE (IV) *

Source	Dock
Build	72 s. / 125 l, 125 W
Hit Points	335
Speed	14
Line of Sight	6
A/D	Galley
Attack	8 (Ms) / 2
Range (AE)	5

GALLEY - BYZANTINE (V) *

Source	Dock
Build	72 s. / 125 l, 125 W
Hit Points	440
Speed	14
Line of Sight	7
A/D	Galley
Attack	9 (Ms) / 2
Range (AE)	6

Sea Stats

GALLEY - MIDDLE AGES (VI)*

Source	Dock
Build	72 s. / 125 l, 125 W
Hit Points	575
Speed	14
Line of Sight	8
A/D	Galley
Attack	11 (Ms) / 2
Range (AE)	7

GALLEON - RENAÏSS. (VII)*

Source	Dock
Build	72 s. / 125 l, 125 W
Hit Points	675
Speed	15
Line of Sight	8
A/D	Galley
Attack	15 (Ms) / 2
Range (AE)	7

GALLEON - IMPERIAL (VIII)*

Source	Dock
Build	72 s. / 125 l, 125 W
Hit Points	825
Speed	15
Line of Sight	8
A/D	Galley
Attack	18 (Ms) / 2
Range (AE)	7

GALLEON - ROYAL (IX) *

Source	Dock
Build	72 s. / 125 l, 125 W
Hit Points	1,100
Speed	15
Line of Sight	9
A/D	Galley
Attack	24 (Ms) / 2
Range (AE)	8

GOLDEN HIND (VII)

Hit Points	1,500
Speed	19
Line of Sight	9
A/D	Destroyer / Ship
Attack	43 (Ms) / 2
Range (AE)	9 (1)
Armor	15 (Ar, Pr), 18 (Gn)

Submarines

SUB - U-BOAT (X) *

Source	Navy Yard
Build	80 s. / 190 l, 190 W
Hit Points	1,000
Speed	13
Line of Sight	8
A/D	Sub
Attack	130 (Ms) / 6
Range (AE)	7

SUB - NAUTILUS (XII) *

Source	Navy Yard
Build	80 s. / 190 l, 190 W
Hit Points	1,350
Speed	13
Line of Sight	9
A/D	Sub
Attack	200 (Ms) / 6
Range (AE)	8

SUB - TRIDENT (XII) *

Source	Navy Yard
Build	120 s. / 600 G, 600 l
Hit Points	800
Speed	13
Line of Sight	3
A/D	BM (Nuclear) Sub
Attack	800 (Ms) / 15
Range (AE)	24 (1)

SUB - HAMMERHEAD (XIV)*

Source	Navy Yard
Build	80 s. / 190 l, 190 W
Hit Points	1,900
Speed	13
Line of Sight	9
A/D	Sub
Attack	250 (Ms) / 6
Range (AE)	8
Armor	50 (Ar, Pr)

EMPIRE EARTH
THE ART OF CONQUEST

SUB - TRITON (XIV) *

Source	Navy Yard
Build	120 s. / 600 G, 600 I
Hit Points	1,000
Speed	13
Line of Sight	3
A/D	BM (Nuclear) Sub
Attack	1000 (Ms) / 15
Range (AE)	24 (1)
Armor	50 (Ar, Pr)

Transports

TRANSPORT RAFT (II) *

Source	Dock
Build	50 s. / 250 W
Hit Points	120
Speed	12 (20)
Line of Sight	4
A/D	NA / Ship
Armor	4 (Ar, Pr)

TRANSPORT - COPPER (III)*

Source	Dock
Build	50 s. / 250 W
Hit Points	200
Speed	14 (20)
Line of Sight	4
A/D	NA / Ship
Armor	6 (Ar, Pr)

TRANSPORT - BRONZE (IV)*

Source	Dock
Build	50 s. / 250 W
Hit Points	360
Speed (Capacity)	13 (24)
Line of Sight	4
A/D	NA / Ship
Armor	7 (Ar, Pr)

TRANSPORT - IMPER. (VIII)*

Source	Dock
Build	50 s. / 250 W
Hit Points	530
Speed (Capacity)	14 (28)
Line of Sight	5
A/D	NA / Ship
Armor	15 (Ar, Pr, Gn)

TRANSPORT - ATOMIC (X)*

Source	Dock
Build	50 s. / 250 W
Hit Points	750
Speed (Capacity)	14 (28)
Line of Sight	5
A/D	NA / Ship
Armor	20 (Ar, Pr), 25 (Gn)

TRANSPORT - LST (XI)

Source	Dock
Build	50 s. / 50 G, 100 I, 100 W
Hit Points	750
Speed (Capacity)	14 (14)
Line of Sight	5
A/D	NA / Ship
Armor	20 (Ar, Pr), 25 (Gn)

TRANSPORT - GARGANTUA (XIII) *

Source	Dock
Build	50 s. / 250 W
Hit Points	920
Speed (Capacity)	8 (28)
Line of Sight	5
A/D	NA / Ship
Armor	20 (Ar, Pr), 30 (Gn, Ls)

WAR RAFT (II) *

Source	Dock
Build	72 s. / 125 I, 125 W
Hit Points	220
Speed	15
Line of Sight	5
A/D	Destroyer / Ship
Attack	12 (Ms) / 3
Range (AE)	3
Armor	4 (Ar, Pr

Air Stats

Air

Balloons

HOT AIR BALLOON (IX) *

Source	Town Center
Build	45 s. / 100 G, 100 W
Hit Points	500
Speed	12
Line of Sight	9
A/D	Hover
Range (AE)	0.5

OBSERVATION BALLOON (X) *

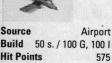

Source	Town Center
Build	45 s. / 100 G, 100 W
Hit Points	700
Speed	16
Line of Sight	11
A/D	Hover
Range (AE)	0.5

Bombers

A-10 ANTI-TANK (XII) *

Source	Airport
Build	50 s. / 100 G, 100 I
Hit Points	575
Speed	22
Line of Sight	8
A/D	AT Air / Aircraft
Attack	14 (Ms) / 0.3
Range (AE)	6

ALBATROS D.V. FIGHTER (X)

Source	Airport
Build	50 s. / 100 G, 100 I
Hit Points	425
Speed	20
Line of Sight	7
A/D	Air Superiority / Aircraft
Attack	17 (Ms) / 0.5
Range (AE)	6

B-122 WYVERN BOMBER (XIII) *

Source	Airport
Build	90 s. / 200 G, 200 I
Hit Points	1,700
Speed	20
Line of Sight	8
A/D	Bomber
Attack	175 (Ms) / 0.5
Range (AE)	5 (1.5)
Armor	50 (Ar, Pr)

B-17 BOMBER (XI) *

Source	Airport
Build	90 s. / 200 G, 200 I
Hit Points	1,200
Speed	19
Line of Sight	8
A/D	Bomber
Attack	135 (Ms) / 0.5
Range (AE)	5 (1.5)

B-2 BOMBER (XII) *

Source	Airport
Build	90 s. / 200 G, 200 I
Hit Points	1,400
Speed	20
Line of Sight	8
A/D	Bomber
Attack	150 (Ms) / 0.5
Range (AE)	5 (1.5)

B-29 BOMBER (XI) *

Source	Airport
Build	150 s. / 700 G, 700 I
Hit Points	750
Speed	18
Line of Sight	8
A/D	Atomic Bomber
Attack	2200 (Sh) / 0.5
Range (AE)	5 (3.5)

B-52 BOMBER (XII) *

Source	Airport
Build	150 s. / 700 G, 700 I
Hit Points	950
Speed	19
Line of Sight	8
A/D	Atomic Bomber
Attack	2800 (Sh) / 0.5
Range (AE)	5 (3.5)

EMPIRE EARTH
THE ART OF CONQUEST

CATALINA (XI)

Source	Navy Yard
Build	60 s. / 100 G, 200 I
Hit Points	1,000
Speed	18
Line of Sight	7
A/D	Anti-Sea / Bomber
Attack	250 (Ms) / 0.5
Range (AE)	6 (1.5)

GOTHA BOMBER (X) *

Source	Airport
Build	90 s. / 200 G, 200 I
Hit Points	850
Speed	18
Line of Sight	8
A/D	Bomber
Attack	100 (Ms) / 0.5
Range (AE)	5 (1.5)

HEINKEL BOMBER (XI) *

Source	Airport
Build	90 s. / 200 G, 200 I
Hit Points	1,000
Speed	18
Line of Sight	8
A/D	Bomber
Attack	120 (Ms) / 0.5
Range (AE)	5 (1.5)

ME110 BOMBER (XI)

Source	Airport
Build	90 s. / 200 G, 200 I
Hit Points	1,300
Speed	19
Line of Sight	8
A/D	Bomber
Attack	135 (Ms) / 0.5
Range (AE)	5 (1.5)

TITAN BOMBER (XIII) *

Source	Airport
Build	150 s. / 700 G, 700 I
Hit Points	1,100
Speed	20
Line of Sight	8
A/D	Atomic Bomber
Attack	3300 (Sh) / 0.5
Range (AE)	5 (3.5)
Armor	50 (Ar, Pr)

TYPHOON ANTI-TANK (XI) *

Source	Airport
Build	50 s. / 100 G, 100 I
Hit Points	450
Speed	20
Line of Sight	7
A/D	AT Air / Aircraft
Attack	11 (Ms) / 0.3
Range (AE)	6

Fighter/Bombers

AVENGER FIGHTER/BOMBER (XIII) *

Source	Aircraft Carrier
Build	25 s. / 60 G, 60 I
Hit Points	740
Speed	23
Line of Sight	7
A/D	Carrier AC / Aircraft
Attack	120 (Ms) / 4
Range (AE)	6
Armor	50 (Ar, Pr)

CORSAIR FIGHTER/BOMBER (XI) *

Source	Aircraft Carrier
Build	25 s. / 60 G, 60 I
Hit Points	496
Speed	22
Line of Sight	7
A/D	Carrier AC / Aircraft
Attack	12 (Ms) / 0.5
Range (AE)	6

F-117 FIGHTER/BOMBER (XII) *

Source	Airport
Build	50 s. / 100 G, 100 I
Hit Points	625
Speed	22
Line of Sight	7
A/D	Strafer / Aircraft
Attack	190 (Ms) / 4
Range (AE)	6

Air Stats

F-14
FIGHTER/BOMBER (XII) *

Source	Aircraft Carrier
Build	25 s. / 60 G, 60 I
Hit Points	610
Speed	22
Line of Sight	7
A/D	Carrier AC / Aircraft
Attack	105 (Ms) / 4
Range (AE)	6

F-80 FIGHTER/BOMBER (XI)

Source	Airport
Build	50 s. / 100 G, 100 I
Hit Points	500
Speed	21
Line of Sight	7
A/D	Strafer / Aircraft
Attack	26 (Ms) / 0.5
Range (AE)	6

FOKKER
FIGHTER/BOMB. (X) *

Source	Airport
Build	50 s. / 100 G, 100 I
Hit Points	350
Speed	20
Line of Sight	7
A/D	Strafer / Aircraft
Attack	18 (Ms) / 0.5
Range (AE)	6

ME109
FIGHTER/BOMB. (XI) *

Source	Airport
Build	50 s. / 100 G, 100 I
Hit Points	425
Speed	20
Line of Sight	7
A/D	Strafer / Aircraft
Attack	22 (Ms) / 0.5
Range (AE)	6

ME262
FIGHTER/BOMB. (XI) *

Source	Airport
Build	50 s. / 100 G, 100 I
Hit Points	500
Speed	21
Line of Sight	7
A/D	Strafer / Aircraft
Attack	26 (Ms) / 0.5
Range (AE)	6

P-38 LIGHTNING (XI)

Source	Airport
Build	50 s. / 100 G, 100 I
Hit Points	500
Speed	22
Line of Sight	7
A/D	Strafer / Aircraft
Attack	26 (Ms) / 0.5
Range (AE)	6

PHOENIX
FIGHTER/BOMBER (XIV) *

Source	Airport
Build	50 s. / 100 G, 100 I
Hit Points	860
Speed	24
Line of Sight	7
A/D	Strafer / Aircraft
Attack	265 (Ms) / 4
Range (AE)	6
Armor	50 (Ar, Pr)

SOPWITH TRIPLANE (X)

Source	Airport
Build	50 s. / 100 G, 100 I
Hit Points	350
Speed	20
Line of Sight	7
A/D	Strafer / Aircraft
Attack	18 (Ms) / 0.5
Range (AE)	6

TALON
FIGHTER/BOMBER (XIII) *

Source	Airport
Build	50 s. / 100 G, 100 I
Hit Points	740
Speed	23
Line of Sight	7
A/D	Strafer / Aircraft
Attack	227 (Ms) / 4
Range (AE)	6
Armor	50 (Ar, Pr)

EMPIRE EARTH
THE ART OF CONQUEST

PRIMA'S OFFICIAL STRATEGY GUIDE

ZERO - STRAFE (XI)

Source	Airport
Build	50 s. / 100 G, 100 I
Hit Points	425
Speed	20
Line of Sight	7
A/D	Strafer / Aircraft
Attack	22 (Ms) / 0.5
Range (AE)	6

Fighters

DAUNTLESS - CARRIER (XI)

Source	Aircraft Carrier
Build	25 s. / 60 G, 60 I
Hit Points	496
Speed	22
Line of Sight	7
A/D	Carrier AC / Aircraft
Attack	12 (Ms) / 0.5
Range (AE)	6

F-15 FIGHTER (XII) *

Source	Airport
Build	50 s. / 100 G, 100 I
Hit Points	660
Speed	22
Line of Sight	7
A/D	Air Superiority / Aircraft
Attack	236 (Ms) / 4
Range (AE)	6

F-86 FIGHTER (XI)

Source	Airport
Build	50 s. / 100 G, 100 I
Hit Points	500
Speed	23
Line of Sight	7
A/D	Air Superiority / Aircraft
Attack	26 (Ms) / 0.5
Range (AE)	6

FW190 FIGHTER (XI)

Source	Airport
Build	50 s. / 100 G, 100 I
Hit Points	502
Speed	20
Line of Sight	7
A/D	Air Superiority / Aircraft
Attack	23 (Ms) / 0.5
Range (AE)	6

JACKAL FIGHTER (XIII) *

Source	Airport
Build	50 s. / 100 G, 100 I
Hit Points	796
Speed	23
Line of Sight	7
A/D	Air Superiority / Aircraft
Attack	285 (Ms) / 4
Range (AE)	6
Armor	50 (Ar, Pr)

MIG-15 FIGHTER (XI)

Source	Airport
Build	50 s. / 100 G, 100 I
Hit Points	500
Speed	21
Line of Sight	7
A/D	Air Superiority / Aircraft
Attack	26 (Ms) / 0.5
Range (AE)	6

NEBULA FIGHTER (XIV) *

Source	Airport
Build	50 s. / 100 G, 100 I
Hit Points	941
Speed	24
Line of Sight	7
A/D	Air Superiority / Aircraft
Attack	338 (Ms) / 4
Range (AE)	6
Armor	50 (Ar, Pr)

P-51 FIGHTER (XI) *

Source	Airport
Build	50 s. / 100 G, 100 I
Hit Points	550
Speed	21
Line of Sight	7
A/D	Air Superiority / Aircraft
Attack	26 (Ms) / 0.5
Range (AE)	6

Air Stats

RED BARON (X)

Source	His plane when flying
Hit Points	5,000
Speed	24
Line of Sight	10
A/D	Red Baron / Aircraft
Attack	50 (Ms) / 0.6
Range (AE)	9
Armor	15 (Ms)

SOPWITH FIGHTER (X) *

Source	Airport
Build	50 s. / 100 G, 100 I
Hit Points	425
Speed	20
Line of Sight	7
A/D	Air Superiority / Aircraft
Attack	17 (Ms) / 0.5
Range (AE)	6

SPITFIRE FIGHTER (XI) *

Source	Airport
Build	50 s. / 100 G, 100 I
Hit Points	502
Speed	20
Line of Sight	7
A/D	Air Superiority / Aircraft
Attack	23 (Ms) / 0.5
Range (AE)	6

ZERO - CARRIER (XI)

Source	Aircraft Carrier
Build	25 s. / 60 G, 60 I
Hit Points	496
Speed	22
Line of Sight	7
A/D	Carrier AC / Aircraft
Attack	12 (Ms) / 0.5
Range (AE)	6

Transport Aircraft

C-47 CARGO PLANE (XI)

Hit Points	600
Speed	22
Line of Sight	7
A/D	Other / Aircraft
Range (AE)	6

PARATROOPER PLANE (X) (ITALY) *

Source	Airport
Build	80 s. / 320 F, 100 G, 320 I
Hit Points	1000
Speed (Capacity)	18 (8)
Line of Sight	7
A/D	NA / Bomber

Helicopters

HELICOPTER ANTI-TANK (XII) *

Source	Airport
Build	65 s. / 200 G, 200 I
Hit Points	850
Speed	21
Line of Sight	6
A/D	Helicopter
Attack	75 (Ms) / 4
Range (AE)	5
Armor	13 (Gn, Ls)

HELICOPTER GUNSHIP (XII) *

Source	Airport
Build	65 s. / 100 G, 100 I
Hit Points	450
Speed	21
Line of Sight	6
A/D	Helicopter
Attack	25 (Gn) / 0.5
Range (AE)	5
Armor	15 (Gn, Ls)

HELICOPTER TRANSPORT (XII) *

Source	Airport
Build	65 s. / 75 G, 75 I
Hit Points	550
Speed	16 (10)
Line of Sight	3
A/D	NA / Helicopter
Armor	15 (Gn)

EMPIRE EARTH
THE ART OF CONQUEST

PRIMA'S OFFICIAL STRATEGY GUIDE

PEGASUS TRANSPORT (XIII) *

Source	Airport
Build	65 s. / 75 G, 75 I
Hit Points	660
Speed	20 (20)
Line of Sight	5
A/D	NA / Helicopter
Armor	50 (Ar, Pr), 15 (Gn)

REAPER GUNSHIP (XIII) *

Source	Airport
Build	65 s. / 100 G, 100 I
Hit Points	600
Speed	22
Line of Sight	6
A/D	Helicopter
Attack	35 (Gn) / 0.8
Range (AE)	5
Armor	50 (Ar, Pr), 15 (Gn), 19 (Ls)

SEA KING (XII) *

Source	Navy Yard or Airport
Build	60 s. / 100 G, 100 I
Hit Points	315
Speed	21
Line of Sight	5
A/D	Anti-Sea / Helicopter
Attack	400 (Ms) / 5
Range (AE)	1 (1.5)

SEA KING II (XIII) *

Source	Navy Yard or Airport
Build	60 s. / 100 G, 100 I
Hit Points	450
Speed	22
Line of Sight	6
A/D	Anti-Sea / Helicopter
Attack	475 (Ms) / 5
Range (AE)	2 (1.5)
Armor	50 (Ar, Pr)

SPECTRE AT HELICOPTER (XIII) *

Source	Airport
Build	65 s. / 200 G, 200 I
Hit Points	1,100
Speed	22
Line of Sight	6
A/D	Helicopter
Attack	100 (Ms) / 4
Range (AE)	5
Armor	50 (Ar, Pr), 15 (Gn, Ls)

UFO (XIV)

Hit Points	1,100
Speed	22
Line of Sight	6
A/D	Hover
Attack	100 (Ls) / 4
Range (AE)	5
Armor	50(Ar, Pr),15(Gn, Ls)

Spacecraft Stats

Spacecraft

PLANETARY FIGHTER (XV) *

Source	Airport
Build	50 s. / 100 G, 100 I
Hit Points	950
Speed	20
Line of Sight	6
A/D	Space Fighter
Attack	230 (Gn) / 2
Range (AE)	5
Armor	10 (Gn, Ls)

SPACE FIGHTER (XV) *

Source	Space Carrier
Build	25 s. / 200 G, 200 I
Hit Points	1400
Speed	24
Line of Sight	6
A/D	Space Fighter
Attack	175 (Gn) / 3
Range (AE)	5 (0.3)
Armor	10 (Gn, Ls)

SPACE CAPITAL SHIP (XV)*

Source	Space Dock
Build	60 s. / 500 G, 500 I
Hit Points	8000
Speed	18
Line of Sight	9
A/D	Space CapShip / Spaceship
Attack	200 (Ms) / 2
Missile	1200 (Gn)
Range	8
Armor	30 (Gn), 20 Ar, Pr, Ls

CAPITAL SHIP YAMATO (XV)

Hit Points	12,500
Speed	18
Line of Sight	9
A/D	Space CapShip / Spaceship
Attack	350 (Ms) / 1.2
Range (AE)	8
Armor	40 (Ls, Ms)

SPACE CARRIER (XV) *

Source	Space Dock
Build	45 s. / 200 G, 200 I
Hit Points	8000
Speed (Capacity)	18 (15)
Line of Sight	9
A/D	NA / Spaceship
Armor	30 (Gn), 20 (Ar, Pr, Ls)

SPACE CORVETTE (XV) *

Source	Space Dock
Build	35 s. / 200 G, 200 I
Hit Points	2500
Speed	18
Line of Sight	9
A/D	Space Corvette
Attack	150 (Ls) / 2
Range (AE)	8
Armor	30 (Gn), 20 (Ar, Pr, Ls)

SPACE TRANSPORT (XV) *

Source	Space Dock
Build	45 s. / 200 G, 200 I
Hit Points	1800
Speed (Capacity)	18 (30)
Line of Sight	7
A/D	NA / Spaceship
Armor	30 (Gn), 20 (Ar, Pr, Ls)

SPY SATELLITE (XIV) *

Source	Town Center
Build	50 s. / 100 G, 100 I
Hit Points	1000
Speed	20
Line of Sight	13
A/D	NA / Spaceship

EMPIRE EARTH
THE ART OF CONQUEST

PRIMA'S OFFICIAL STRATEGY GUIDE

Animals

CHICKEN

Hit Points	8
Speed	6
Line of Sight	2
A/D	NA / Animal
Range (AE)	0.5

DEER

Hit Points	12
Speed	12
Line of Sight	2
A/D	NA / Animal
Range (AE)	0.5

EAGLE

Hit Points	99
Speed	10
Line of Sight	1
A/D	Animal
Attack	(Gn) / 1
Range (AE)	0.5

ELEPHANT

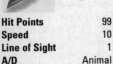

Hit Points	40
Speed	8
Line of Sight	2
A/D	Animal
Attack	12 (Sh) / 4
Range (AE)	0.6

GIRAFFE

Hit Points	20
Speed	10
Line of Sight	2
A/D	NA / Animal
Range (AE)	0.6

GOAT

Hit Points	12
Speed	8
Line of Sight	2
A/D	NA / Animal
Range (AE)	0.6

HIPPOPOTAMUS

Hit Points	30
Speed	14
Line of Sight	2
A/D	Animal
Attack	8 (Sh) / 2
Range (AE)	0.6

HORSE

Hit Points	12
Speed	14
Line of Sight	2
A/D	NA / Animal
Range (AE)	0.6

OSTRICH

Hit Points	12
Speed	10
Line of Sight	2
A/D	NA / Animal
Range (AE)	0.6

TIGER

Hit Points	16
Speed	14
Line of Sight	5
A/D	Animal
Attack	10 (Sh) / 2
Range (AE)	0.6

WALRUS

Hit Points	30
Speed	8
Line of Sight	2
A/D	Animal
Attack	8 (Sh) / 2
Range (AE)	0.6

WOLF

Hit Points	16
Speed	14
Line of Sight	3
A/D	Animal
Attack	10 (Sh) / 2
Range (AE)	0.5

OPPER AGE	DARK AGE	RENAISSANCE	INDUSTRIAL AGE	INFORMATION
BC 2000 BC 500 BC	0AD 900 AD 1300 AD	1500 AD 1700 AD	1900 AD	2000 AD
BRONZE AGE	MIDDLE AGES	IMPERIAL AGE	ATOMIC AGE	

Attack Multipliers

∞ Attack Multipliers ∞

The unit relationship diagrams show which units have advantages over other units. Some advantages come from a unit being less expensive, doing more damage, or having the appropriate armor to defend against the other unit. All of this information is included in the individual unit stats. However, another major factor is whether one unit's attack damage is multiplied when it attacks the other unit.

The table on the next two pages lists each unit's attack multipliers for each possible unit it can attack. For the most part, the listed multiplier is "1" (meaning its attack damage isn't multiplied). However, the damage for some attacks is multiplied by 1.5, or 2, or more. In other cases, damage is reduced — any multiplier below 1 means that the attacker does less than its normal damage.

Row heads match the attack class of the individual unit stats (the "A" part of the "A/D" line). Column heads match the defense class of the individual unit stats (the "D" part). For example, looking at the ships on pages 208 and 213, we see that the royal galleon (IX) has "A/D: Galley," while the battleship – Agincourt (IX) has "A/D: Destroyer/Battleship." In a battle between the two, the galleon's damage is multiplied by 3.8 (found by matching the galleon's "Galley" attack class row with the Agincourt's "Battleship" defense class column, on page 227), while the Agincourt's damage is neither increased nor decreased (matching the "Destroyer" attack class with the "Galley" defense class, on the same page).

When an intersection is blank, it means that units in the attack class can't attack units in the defense class — they ignore them.

NEW EXPANSION ATTACK MULTIPLIERS

The Art of Conquest introduces several new unit types. They wouldn't fit on the original chart, so they are listed below, following the same format.

When a Fishing Boat Attacks a Fish
The multiplier is x1. No other units can attack fish.

When an Anti Missile Battery Attacks an ICBM
The multiplier is x0.5. No other units can attack an ICBM.

When Space Fighters Defend

ATTACKER	MULTIPLIER
AA	1.5
Air Superiority	1
Carrier AC	1
Strafer	1
Primitive AA	1.5
Red Baron	1
Space CapShip	0.5
Space Fighter	1
Space Corvette	1.5
Nuclear Missile	1
Anti-Space	1
All Others	0

When New Units Attack

ATTACKER / DEFENDER	AA Building	Building	Land-AA	Mine	Space Corvette	Space Fighter	Spaceship	Sub/Nuclear Sub	Space Turret	Tower	Fish, ICBM	All Others
Space CapShip	1	1			1.3	0.5	1		1	1		
Space Fighter	0.3	1	0.3		0.5	1	2		0.5	0.8		1
Space Corvette					1	1.5	1		0.8			
Nuclear Missile	1	1	1	1	1	1	1	1	1	1		1
Anti-Space					1	1	1					

EMPIRE EARTH
THE ART OF CONQUEST

PRIMA'S OFFICIAL STRATEGY GUIDE

ATTACKER \ DEFENDER	Citizen	Animal	Human/Canine Scout	Priest	Hero	Foot Shock/Barbarian	Spear	Spear Thrower	Archer	Mounted Shock	Mounted Spear	Ranged Cav	Elephant Archer	War Elephant	Tower	Wall/Gate	Building	Ram	Siege	Field Piece	Persian Cav	Viking	Musket/Rifle	Mounted Gun	Elite Guard	Machine Gun
Citizen	3	1	1	1	1	1	1	1	1	1.3	1.5	1	1	1	1	1	0.3	1	1	1	1	1	1	1	1	1
Animal	1	1	1	1	1	1	1	1	1	1	1	1	1	1				1	1	1	1	1	1	1	1	1
Priest	1		1	1	1	1	1	1	1	1	1	1	1	1	1	1	1	1	1	1	1	1	1	1	1	1
Hero	1	1	1	1	1	1.3	1	1	1	1	1.5	1	1	2	1	0.3	0.5	1	1	1	1	1.5	1	0.9	0.8	1
Foot Shock	2	1	1	1	1	1.5	1	0.8	1	1.5	1	1	2	1	0.8	0.3	0.3	1	1	1	1	1.3	1	0.9	1	1
Foot Spear	1	1	1	1	1	1	1	0.6	1	1.4	1	1	2	1	1	0.3	0.3	1	1	1	1	1	1	0.7	1	1
Primitive Ranged	1	1	1	1	0.9	1	1	1	1	1	1	1	3	0.3	0.1	0.2	0.1	1	0.2	1	0.2	1	1	1	1	1
Mounted Shock	1.3	1	2	1	1	1	1	1	1.5	1	1	1.8	2	0.8	1	0.3	0.3	1	1	1	1.3	1	1.3	2	1	2
Mounted Spear	1.3	1	1	1	1	2	1	1.7	1	1	1.5	1	1	2	1	0.3	0.3	1	1	1	1	1.5	2	1	1	1
Ranged Cav	1	1	1	1	0.5	1	1.4	1.4	1	1	1	1	3	0.3	0.1	0.2	0.1	1	0.2	1	1.1	0.2	0.9	0.7	1	1
Tower	1	1	0.6	1	1	1	†	1	1	1	1	1	1	1	0.1	0.1	0.1	0.1	0.2	1	1	0.6	1	0.6	1	0.5
Ram																1	1									
Siege	1	1	1	1	0.5	1	1	1	1	1	1	1	1	1	3	3.5	1.5	1	1	1.4	1	1	1	1	1	1
Field Piece/Field Can.	1	1	1	1	1	1	1	1	1	0.5	0.8	1	1	1	1	1	1	0.7	1	0.8	1	1	1	1	1	0.7
Persian Cav	2	1	1	2	0.5	1.8	1.3	0.9	1	1.8	1	1	2.5	1	1	0.4	0.3	1	1	1	1	1	0.5	1	1	1
Barbarian	1	1	1	1	1	1.8	1.3	1	2.5	1	1	2.5	2	1	1	1	0.3	1	1	1	1	1	1	1	1	1
Viking	2	1	1	1	1	1	1	3	4	1	1	4	3	1	1	0.3	0.3	1	1	1	1	1	3	1	1	1
Halberdier	2	1	1	1	1	1	1	1	1	2.2	2.3	1	1.3	1	1	0.3	0.3	1	1	1	1	2.3	1	1	1.8	1
Primitive Gun	1	1	1	0.8	1	3	1.7	1	1	1	1.5	1	1	0.8	0.1	0.2	0.2	1	0.3	1.5	1.5	0.9	1.5	0.8	1	0.5
Mounted Gun	0.8	1	1	1	1	2.5	1.5	1	1	2.5	2	1	2.5	1	0.1	0.1	0.2	1	1.5	2	1	0.7	1	1	1	1
Elite Guard	0.5	1	1.8	1	1	1.8	1.8	1.8	1	1	1	1	1	1	0.5	0.2	0.2	1	0.1	1	1	1.8	1.8	0.7	1.8	1
Hand Cannon	1	1	1	1	1	1	1	1	1	1	1	1	1	1	1	0.3	0.5	1	1	1	1	1	1	1	1	1
Sniper	3	1	12	12	3	12	12	12	12	1	1	1	1	1	1	1	1	1	1	0.2	1	1	12	12	1	12
Partisan	1	1	1	1	1	1	1	1	1	1	1	1	1	1	1	0.3	0.5	1	1	1	1	1	1	1	1	1
Rifle	1	1	1	0.8	0.9	1.8	1	1	1	1	1	1	1	1	0.5	0.2	0.1	0.2	1	1	1	1.8	0.9	1.8	1	1
Machine Gun	1	1	3	3	1.5	3	3	3	1	3.5	3.5	1	3.5	1	0.5	0.2	0.1	1.5	1	3.5	3	3	4	3	1	2.1
Bazooka	1	1	1	1	1	1	1	1	1	1	1	1	1	1	1	0.3	0.5	1	1	1	1	1	1	1	1	0.5
Mortar	1	1	1	1	1	1	1	1	1	1	1	1	1	1	1	0.3	0.5	1	1	1	1	1	1	1	1	1.5
Modern Siege	1	1	1	1	1	1	1	1	1	1	1	1	1	1	3	3.6	1.5	1	1	1	1	1	1	1	1	1
AT Gun	1	1	1	1	1	1	1	1	1	2	1	1	1	2	0.5	0.4	1	1.5	1	1	1	1	1.5	1	1	1.1
Tank	1	1	2	2	1.5	1	2	1	1.8	1.5	1	1.5	1.7	1	0.3	0.5	1	0.3	1.5	1	2	1	1.5	2	1	2
Tank (German)	1	1	2	2	2	1	2	1	1.8	1.5	1	1.5	1.7	1	0.2	0.2	1	0.3	1.5	1	2	1	1.5	2	1	2
Fishing Boat																										
Galley	1	1	2	2	0.5	2	2	2	2	2	2	2	2	2	2	2	4	0.1	1	2	2	2	2	2	2	2
Destroyer	1	1	1	1	1	1	2	2	1	1	2	2	1	1	0.4	0.4	0.5	0.1	0.3	1	1	2	1	1	1	1
Battleship	0.8	1	1	1	1	1	1	1	1	1	1	1	1	1	1	0.4	1	1	0.3	1	1	1	1	1	1	1
Sub																										
BM (Nuclear) Sub	1	1	1	1	1	1	1	1	1	1	1	1	1	1	1	0.5	1	1	1	1	1	1	1	1	1	1
Anti-Sea																										
Helicopter/Hover	1	1	1.5	1.5	0.8	1.5	1.5	1.5	1.5	1.5	1.5	1.5	1.5	1.5	0.1	0.1	0.1	1	0.8	1	1.5	1	1.5	1.5	1.5	1.5
AA																										
Air Superiority																										
Strafer	1	1	1	1	0.5	1	1	1	1	1	1	1	1.5	1	0.2	0.2	0.2	1	1	1	1	1	1	1	1	1
Red Baron	1	1	1	1	0.5	1	1	1	1	1	1	1	1.5	1	0.2	0.2	0.2	1	1	1	1	1	1	1	1	1
Bomber/Atomic Br.	1	1	1	1	2.5	1	1	1	1	1	1	1	1	1	2	2.5	3	1	1	1	1	1	1	1	1	1
Carrier AC	1	1	1	1	0.5	1	1	1	1	1	1	1	1	1	0.2	0.2	0.2	1	1	1	1	1	1	1	1	1
AT Air	1	1	1	1	1	1	1	1	1	1	1	1	1	1	1	1	1	1	1	1	1	1	1	1	1	1
Ares	0.8	1	1	1	1	2	2	2	1	2	1	1	2	2	0.5	1	0.1	1	1	1	2	2	2	1	2	1
Hades/Poseidon																										
Hyperion	1	1	1	1	1.5	2	2	2	2	3	2	2	3	3	0.5	1	0.3	1	1	2	3	2	1	3	1	1
Minotaur	1	1.5	1	1.5	1	2	2	2	1.5	2	2	1.5	2	1	0.5	1	0.4	1	1	2	2	2	1	2	1	1.5
Pandora	1	1	1.3	1	1	2	2	2	2	2	2	2	2	2	0.5	1	0.4	1	1	2	2	2	1.3	1	1.3	1
Zeus	1	0.4	0.4	0.4	1.5	1	1	1	1	1	1	1	1	1	1	1	0.2	1	1	1	1	1	0.4	1	0.4	1
Other	1	1	1	1	1	1	1	1	1	1	1	1	1	1	1	0.3	0.5	1	1	1	1	1	1	1	1	1

ATTACKER / DEFENDER	Field Cannon/Car	AT Gun	Artillery	Tank	Tank (German)	Land AA	AA Building	Ship	Galley	Battleship	Aircraft Carrier	Sub/BM (Nuclear) Sub	Helicopter/Hover	Aircraft	Bomber	Atomic Bomber	Apollo/Ares	Furies/Hades	Hyperion/Poseidon	Minotaur	Pandora/Tempest	Zeus
Citizen	1	1	1	0.2	0.2	1	1	1	1	1	1							1	1	1	1	1
Animal	1	1	1	1	1	1	1											1		1	1	1
Priest	1	1	1	1	1	1	1	1	1	1	1											
Hero	1	0.4	1	0.3	0.5	1	1	1	1	1	1							0.5	1	0.5	0.8	0.5
Foot Shock	1	1	1	1	1	1	1	1	1	1	1							1	1	1	1	1
Foot Spear	1	1	1	1	1	1	1	1	1	1	1							1	1	1	0.8	1
Primitive Ranged	0.1	1	1	0.1	0.1	1	1	1	1	1	1							1	1	1	1	0.3
Mounted Shock	1.3	1	1.3	0.8	0.8	1	1	1	1	1	1							1	1	1	1	1
Mounted Spear	1	1	1	1	1	1	1	1	1	1	1							1	1	1	1	1
Ranged Cav	0.1	1	1	0.1	0.1	1	1	1	1	1	1							1	1	1	1	0.3
Tower	0.3	0.5	0.1	0.3	0.3	1	1	1	1	1	1	1						1	1	1	0.5	0.3
Ram							1.5															
Siege	1.4	0.5	1	0.9	0.9	1	1	1	1	4.5	1							1	1	1	1	1
Field Piece/Field Can.	1	0.5	1	0.9	0.9	1	1	1	1	1	1							1	1	1	1	1
Persian Cav	0.1	1	1	1	1	1	1	1	1	1	1							1	1	1	1	1
Barbarian	1	1	1	1	1	1	1	1	1	1	1							1	1	1	1	1
Viking	1	1	1	1	1	1	1	1	1	1	1							1	1	1	1	1
Halberdier	1	1	1	1	1	1	1	1	1	1	1							1	1	1	1	1
Primitive Gun	1.1	1.3	1	1	1	1	1	1	1	1	1							0.4	0.4	0.4	0.4	0.4
Mounted Gun	1	0.5	1	1	1	1	1	0.4	0.4	1	0.4							0.4	0.4	0.4	0.4	0.4
Elite Guard	1	1	1	1	1	1	1	1	1	1	1							1	1	1	1	1
Hand Cannon	1.4	1	1	2.3	2.3	1	1	1	1	1	1							1	1	1	0.8	1
Sniper	0.2	0.9	1	1	1	1	1	1	1	1	1							1	1	1	1	0.7
Partisan	1	1	1	1	1	1	1	1	1	1	1	2	0.8	2.3	1.8		1	1	1	1	1	1
Rifle	1	1.3	1	0.9	0.9	1	1	1	1	1	1		0.4				1	1	1	1.1	1	1
Machine Gun	1	1.3	1.5	1	1	2	1	1	1	1	1							1	1	1	1	1
Bazooka	1	0.8	1	2	2	1	1	1	1	1	1							1	1	1	0.8	1
Mortar	1.4	1.5	1	1	0.8	1	1	1	1	1	1							1	1	1	0.8	1
Modern Siege	1	0.5	1	0.2	0.2	1	1	1	1	5	1							1	1	1	0.8	1
AT Gun	1	1.8	1.5	2.7	4.5	1	1	1	1	1	2	1						2.6	3.5	2.1	1.7	0.7
Tank	1	0.6	1	1.3	1	2	1	1	1	1	1							1.2	1.2	0.4	1	1
Tank (German)	1	0.5	1	1.9	1.8	1	1	1	1	1	1							1.2	1.2	0.5	0.8	1
Fishing Boat								1	1	1	1											
Galley	2	1	1	1	1	2	1	1	1	3.8	1							2	2	2	2	2
Destroyer	1	1	0.3	0.2	0.2	1	1	1	1	1	1	1						1	1	1	1	1
Battleship	1	0.5	0.3	0.4	0.4	1	1	1	0.3	1	1							1	1	1	0.4	1
Sub								1	1	3.5	1	1							3.5			
BM (Nuclear) Sub	1	1	1	1	1	1	1											1	1	1	1	1
Anti-Sea											1											
Helicopter/Hover	1	0.7	0.8	1	1.5	0.4	0.4	1	1	1	1		1				1.5	1	2	1	1	1
AA												1.4	1	1.5	2	4						
Air Superiority													1	1.3	1.4	1.4	1.5					
Strafer	1	0.7	0.3	0.4	0.4	0.1	0.1	0.8	1	0.8	1		0.8	0.5	1.4	1.4	1.5	1	1	1	1	1
Red Baron		0.7	1	0.4	0.4	0.1	0.1	1	1	1			1	1	1	1	1.5	1	1	1	1	1
Bomber/Atomic Br.	1	0.8	1	0.5	0.5	1	1	1	1	4	1							1	1	1	0.6	1
Carrier AC	1	1	1	0.5	0.5	0.1	0.1	1.9	1.5	3	1.5		0.8	1.3	1.4	1.4	2.3	1	1	1	1	1
AT Air	1	1	1	1.5	1.5	1	1	1	1	1								1	1	1	1	1
Ares	1	1.3	1	1	1	0.2	0.3	1	1	1	1		0.5				1.4	1	1.5	2	1.4	0.6
Hades/Poseidon																	1	1	1	1	1	1
Hyperion	1	0.7	1	1	1	1	1	1	1	1	0.1	0.2						1.2	1.4	2	1.3	0.5
Minotaur	1	1	1	2.1	2.1	1	1	1	1	1*	1							1	1	1	1	0.7
Pandora	1	0.6	1	1.2	1.2	1	1	1	1	1	1						1	1.1	1.1	1.7	1.2	1
Zeus	1	1.1	1	0.1	0.1	0.5	1	1	1	1	1					2		2	2.2	1	0.6	1
Other	1	1	1	1	1	1	1	1	1	1	1							1	1	1	0.8	1

EMPIRE EARTH
THE ART OF CONQUEST

Unit Relationship Diagrams

The first set of parentheses lists the epoch in which the unit first becomes available. The second set of parentheses describes the attack type (Ar = Arrow / Gn = Gun / Ms = Missile / Sh = Shock / Pr = Pierce / Ls = Laser).

Only units that have offensive advantages or disadvantages against other units appear here. Siege weapons, civilians and heroes, buildings, towers, unarmed aircraft, animals, unarmed vessels and non-offensive units are not listed.

Units marked with an asterisk (*) are available in all epochs.

LAND: PREHISTORY (I) — MIDDLE (VI)

Shock
(Gun/Sword)

Clubman (I) (Sh)
Rock Thrower (I) (Sh)
Sampson (II) (Gn)
Horseman (III) (Sh)
Maceman (III) (Sh)
Royal Guard (IV) (Sh)
Short Sword (IV) (Sh)
Trojan Horse (IV) (Sh)
Barbarian (V) (Sh)
Cataphract (V) (Sh)
Moorish Cavalry (V) (Sh)
Moorish Infantry (V) (Sh)
Ashikagu Arquebus (VI) (Gn)
Huskarl (VI) (Sh)
Long Sword (VI) (Sh)
Samurai (VI) (Sh)

Pierce (Spear)

Spearman (II) (Pr)
Bronze Cavalry (IV) (Pr)
Chinese Infantry (IV) (Pr)
Companion Cavalry (IV) (Pr)
Javelin (IV) (Pr)
Persian Immortal (IV) (Pr)
Phalanx (IV) (Pr)
Persian Cavalry (V) (Pr)
Pilum (V) (Pr)
Knight (VI) (Pr)
Pikeman (VI) (Pr)

Arrow/Missile

Slinger (II) (Ar)
Incan Warrior (III) (Ar)
Simple Bowman (III) (Ar)
Chariot Archer (IV) (Ar)
Elephant Archer (IV) (Ar)
War Elephant (IV) (Ms)
Composite Bow (V) (Ar)
Crossbow (V) (Ar)
Viking (V) (Ms)
Cavalry Archer (VI) (Ar)
Long Bow (VI) (Ar)

Unit Relation Diagrams

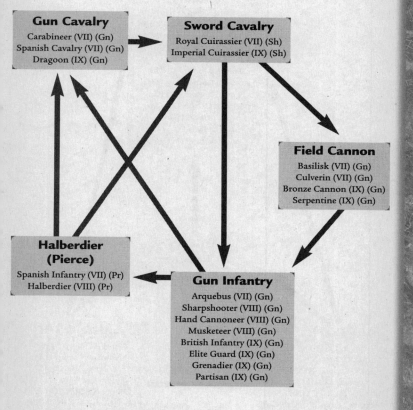

LAND: RENAISSANCE (VII) — INDUSTRIAL (IX)

Gun Cavalry
Carabineer (VII) (Gn)
Spanish Cavalry (VII) (Gn)
Dragoon (IX) (Gn)

Sword Cavalry
Royal Cuirassier (VII) (Sh)
Imperial Cuirassier (IX) (Sh)

Field Cannon
Basilisk (VII) (Gn)
Culverin (VII) (Gn)
Bronze Cannon (IX) (Gn)
Serpentine (IX) (Gn)

Halberdier (Pierce)
Spanish Infantry (VII) (Pr)
Halberdier (VIII) (Pr)

Gun Infantry
Arquebus (VII) (Gn)
Sharpshooter (VIII) (Gn)
Hand Cannoneer (VIII) (Gn)
Musketeer (VIII) (Gn)
British Infantry (IX) (Gn)
Elite Guard (IX) (Gn)
Grenadier (IX) (Gn)
Partisan (IX) (Gn)

LAND: ATOMIC WWI (X) — MODERN (XII)

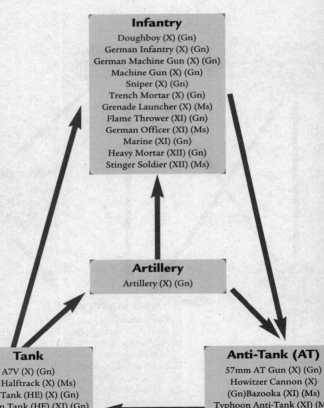

Infantry

Doughboy (X) (Gn)
German Infantry (X) (Gn)
German Machine Gun (X) (Gn)
Machine Gun (X) (Gn)
Sniper (X) (Gn)
Trench Mortar (X) (Gn)
Grenade Launcher (X) (Ms)
Flame Thrower (XI) (Gn)
German Officer (XI) (Ms)
Marine (XI) (Gn)
Heavy Mortar (XII) (Gn)
Stinger Soldier (XII) (Ms)

Artillery

Artillery (X) (Gn)

Tank

A7V (X) (Gn)
Flak Halftrack (X) (Ms)
MkV Tank (HE) (X) (Gn)
Sherman Tank (HE) (XI) (Gn)
Panzer Tank (AP) (XI) (Gn)
Leopard Tank (AP) (XII) (Gn)
M1 Tank (HE) (XII) (Gn)

Anti-Tank (AT)

57mm AT Gun (X) (Gn)
Howitzer Cannon (X)
(Gn)Bazooka (XI) (Ms)
Typhoon Anti-Tank (XI) (Ms)
120mm AT Gun (XII) (Gn)
A-10 Anti-Tank (XII) (Ms)
Helicopter Anti-Tank (XII) (Ms)

Unit Relation Diagrams

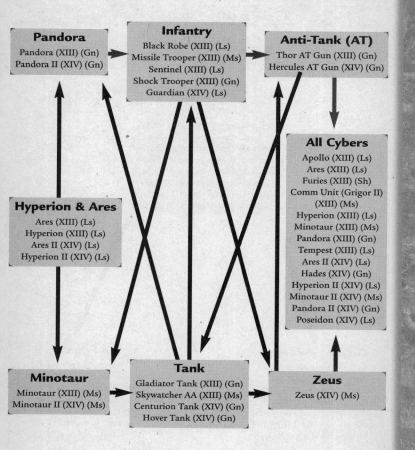

LAND: DIGITAL (XIII) — NANO (XIV)

Pandora
Pandora (XIII) (Gn)
Pandora II (XIV) (Gn)

Infantry
Black Robe (XIII) (Ls)
Missile Trooper (XIII) (Ms)
Sentinel (XIII) (Ls)
Shock Trooper (XIII) (Gn)
Guardian (XIV) (Ls)

Anti-Tank (AT)
Thor AT Gun (XIII) (Gn)
Hercules AT Gun (XIV) (Gn)

All Cybers
Apollo (XIII) (Ls)
Ares (XIII) (Ls)
Furies (XIII) (Sh)
Comm Unit (Grigor II) (XIII) (Ms)
Hyperion (XIII) (Ls)
Minotaur (XIII) (Ms)
Pandora (XIII) (Gn)
Tempest (XIII) (Ls)
Ares II (XIV) (Ls)
Hades (XIV) (Gn)
Hyperion II (XIV) (Ls)
Minotaur II (XIV) (Ms)
Pandora II (XIV) (Gn)
Poseidon (XIV) (Ls)

Hyperion & Ares
Ares (XIII) (Ls)
Hyperion (XIII) (Ls)
Ares II (XIV) (Ls)
Hyperion II (XIV) (Ls)

Minotaur
Minotaur (XIII) (Ms)
Minotaur II (XIV) (Ms)

Tank
Gladiator Tank (XIII) (Gn)
Skywatcher AA (XIII) (Ms)
Centurion Tank (XIV) (Gn)
Hover Tank (XIV) (Gn)

Zeus
Zeus (XIV) (Ms)

EMPIRE EARTH
THE ART OF CONQUEST

SEA: STONE (II) — INDUSTRIAL (IX)

Battleship
Battleship - Copper (III) (Ms)
Battleship - Bronze (IV) (Ms)
Battleship - Byzantine (V) (Ms)
Battleship - Middle Ages (VI) (Ms)
Battleship - Renaissance (VII) (Ms)
Battleship - Imperial (VIII) (Ms)
Battleship - Agincourt (IX) (Ms)
Battleship - Royal (IX) (Ms)

Galley / Galleon
Galley - Copper (III) (Ms)
Galley - Bronze (IV) (Ms)
Galley - Byzantine (V) (Ms)
Galley - Middle Ages (VI) (Ms)
Galleon - Renaissance (VII) (Ms)
Galleon - Imperial (VIII) (Ms)
Galleon - Royal (IX) (Ms)

Frigate
Frigate - Copper (III) (Ms)
Frigate - Bronze (IV) (Ms)
Frigate - Byzantine (V) (Ms)
Frigate - Middle Ages (VI) (Ms)
Frigate - Renaissance (VII) (Ms)
Frigate - Imperial (VIII) (Ms)
Frigate - Royal (IX) (Ms)

Unit Relation Diagrams

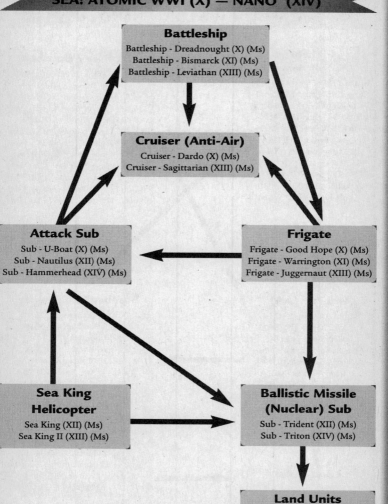

SEA: ATOMIC WWI (X) — NANO (XIV)

Battleship
Battleship - Dreadnought (X) (Ms)
Battleship - Bismarck (XI) (Ms)
Battleship - Leviathan (XIII) (Ms)

Cruiser (Anti-Air)
Cruiser - Dardo (X) (Ms)
Cruiser - Sagittarian (XIII) (Ms)

Attack Sub
Sub - U-Boat (X) (Ms)
Sub - Nautilus (XII) (Ms)
Sub - Hammerhead (XIV) (Ms)

Frigate
Frigate - Good Hope (X) (Ms)
Frigate - Warrington (XI) (Ms)
Frigate - Juggernaut (XIII) (Ms)

Sea King Helicopter
Sea King (XII) (Ms)
Sea King II (XIII) (Ms)

Ballistic Missile (Nuclear) Sub
Sub - Trident (XII) (Ms)
Sub - Triton (XIV) (Ms)

Land Units

EMPIRE EARTH
THE ART OF CONQUEST

AIR: ATOMIC WWI (X) — NANO (XIV)

Fighter
(Air Superiority)

Albatros D.V. Fighter (X) (Ms)
Sopwith Fighter (X) (Ms)
F-86 Fighter (XI) (Ms)
FW190 Fighter (XI) (Ms)
MiG-15 Fighter (XI) (Ms)
P-38 Lightning (XI) (Ms)
P-51 Fighter (XI) (Ms)
Spitfire Fighter (XI) (Ms)
F-15 Fighter (XII) (Ms)
Jackal Fighter (XIII) (Ms)
Nebula Fighter (XIV) (Ms)

Fighter / Bomber

Fokker Fighter/Bomber (X) (Ms)
Red Baron (X) (Ms)
Sopwith Triplane (X) (Ms)
Corsair Fighter/Bomber (XI) (Ms)
F-80 Fighter/Bomber (XI) (Ms)
ME109 Fighter/Bomber (XI) (Ms)
ME262 Fighter/Bomber (XI) (Ms)
F-117 Fighter/Bomber (XII) (Ms)
F-14 Fighter/Bomber (XII) (Ms)
Avenger Fighter/Bomber (XIII) (Ms)
Talon Fighter/Bomber (XIII) (Ms)
Phoenix Fighter/Bomber (XIV) (Ms)

Anti-Air (AA)

88mm AA Gun (X) (Ms)
Flak Halftrack (X) (Ms)
Carrier - Enterprise (XI)
Stinger Soldier (XII) (Ms)
AA Missile Tower (XIII) (Ms)
Carrier - Nexus (XIII)
Skywatcher AA (XIII) (Ms)
Missile Trooper (XIII) (Ms)

Bomber & Helicopter

Gotha Bomber (X) (Ms)
B-29 Bomber (XI) (Sh)
B-17 Bomber (XI) (Ms)
Heinkel Bomber (XI) (Ms)
ME110 Bomber (XI) (Ms)
Typhoon Anti-Tank (XI) (Ms)
A-10 Anti-Tank (XII) (Ms)
B-2 Bomber (XII) (Ms)
B-52 Bomber (XII) (Sh)
Helicopter Anti-Tank (XII) (Ms)
Helicopter Gunship (XII) (Gn)
B-122 Wyvern Bomber (XIII) (Ms)
Reaper Gunship (XIII) (Gn)
Spectre AT Helicopter (XIII) (Ms)
Titan Bomber (XIII) (Sh)
UFO (XIV) (Ls)

Land Units

Unit Relation Diagrams

SPACE (+LAND, AIR): NANO (XIV) — SPACE (XIV)

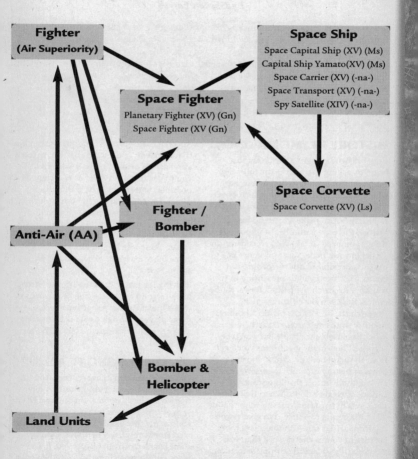

COPPER AGE		DARK AGE		RENAISSANCE		INDUSTRIAL AGE	
BC	5000 BC	2000 BC	500 BC	0 AD	900 AD	1800 AD	1500 AD	1700 AD	1900 AD
STONE AGE		BRONZE AGE		MIDDLE AGES		IMPERIAL AGE		ATOMIC AG

PRIMA'S OFFICIAL STRATEGY GUIDE

EMPIRE EARTH
THE ART OF CONQUEST

The Theory of
∼ Scenario Design ∼

By Gordon Farrell

Gordon Farrell is an award-winning scenario designer who created The Greek Campaign, The Tutorials and scenarios about the Napoleonic wars for *Empire Earth*. His previous design work includes many of the most highly-rated RTS scenarios on the web. *PC Gamer Magazine* included his work on their compilation CDs (*Extended Play 2* and *Online Arena: Best Add-On Levels of 1999*). *Computer Gaming World* has cited his add-on levels as being among the best on the web. A professional screenwriter and playwright, Gordon holds an MFA in Playwriting from the Yale School of Drama. His new book *The Power of the Playwright's Vision*, was recently published by Heinemann Press.

HISTORY IN THE MAKING ...

Everyone who designs a scenario must begin by asking themselves the following question: Am I going to design a scenario which will recreate events from history? Or will I make up my own story from scratch?

If you choose to make a scenario based on history, there are a number of important things you need to take into consideration. To begin with, make sure you know as much as possible about the people and events which you will be presenting in your scenario. Research the period. Research the events. Research the cultural setting. Research the lives of the historical figures. In other words: research, research, research. Why? Because right off the bat, you'll be surprised how many great ideas you'll get from the actual events. Often, the incidents of history organize themselves easily and naturally into a thrilling story. Of course, often they don't. When that happens, you have to find creative ways to link all of the events together. As a result, working from actual facts can make you more creative in your scenario work than you would be if you had the complete freedom to tell the story any way you wanted.

Another major reason for doing research is that once you've declared that you're recreating actual history, players will expect you to get as many of the details right as possible. And they will be resoundingly disappointed if you don't. Look at it this way: the game artists have lavished hours and hours researching and creating historically accurate units and buildings. If accurate-looking armies and cities make the game more exciting, why wouldn't an accurate story?

Striving for historical accuracy can extend to the terrain and the shape of the map as well. One of the ways that I made my name as a scenario designer is by making sure my maps correlate closely with the real world.

... OR MAKING IT ALL UP

Of course, you don't have to work from history. You can create your own story, something completely original that no one has seen or heard before. If this is the route you choose, my first piece of advice is this: Make your story completely fictitious. Don't use some characters from history, like Robin Hood or Winston Churchill, and then tell a story about how they were members of the King's Musketeers who set sail to start a colony in North America. This is the sure sign of a designer who lacks imagination.

The fact is, if you're going to create your own story, it takes as much work as researching history. It's just work of a different kind. When you create an alternate world, you make it seem real to us by filling it with well-thought out details, details that are apparent in every aspect of the game — the shapes and textures of the mountains, the layout of the farms and cities, the placement of ambient animals like chickens and deer.

But it's not enough just to create a map and place some units on it. You have to create detailed situations which the player feels are very much like the kinds of complexities we experience in real life.

Whether your scenario is a fictitious story set in ancient Rome or on the Planet Xzzyl, it will only be believable if the different characters who are represented in your story, the people they have relationships with, and their motives for undertaking the actions necessary to win the scenario are conceived and presented with as much detail as possible. You must make sure the player is faced with choices that are not simple, and which will carry with them significant repercussions.

THE END COMES FIRST

Next you must ask yourself what event will occur at the end of the scenario that will make it fun, memorable and worth playing. An example of an "event" would be a huge battle that occurs at the end of the scenario. On the other hand it might be a surprise attack by a handful of assassins. The memorable event might be a run-for-your-life chase sequence. It might be the discovery of some beautiful city or natural location. Or it might be an unexpected insight into a famous person from history, or possibly a fresh way of looking at a famous moment in history.

Theory of Scenario Design

If you're going to design a scenario where the Duke of Wellington defeats Napoleon Bonaparte at the Battle of Waterloo, then you have to ask yourself, where's the surprise? This was the problem I faced in the British Campaign in *Empire Earth*. I tried to solve it by providing a surprise in Wellington's recognition that Napoleon was simply trying to usher in a new era. Wellington knows it's inevitable, and that he's defending a dying aristocracy. As the battle ends, Wellington acknowledges Napoleon's wisdom. That's a relatively subtle kind of surprise.

I used another kind of surprise in add-on levels I designed for *Age of Empires*. One is a scenario based on the Battle of Thermopylae in which you can only win by dying. People got a kick out of the fact that you had to inflict a certain amount of damage on the enemy before you die, but then you had to die in order to win the scenario. (This was based on the actual fate of King Leonidas and the 300 Spartans who died with him.)

Or there can be a visual surprise ... you can arrive at a magnificent city after you travel across the globe. (Of course then you have to provide the "eye-candy" — the magnificent city — at the end!)

Every scenario has in its core an event like this. In a sense the scenario has to be constructed backwards. You have to decide what event/revelation/surprise is going to occur at the end of the scenario. Then you decide how the player will arrive at it.

Another way to think of this is that a scenario is a goal preceded by a series of obstacles. The goal contains the surprise or the memorable event. The obstacles are what must be overcome for the player to earn the surprise.

A common failure of people who do this for the first time is they'll say they want to recreate a famous battle from history. They'll create a map, put the units in the historically correct places. The scenario commences, the battle is fought, no one

EMPIRE EARTH
THE ART OF CONQUEST

enjoys it because there were no obstacles enroute to the battle. Fighting the famous battle is the payoff, the reward that should come at the end of the scenario. Gathering your army, coping with trigger-based events, locating the enemy and deploying your forces effectively are the obstacles that must be overcome before you get to fight the battle.

PICK A PROCESS

The body of the scenario is made up of a process. A process is the activity that the player is occupied with throughout the scenario and the one that he or she must complete in order to arrive at the surprise.

In real-time strategy (RTS) games, the type of process everyone's most familiar with is gathering/harvesting resources, constructing buildings, creating an army, locating and destroying an enemy. This is the traditional process that lies at the heart of all RTS games like *Empire Earth*. But you don't want to use this process in every scenario you create. Remember that people who've played all the scenarios in the game, per force, played many scenarios based on this process already. So they might get bored if you don't offer them something different.

Try to come up with other types of process.

For example, traveling across terrain — getting from point A to point B — can be a very satisfying process. The experience of traveling is enriched by placing obstacles in the path of the player's units. Those obstacles can be enemies, terrain features, natural events or story-based events. By story-based events, I mean having unexpected developments in the story occur. Members of your party might desert you, or your allies might change into enemies.

WHAT'S YOUR PROCESS?

Building an army

Traveling across the map

Locating another tribe

Accomplishing specific goals

Prosecuting a war with fixed forces

In addition to these obstacles, there can be requirements that have to be met for the units to be sustained along the way. For example, you can write triggers that require that you supply your units with food, pay them wages, or provide medicine to a unit that has been designated as sick. The process of the journey is complicated by the need to satisfy whatever additional burdens you've invented to put on your units.

Another process is where you need a unit or small group of units to accomplish certain tasks. For instance, securing an area of the map, and then constructing certain specified buildings there. Or capturing an artifact. Or liberating a unit being held prisoner by enemy forces. This is similar to the kind of experience you have in role-playing games (RPGs). In *Empire Earth* we decided to make some of the scenarios like this. We call them focused scenarios. Focused means you concentrate on a small number of units over a limited period of time. The events may occur over the course of a day, or a week, or even a few weeks. That's as opposed to the traditional scope of the RTS world which usually unfolds over centuries or epochs. It's quite different from the harvest/build/destroy-type scenarios that are so central to RTS games.

Locating another tribe, town or kingdom on the map can be a process.

Theory of Scenario Design

Yet another process can be successfully conducting a war with fixed resources. You're given an army, you can't build any more units ... now you have to figure out how to defeat an opponent who greatly outnumbers you. We call that a "fixed forces" scenario.

Once you have decided whether you're recreating history or weaving fiction, and you know what the surprise will be at the end as well as the process by which the player will arrive at the surprise, you must make certain they all connect to each other in a story that feels plausible and satisfying to the player.

At this point — weaving and telling a story — scenario design rises above technical craft and becomes an art. Without a story, the events and the challenges within the scenario will feel completely random and meaningless. But when they're connected by a thoughtful story, the events within your scenario will become an unforgettable experience that will linger in the player's memories long after the game is finished.

Ultimately, the art of good scenario designing is synonymous with the art of good storytelling. How do you tell a good story? By making sure that every goal and every obstacle grows out of the kinds of needs that people have in the real world — by connecting the events together in a way that reflects our shared memories of human experience.

Let me show you what I mean.

A typical scenario created by a beginner might start out with a city and an army. The player is told to go and conquer another city and army. After he has done so, a third army appears and attacks his home base. He must rush home and defend his own city.

These are essentially random, unconnected events. But if they were woven together into a story, it might go something like this:

The player is told he's the king of a specific city. He has received a secret message

from his brother informing him that a neighboring kingdom is planning an attack. According to your brother, your only hope is to strike first. So you take your army out and conquer the neighboring city. Suddenly you learn that in your absence your brother's army has invaded your home base. The neighbor you attacked and destroyed was never a threat to you — you were tricked by your brother. You rush home to defend your first city, and in the course of the battle you kill your brother.

Now you have the beginnings of a story. With a few more complications and obstacles, it can become a truly memorable experience for the player.

DESIGNING THE MAP

Terrain needs to have rich details. Take advantage of everything in the editor: little plants, different rocks, etc. Each pocket of the map should be fresh and unique. Part of a swampy area might be dotted with flowers, for example, and another part could have dead animals. Marsh, plants and different kinds of soil can be used to texture the edges of rivers. Mountains can be snowy with patches of grass sticking through. Don't underestimate the degree to which a rich environment will affect your enjoyment of playing a scenario.

In a similar vein, cities should look like they are inhabited by people. Paths should be worn between buildings, buildings should be clustered around highways, docks will be in sheltered coves. These things will add a kind of recognizable human logic ... they increase the air of reality.

When you're designing the map terrain, avoid using straight lines. You should never be able to get from point A to point B in a straight line. You should have to go around forests, volcanoes, canyons, etc. It's tremendously important to make the terrain a challenge.

EMPIRE EARTH
THE ART OF CONQUEST

Give a great deal of thought to resources and how you place them on the map. One of the ways to control the difficulty level of a scenario is by giving the player as few resources as possible. Too many resources will make the scenario too easy.

When doing the terrain, I sketch the continent edges, then place the terrain. I make sure the map is visually interesting, but I also know where I want home base and enemies to be.

GETTING DOWN TO WORK

When I'm creating the story for a scenario, I usually write it down in outline form. I spend as much as a week just planning out the story. I begin by asking myself, "How long do I want the game to take? 45 minutes? Saved and returned to for a few days? Is it going to be quick, or an immersive, long-term experience?" In a 45-minute scenario, you want at least two major obstacles between you and the climactic events. If you're recreating an historical battle, there should be two or three major obstacles that have to be overcome before the battle begins. That might give you about an hour's playing time. Conversely, if you want the player to get completely immersed in the game, you may want to sustain the experience for 2-5 hours. You'll need to put in more obstacles. A dozen obstacles might make for five hours of gameplay.

I work on several scenarios at the same time. I can create a basic scenario in anywhere from a week to a month, and that includes about 15 hours working on the terrain alone. Then, when all the triggers are written, it takes at least another month to get the bugs worked out.

You should try to make your scenarios as polished and as complete as the ones that came with the game. If you'd like to do this work professionally some day, there's no better way to prepare yourself. When I created scenarios for *Empire Earth*, I would polish every aspect of the scenario as completely as possible. Because of production deadlines, however, the staff in Cambridge would take over at some point and make all the necessary changes. The art department would finalize the terrain. The document specialist would revise the dialogue and the intro. The staff in Cambridge would fix any new bugs or glitches that popped up. But you shouldn't assume that this is ever going to be the case for you. Learn to do all of this stuff yourself. It makes amateur production good practice for becoming a pro.

Test your scenario twenty or thirty times before you give it to anyone else to play. If you find you need to make a small change in the triggers, then you have to play the whole thing over again, because later events in the scenario may be affected in ways you didn't anticipate. For example, you may have a hostile force, and there's a trigger that will cause the hostile force to attack the player's city. You decide the hostile force is too easy to defeat, so you increase the number of units that attack. Later on in the scenario the player is expected to invade the enemy force's home base, and suddenly there are too few left to defend it, so now the final victory is too easy. But you wouldn't have discovered this if you hadn't played it through to the end.